Excelling at University

How do you excel at university? What do you need to do in order to exceed your own expectations when it comes to your academic performance? How do you make the most of your learning experience at university so that you can develop the most valuable attributes employers look for in graduates?

This book provides a wealth of guidance on how to excel at university by engaging effectively with all aspects of the university learning experience. Covering tutors' expectations for how you learn on your programme of study, understanding the role of assessment in learning, the need to engage critically with academic sources, and effective research practice, it offers practical support on how to get the most out of the learning experience. It also includes guidance on different modes of learning, such as collaborative work on group projects, and practice- and work-based learning. Chapters adopt a fresh approach to the traditional guidance by moving beyond the 'how' to do something to explore the 'why', addressing such questions as why your tutors want you to be able to write confidently across different genres of writing, and why these competencies have an influence on your ability to excel.

This must-read guide will open up your tutors' expectations for how you should engage with the learning on your course. It offers a fresh, up-to-date, and innovative perspective on learning at university for all those new to or already engaged in higher education.

Chris Dennis is an Academic Skills Specialist at Cardiff Metropolitan University, UK.

Stuart Abbott is an Academic Skills Specialist at Cardiff Metropolitan University, UK.

Routledge Study Skills

Excelling at University
Academic Literacies and the Development of Graduate Identity
Chris Dennis & Stuart Abbott

The Mature Student's Companion for Successful Undergraduate Study
David Allan

The Mature Student's Guide to Completing a Doctorate
Sinéad Hewson

The Student Wellbeing Toolkit
Preparing for Life at College, University and Beyond
Camila Devis-Rozental

Writing a Postgraduate Thesis or Dissertation
Tools for Success
Michael Hammond

Studying Online
Succeeding through Distance Learning at University
Graham Jones

For more information about this series, please visit: https://www.routledge.com/Routledge-Study-Skills/book-series/ROUTLEDGESS

Excelling at University

Academic Literacies and the Development of Graduate Identity

Chris Dennis and Stuart Abbott

LONDON AND NEW YORK

Designed cover image: © Getty Images

First published 2026
by Routledge
4 Park Square, Milton Park, Abingdon, Oxon OX14 4RN

and by Routledge
605 Third Avenue, New York, NY 10158

Routledge is an imprint of the Taylor & Francis Group, an informa business

© 2026 Chris Dennis and Stuart Abbott

The right of Chris Dennis and Stuart Abbott to be identified as authors of this work has been asserted in accordance with sections 77 and 78 of the Copyright, Designs and Patents Act 1988.

All rights reserved. No part of this book may be reprinted or reproduced or utilised in any form or by any electronic, mechanical, or other means, now known or hereafter invented, including photocopying and recording, or in any information storage or retrieval system, without permission in writing from the publishers.

For Product Safety Concerns and Information please contact our EU representative GPSR@taylorandfrancis.com. Taylor & Francis Verlag GmbH, Kaufingerstraße 24, 80331 München, Germany.

Trademark notice: Product or corporate names may be trademarks or registered trademarks, and are used only for identification and explanation without intent to infringe.

British Library Cataloguing-in-Publication Data
A catalogue record for this book is available from the British Library

ISBN: 978-1-032-10240-5 (hbk)
ISBN: 978-1-032-10889-6 (pbk)
ISBN: 978-1-003-21752-7 (ebk)

DOI: 10.4324/9781003217527

Typeset in Galliard
by KnowledgeWorks Global Ltd.

Contents

List of figures vii
List of tables viii
Acknowledgements ix
Glossary x

1 Introduction 1

2 Excelling at university: Mindset, motivation, and goals 9

3 Defining 'learning' at university 27

4 Becoming a self-regulating learner 44

5 Understanding assessment 59

6 Making effective use of feedback 75

7 Research: Developing effective search strategies 95

8 Critical thought and developing a critical edge in writing 113

9 Writing for assessment 135

10 Academic integrity and referencing 184

11 Creating effective presentations and working in groups 200

12 Learning by doing: Practice- and work-based learning	220
13 Revision and exam strategies	231
14 Conclusion: Becoming a graduate	246
Index	252

Figures

3.1	The discourse community and a student's learning journey	29
3.2	Jess' mind-map relating to the use of Instagram by clothing retailers	34
3.3	The learning framework (simplified version)	40
4.1	A three-stage reflective cycle	53
6.1	The feedback cycle	82
9.1	The writing cycle	166
12.1	Kolb's experiential learning cycle	226
13.1	Active revision techniques	238
14.1	Tomlinson's graduate capital framework	248

Tables

5.1	Simplified marking criteria used for assessment at Level 4	72
6.1	Simplified marking criteria used for assessment at Level 4	87
6.2	Positive and negative comments identified in tutor's feedback	88
6.3	Links between positive comments and marking criteria	88
6.4	Links between negative comments and marking criteria	88
8.1	Structural elements of a journal article	121
8.2	Examples of the language of criticality	131
9.1	Topic areas and research questions	152
9.2	Report structure	160

Acknowledgements

This book has taken longer than expected to write. In part, this is because of the disruption caused by the pandemic; but it is also because of other commitments we've taken on as our roles have evolved with the shifts in the higher education landscape in recent years. We would like to thank Routledge, first of all, for their patience and support in getting the book to publication. A number of people have helped both of us over the years as our ideas and approach to academic literacies provision have taken shape. Among our colleagues at Cardiff Metropolitan University, we would like to thank Aimee Jones for ringfencing the time needed to complete the manuscript and Marie Lancaster for her interest in and support for the project. Rebecca Evans kindly read through the chapter on research and was on hand to answer questions on all library-related things. Finally, it's important to acknowledge the role played by our students in the evolution of the ideas found within this work. It is by teaching and engaging with them that we have been able to create this book; it is therefore to our students – and those we're yet to teach – that we offer this work in the hope that it can encourage them to excel at university before making their mark on the world.

Glossary

academic literacy a collective term referring to all individual literacies needed to contribute effectively to the work of a discourse community.
active learning learning based on the student's direct participation in the learning process.
add-on provision extra-curricular, opt-in learning activities – like workshops on developing search strategies offered by academic librarians – that complement formal elements of the learning framework, like lectures.
analysis breaking down an interpretation, body of evidence or data set through close examination.
asynchronous learning learning activities that aren't live; you can engage with them at a time that is convenient to you (e.g. an e-lesson on Moodle or Blackboard, or a video hosted on YouTube).
behaviourism a learning theory based on the principle that effective behaviours can be taught through training and repeated actions.
citation searching the process of looking for citations (i.e. references) to, for example, a specific journal article, book, or book chapter in other academic sources.
cognitive resilience the ability to stay focused on objectives while managing external pressures, some of which may be academic in nature (e.g. exams).
constructivism a learning theory which emphasises the role of the individual (i.e. you, as a student) in constructing knowledge and developing understanding by participating in the learning activities on your course, by interacting with your tutors and fellow students, and by reflecting on prior learning.
conventions characteristic features of writing within a particular discipline.
criticality the quality of 'being critical'; an ability to think critically and to then communicate that critical thought.
curriculum components of a course of study for a degree or similar qualification; a framework used to structure the learning undertaken at a university.

databases collections of indexed references; a tool used to extend search strategy.

deep-level learning learning focused on developing understanding of how knowledge is applied, its context, and how it is linked to other knowledge; the opposite of surface-level learning.

discourse academic debate or discussion within a specific discipline found in a variety of different academic source types; most closely associated with academic journals and journal articles.

discourse community a group of academics brought together by a shared interest in a discipline who together contribute to the creation and development of discourse within that discipline community.

discovery service the search system or service used to find books, journal articles, and other academic sources held by your university's library.

epistemology the study of the nature and foundation of knowledge; how something is known.

evaluation assessing the relative value of a factor (relative to that of other factors).

flow [in writing] the sense of progression in writing; the connectedness of sentences within a paragraph.

formative assessment assessment that doesn't contribute towards your final mark for a module; its purpose is to allow both you and your tutor to assess your progress up to that point, with a view to helping you to identify areas for development prior to the submission of a summative assessment.

graduate attributes personal attributes, skills, or competencies which a student can expect to develop throughout the course of a programme of study (i.e. a degree).

graduate capital resources, skills, and personal attributes valued by employers in graduates.

graduate identity an identity defined by the competencies and capabilities associated with being a graduate.

intended learning outcomes (ILOs) statements reflecting the objectives of a learning activity, often phrased using verbs; what you, as a student, can expect to take away from engaging in such activities.

keywords words or phrases used in the practice of searching.

knowledge broadly defined here as the interpretations of data, facts, evidence, understanding, and insights which emerge out of the discourse. Knowledge is the currency of the discourse community.

language of criticality words or phrases used to flag up critical use of academic sources, usually in writing.

learning framework the organisation of the different elements of your learning experience that build towards the completion of an assessment task.

lifelong learner (and learning) a person who willingly engages in learning – in academic or professional contexts – beyond compulsory education.

limiter(s) filters incorporated into a discovery service which can be applied in order to refine search results.

literacies defined here as skills combined with an understanding of why each one is important within the context of learning at university.

marking criteria what tutors look for in assessed work; the measures used to determine your overall mark for an assessed piece of work.

mastery expert-level knowledge and understanding.

mindset a set of attitudes held by someone.

peer-reviewed the editorial process through which journal articles pass prior to publication; work is checked by other academics working in the discipline.

plagiarism the practice of presenting the work of another author as your own without properly acknowledging its source.

rationale the reasons for something (i.e. a decision; the choice of research question).

reading list a list of recommended sources relevant to an assessment or module; this list is often 'indicative', which means it is meant to support your learning or preparation – it's not compulsory to read all the sources on the list.

reflective practice to look back critically at past performances, including actions and decisions taken, in order to bring about an improvement in performance by gaining greater understanding of the self (i.e. you).

search strategy a structured and carefully planned approach to searching built around the use and refinement of keywords.

self-efficacy a belief in your ability to do something.

self-regulated learning (and self-regulating learner) an approach to learning in which a student directs their own learning, monitors their performance, reflects on it, and then takes practical steps to bring about an improvement.

sense-making understanding developed by linking newly learnt knowledge to knowledge already held.

student-centred learning learning that is shaped around an awareness of each student's ability and learning style; tutors act as the facilitator of learning within such an approach.

summative assessment an assessment task designed to evaluate your performance; the mark you receive contributes towards your overall mark for the module or degree programme.

surface-level learning a narrow approach to learning focused only on what is needed in the short term; there is little attempt to understand how such knowledge might be applied; the opposite of deep-level learning.

synchronous learning learning activities in which you engage at the same time as the tutor and other students; for example, a lecture.

synonym a word that means the same as another word; often used in searching to enhance search results.

synthesis (synthesising) the ability to draw evidence together – or different and often contradictory interpretations – in expressing your own view.

systematic review a structured search that involves reviewing all existing research on a specified topic with a view to gaining an overview of the relevant discourse.

transferable skills skills or competencies that can used across a variety of professional contexts.

tutor-centred learning learning that is centred on the tutor: the tutor determines what to learn and when, as the expert in the discipline; students have little choice in this approach and are expected to follow the instructions of the tutor.

Chapter 1

Introduction

This book is about *excelling* at university. By *excelling*, we're not just talking about finding success – getting those really high marks you're looking for so that you can leave university with a good degree. We're talking about exceeding your expectations, making the most of the learning experience at university, and maximising your potential, so that when you leave higher education as a graduate, you can make a meaningful impact on the world through your chosen career path.

The last part of that definition – about making an impact on the world – seems quite daunting, doesn't it? But this book is about more than simply 'study skills' or learning about tricks and techniques to help you study *in the right way*. This book is about your personal development, your growth as an individual as you move through the experience of learning at university, developing the competencies and expertise that sit at the heart of your identity as a graduate. *Excelling* at university, therefore, is about *becoming a graduate*.

All of this might seem beyond what you were expecting when you picked up a book that, at first glance, is about studying. But we are very deliberately positioning this book outside the field of traditional 'study skills' textbooks. A lot of what's in this book will overlap with the content of these titles, but we have a different, fresher, more authentic perspective on what you need to know to excel at university. While it's certainly important to offer you practical guidance on effective practices related to studying – as we do throughout this book – we also feel that to give you that extra bit of insight and understanding, that additional push needed to excel, you need to appreciate *why* you are expected to do things in a certain way, what the rationale is for doing so, and what objectives your tutors are working towards as they design and deliver your learning experience. Our aim, therefore, is to open up the practice of studying at university by exploring what tutors expect of you, as learners, as you participate in the learning experience. This will allow you to see the practice of learning at university from a tutor's perspective; as such, it will allow you to build an awareness of the value of what we call the *literacies* associated with academic excellence to your personal development.

DOI: 10.4324/9781003217527-1

If you're new to studying at university, this book will give you a head start; if you've already started, it will give you a boost. Either way, there's something in here for everyone, whether you want to read it cover to cover or dip in and out as and when you need some guidance.

Why read this book?

Why should you spend time reading this book when there are many other titles available in your university's virtual library? Well, as we've already said, this book stands apart from similar titles that look at studying at university. The majority of these books can be described as 'study skills' textbooks, which often provide bits of useful advice on *how* to do certain things, such as writing an essay. However, many of these books only scratch the surface of these topic areas; less time is spent on explaining to the student reader *why* a particular 'skill' is important within your tutors' conception of learning at university. Our approach has other distinguishing features:

It is aspirational

A problem with some 'study skills' books is that they are pitched at a lower level. This is not meant to be a criticism. Some students, for example, who are either entirely new to studying at university or have come back into education after a long break away worry a great deal about whether they're going to pass their course; excelling is not in their minds to begin with! Practical advice on planning a piece of written work, for example, or prompts on where to get help on financial support is vital for many students. While books pitched at this level can therefore have a great impact on student learning, they are less useful for the many students who already possess this knowledge and feel fairly confident about much of the work they're doing. Our book is pitched at a level to help both new students and those students who are already doing well but want to do even better. This is why its approach – to explain *why* each skill area is important within the idea of excelling in your studies – is key; the insights it yields will give you a sharper understanding of what tutors are looking for in assessed pieces of work. In other words, we're looking up!

Literacies rather than 'study skills'

In keeping with its aspirational approach, we conceive of the competencies usually referred to collectively by tutors as 'study skills' as *literacies. Literacies is an over-used term among academics working in the field of learning and teaching at university; its use here is potentially problematic, since it might confuse rather than clarify the objectives of this book (Lillis

& Scott, 2007). Here, we effectively extend the definition of 'academic literacy' offered by Ursula Wingate as a collection of competencies you, as a student, need to acquire when beginning to study a new academic discipline. She adds that these competencies 'require knowledge of the community's *epistemology, of the genres through which the community interacts, and of the conventions that regulate these interactions' (Wingate, 2018, p. 350). It is these *conventions in particular that we are concerned with in this book: the expectations of tutors, often unseen, that you need to meet if you're going to excel.

We use literacies here to describe a particular skill (e.g., searching for academic sources via a library discovery service) combined with an understanding of its significance in relation to assessment criteria and effective studying, as well as its broader value as a formative element of graduate identity. What does this mean? The skill is the *how* to do something, understanding its significance is the *why*, while the awareness of its place within graduate identity is its *value*. Conceiving of the skills traditionally associated with studying as *literacies* is important since it will deepen your understanding of tutors' expectations, particularly when it comes to assessed work. In addition, it helps you to see the broader value of your learning experience in higher education to your personal development as you seek to become a graduate.

Taking a longer view of the learning experience

Whereas many 'study skills' textbooks focus largely on the here and now of studying at university – the day-to-day tasks in which you engage as you tackle the requirements of your course – we take a longer view of the learning experience by setting our guidance within a personal development context. This aspect of our approach aligns it quite closely with the overriding objectives of degree-level courses, since curricula at universities are now designed quite deliberately to develop specific characteristics and qualities within each student. In other words, universities are working towards helping you to *become a graduate*, just as much as we are in this book (Holmes, 2015; Yorke, 2004). We include reflective exercises which at first glance you might be tempted to dismiss; but engaging with these exercises is vital to your personal development since they encourage you to think more deeply about *what* you do, *how* you do it, and *why* you need to do it.

Opening up the practice of studying by exploring tutors' expectations of you, as a learner

Opening up the practice of studying by exploring tutors' expectations forms one of this book's key features. If we are taking a longer view of the learning experience that is less apparent in many 'study skills' textbooks, and if we conceive of these skills as 'literacies', then it makes perfect sense to open up for you the practice of studying by looking at it from the perspective of tutors. If you have a better understanding of the importance of learning outcomes in the process of designing a module, of the rationale behind setting an assessment task within a professional scenario, and of how tutors conceive the assessment and feedback process more broadly, then it will undoubtedly help you to excel and to draw more benefit out of the learning experience for your own personal development.

How does this book work?

The book is structured logically, beginning with some chapters that explore the nature of learning at university, its structure, and how you, as a student, are expected to engage with the 'learning framework'. These chapters provide the foundation on which the rest of the book sits, and so even if you're a more experienced student, you might find it helpful to review them.

To begin with, in Chapter 2, we set out to define what we mean by 'excelling' at university. The notion of 'excelling' – in the sense of surpassing your expectations as to what you might gain from the learning experience at university – should be interpreted in two ways: (i) in relation to your academic performance, particularly in assessed work, and (ii) as it might be applied to your personal development, as you seek to become a graduate. One of the key themes of this book is the need to recognise the broader value of the learning experience to the formation of your graduate identity. This involves acknowledging the significance of each of the literacies discussed here to the development of the attributes associated with that identity. Thus, writing for assessment clearly holds value in terms of academic performance, but it also supports the development of an ability to write for different audiences, something graduates are expected to be able to do. And so, in this chapter, we explore the importance of mindset, motivation, and goal setting, aspects of a successful approach to learning that will help you to excel.

In Chapter 3, on learning at university, we broaden the scope of the discussion by looking in more detail at how learning is conceived by tutors. We look at the idea of the discourse community, for example, which helps to explain what we mean by the 'journey' you embark on as a new student. We look at the nature of learning within this context and discuss how tutors go about designing learning with a view to helping you better understand their expectations. The chapter also includes an overview of what we call the 'learning framework', a model which sets out the different elements of learning and highlights the links between them. This chapter, together with Chapter 2, helps to set the scene for Chapter 4, on 'self-regulated learning'. Here, we set out an approach to learning, which builds on our discussion of mindset, motivation, and goal setting in Chapter 2. Self-regulated learning requires you, as a learner, to engage actively in all elements of learning, as they are set out in the learning framework. It is driven by a process of self-reflection, which we discuss in the chapter through examples.

As we've noted, these chapters form the foundation on which the discussion of individual literacies in the rest of the book sits. Having established this foundation, the starting point for our discussion of literacies has to be assessment, since it provides the context for much of the guidance offered. Chapter 5, therefore, on 'understanding assessment', explores the role of assessment in your learning journey, its value to both you and your tutors as a driver of learning, the different forms it takes, and how it is designed by tutors. We also look more closely at marking criteria, the measures used by tutors to assess your work. Doing so helps to bring into sharper focus what tutors look for when they assess your work and, as a consequence, the importance of developing the literacies we discuss. Chapter 5 is very closely linked to Chapter 6, on 'making effective use of feedback'. Feedback on assessed work, provided by tutors, is meant to be used by you, as a learner; in the context of self-regulated learning, feedback holds special value as a means of better understanding how you might go about improving your performance. It is this point that we stress throughout this chapter.

With a greater awareness of assessment practice and the role played by assessment and feedback within learning at university, in Chapter 7, we turn to 'research' and the importance of developing effective search strategies as you go about engaging with discourse. Here, we set out the principles of effective searching using your university library's discovery service. The key point is that searching is more complex than you might think. If it is to be effective, it requires planning and careful consideration. Moreover, it is at the research stage when you begin to engage critically with the discourse, a point we highlight in the chapter through exemplars of students conducting searches. In this way, the chapter segues neatly into Chapter 8, on 'critical thought and writing'. Successful academic performance in the majority of assessments will depend on how effectively you've engaged with academic sources. In this chapter, we explore what 'critical thought' means – and what it looks like in writing – and how it is developed by carefully engaging with the discourse and gradually building up a plan for your written work. In the second half of the chapter, we look at some of the techniques you can use to flag up to your reader where you are engaging critically with these sources. What we call the 'language of criticality' is particularly important here, for it highlights how 'being *more* critical' (e.g., as tutors often note in feedback) is often about the way you present the interpretations you find.

'Writing for assessment', the subject of Chapter 9, provides an overview of (i) the theory that underpins effective writing for assessment and (ii) the practice of writing. In the first aspect, we examine the idea of 'writing within disciplines', the notion that writing conventions differ across disciplines and that one of the main challenges for new students is to familiarise themselves with these conventions. Tutors' expectations, of course, are shaped by these conventions. The second aspect of theory we discuss is that there are a number of different genres of writing underneath the more general term 'academic writing'. A second challenge therefore is about recognising these different genres and tailoring your writing so that it meets the requirements of each one. Developing an ability to write successfully across different genres helps to develop a writing agility which will only enhance the communication element of your graduate identity. In the second part of the chapter, we look in more detail at the process of creating assessed written work, from understanding the assessment question or task, through to editing and proofreading. In between, we consider such things as the importance of structure, how to write introductions and conclusions, and the importance of offering relevant judgements.

In Chapter 10, we look at referencing within the broader context of 'academic integrity'. Referencing itself is clearly an important part of academic practice at university. Here, we stress its broader value as a means for you, as a learner, to demonstrate your engagement with the relevant discourse. Academic integrity, as a topic, is more important now than ever before, with many students considering how to make use of generative AI. It's therefore important to situate referencing and the anxiety it can cause within this broader context. In addressing academic integrity, we set out the values associated with it. Such values are directly related to your graduate identity and so careful consideration of them supports your efforts to become a graduate.

Chapter 11 is about presentations and group work, two modes of assessment that are widely used across a number of disciplines, often to imitate real scenarios in the professional world. In our discussion of each type of assessment, we put the experience of completing it first. We look, for example, at the anxiety you might feel when presenting and the frustration working with others can sometimes provide. Guidance offered here therefore concerns not only how to put together and deliver an effective presentation and how to engage successfully in group work; it also addresses ways of overcoming the challenges associated with each assessment type. Chapter 12, on 'practice and work-based learning', adopts a similar approach. We begin by considering the value of such learning to your personal development and to the process of becoming a graduate. We discuss the importance of reflecting on such experiences as a driver of personal development; we do this by looking at an example of reflective writing concerning a student teacher's lesson on digital communities. Revision and strategies for optimising your performance in exams are considered in Chapter 13. We begin by addressing the experience of taking exams, as we did in Chapter 11 with presentations and group work, focusing on the anxiety many students feel, and we look at ways of offsetting stress by adopting an organised approach to exam management. In addition, we set out a variety of active learning revision techniques which will help you to develop deep-level knowledge in preparation for exams. Such techniques also work towards alleviating any anxiety you might feel. We conclude the book by encouraging you to reflect on the value of your learning experiences to the build-up of your 'graduate capital'. Identifying how the learning experience at university has enriched your personal development is a key part of preparing to enter the workplace as a graduate. It's therefore important for you to have a good sense of what you would bring to a graduate position before you begin the process of applying such roles.

We've included objectives at the start of each chapter, to help focus your attention on what we think are the key points relating to each literacy, and keywords, which correspond to a glossary. Each term marked in the text with an asterisk (*) is defined in the glossary. Many of these terms will be used by your tutors; you'll even find some of them in the feedback you get on assessed work. This part of the book therefore provides a useful reference point for you whenever you come across a term you don't fully understand. You'll find examples and exercises to help illustrate key points, and each chapter includes reflective tasks aimed at focusing your attention on personal development. You might be inclined to skip these exercises, but don't! Reflective practice, as we'll go on to stress, forms a key part of learning at university and – by extension – excelling in your studies, and so it's really important for you to engage with them.

The onus, throughout all of this, is on you, the learner. It's up to you how far you engage with the guidance on offer. If you want to get the most out of this book as possible, we recommend doing as many of the exercises as possible. If you just want to refresh your mind on aspects of the writing process then you can just read through the relevant guidance. But for the learning to stick, we urge you to complete the tasks.

The learning challenge

It goes without saying that not every reader of this book will be studying on the same degree programme. Some of you will be studying disciplines in the humanities, while others will be working in the sciences, business and management, or practice-based disciplines like social work. The examples we use may not on the surface look immediately relevant to you, but many of the principles we are illustrating will be. The challenge to you, as the learner, is to identify, understand and then reflect on these principles, before considering how they might be applied in your own discipline, and how you might use them to bring about an improvement in your approach to assessed work. Much of this book, as you will see, is about building up your awareness of the principles that underpin successful academic study at university. It's up to you to determine how you can use these principles in your own work.

References

Holmes, L. (2015). Becoming a graduate: The warranting of an emergent identity. *Education & Training*, 57(2), 219–238.

Lillis, T., & Scott, M. (2007). Defining academic literacies research: Issues of epistemology, ideology and strategy. *Journal of Applied Linguistics*, 4(1), 5–32.

Wingate, U. (2018). Academic literacy across the curriculum: Towards a collaborative instructional approach. *Language Teaching*, 51(3), 349–364.

Yorke, M. (2004). Employability in the undergraduate curriculum: Some student perspectives. *European Journal of Education*, 39(4), 409–427.

Chapter 2

Excelling at university
Mindset, motivation, and goals

The starting point for this book must be a chapter exploring what we mean by *excelling* at university. You're probably expecting us to talk here about what it means to be *successful* on your degree programme. We'll do some of that in this chapter, but we want to push this discussion beyond what you might already be thinking about success by setting it in a broader context, one that considers your approach to learning, your mindset, what motivates you, and how confident you feel about your own abilities. All of these factors influence your chances of finding success – and therefore excelling – in your studies, but they're also of critical importance to your development as an individual.

Success is often seen in terms of results: a certain percentage that might represent 'a good mark' or a degree classification that reflects above average academic performance. Success is, of course, about these things, but, at the same time, in higher education today, it's about much more than that. Universities seek to prepare you for the workplace: a degree programme is meant to help you to *become a graduate*. Success is therefore measured not just in terms of the marks you get but also in your growth as an individual, as you develop the attributes associated with *graduate identity by engaging with the different elements of your degree programme.

This chapter is therefore more concerned with the psychology of effective learning than with the criteria you need to meet in order to find success in your academic work. We define success and consider what excelling means in light of this definition, but we're also going to focus on you, as an individual, and your approach to studying. This involves some self-reflection, the results of which will be really useful to you as you look for more effective ways of working.

Learning Objectives

By the end of this chapter, you will have gained:

- a clear understanding of what we mean by excelling at university and its relationship to success;
- an appreciation of the importance of assessing success in terms of academic performance, but also in relation to personal growth and the process of becoming a graduate;
- an awareness of the importance of developing a mindset geared to success;
- an understanding of the significance of self-efficacy beliefs to excelling;
- greater awareness of the importance of understanding your motivation and how it relates to your chances of finding success and of excelling;
- an appreciation of the importance of setting goals in building confidence and maximising your chances of excelling.

Keywords

assessment criteria; self-efficacy; self-regulated learning; mastery experiences; graduate attributes; mindset; motivation; goal setting

Defining success and the notion of 'excelling'

If we were to ask three different undergraduate students on the same degree programme what 'success' in relation to their experience of studying at university means to them, we would almost certainly get three different answers. That's because notions of success are subjective – they're personal, in that everyone faces different challenges, has different conceptions of their own abilities (something called *self-efficacy, which we'll come back to shortly), different levels of confidence when it comes to engaging with their course, and different personal goals. Our understanding of success is also determined by the timeframe in which it sits: short-term success might include contributing in a meaningful way to a workshop or tutorial; medium-term success might be reflected in the mark attained for a piece of formative assessment; and long-term success might be found in the degree classification you end up receiving. Setting aside these nuances, success at university can be seen broadly in two different ways: (i) in relation to academic performance (i.e., specifically, the marks you get); and (ii) in relation to personal development, as you seek to develop the attributes associated with graduate identity by engaging in the different learning experiences associated with your course.

Success: Academic performance

Success in relation to academic performance can take many forms because the learning experience associated with your degree programme has lots of different elements. We've already referred to the example of participating effectively in a workshop or tutorial. For new students in particular, such an experience might represent a significant academic challenge. Taking on such a challenge and performing well therefore represents a considerable achievement for these students. Other tasks associated with the literacies we're going to talk about in this book might represent similar challenges for some. Research, for example, is an aspect of studying which some students find difficult early on in their course, as is writing for assessment. A challenge facing all students is recognising the situations that represent learning challenges, however big or small, which need to be overcome to find success. It's not just new students who face such challenges. A final year undergraduate, for example, will meet lots of them as they work on a dissertation. Similarly, studying on a postgraduate course will throw up a variety of new challenges. Acknowledging when you have successfully overcome such challenges is key to building confidence. The point is that success isn't just about the marks you get for assessments; it's about how effectively you engage with all elements of the learning experience on your course.

That said, success in relation to academic performance is for many students about how well they do on assessed tasks. Clearly, marks are important because they give you an immediate sense of how well you're doing. Good marks – or marks that are higher than expected – build confidence; disappointing marks can undermine confidence. When seen in the context of learning within a *discourse community, a community focused on a particular discipline (e.g., English literature or human resource management) in which your degree programme represents the journey you take as you move from 'beginner' to 'expert', good marks point towards your growing *mastery of the discipline (Lave & Wenger, 1991). In other words, you're on the right track. Disappointing marks suggest the opposite: that you're finding it difficult to develop this sense of mastery.

Success in relation to academic performance can therefore be seen as the steps you take on that journey as you work towards mastery of your discipline. It's about setting goals and achieving them. The goals can be quite specific: attending a particular lecture, gaining a good understanding of a particular topic, or identifying areas for improvement based on the feedback you receive for an assessment. As long as each one represents a step forward in relation to the development of your knowledge and understanding in relation to your discipline then achieving it represents a success.

Task: Success and academic performance

What tasks are you facing this week? Which tasks are the most challenging? What does success look like in relation to each of these challenges?

To help you, let's have a look at an example. Jess has a busy week ahead of her: lectures on Monday and Wednesday, a tutorial on Tuesday, and she intends to go to a workshop on Thursday about advanced searching for academic sources using databases. This workshop, she thinks, will be really important as she works on her next assessment.

Jess looks at her timetable for the week ahead. Her goal for this week is to get a good understanding of how she can use databases in her research to find a broader range of suitable academic sources for her next assessment. Getting the most she can out of the workshop therefore represents the most significant challenge she faces this week. She reasons that success in relation to this goal can be measured by looking at the number of relevant sources she finds after the session by using a relevant database which she didn't know about already. She makes a list of questions she'd like answers to before the workshop. In the workshop, she notes down some of the guidance offered by the librarian and has a go at using the database. Using it provides her with an opportunity to ask some of those questions on her list; she does, and she makes a note of the librarian's replies. In her own time, she practises using the database. Not only does she find a broader range of sources; she also finds recently published sources that provide her with an entirely new perspective on the topic. This represents a great success for her.

Jess identifies the greatest challenge she's facing this week by considering what she wants to achieve by the end of the week. Because she has a clear goal, it's easier for her to recognise what success might look like in relation to that challenge. She wants to develop her research skills; the effectiveness of these skills can be measured by considering what sources she finds using a database. In the end, she achieves more than she had expected: she finds recently published sources which open up for her another way of looking at the topic. All of this represents a huge success for Jess.

> Over to you. Here are some questions to help you structure your thinking:
>
> - What tasks are you facing this week?
> - What is your goal for the week ahead?
> - Which task represents the most significant challenge?
> - What does success look like in relation to that challenge?
>
> Write out your thoughts as a diary entry. Explain your responses to the above questions. Try to be as clear as possible when it comes to explaining what success might look like. Although this might seem like a lot of work, if you get into the habit of noting down tasks, establishing goals and identifying potential challenges, you'll gradually build up your confidence.

Success: Personal development

As this discussion of overcoming challenges suggests, success is about more than just your academic performance; it's about your development as an individual, as you work towards becoming a graduate. Learning at university is shaped by an employability agenda. Employability has been defined by one leading academic as a set of 'achievements': the development of skills, understanding and personal attributes which when combined make it more likely that you, as a graduate, will find the sort of employment you're looking for (Yorke, 2006). What this means is that the learning activities (such as assessments) which make up your degree programme are intended to develop both discipline-specific literacies (i.e., those that are directly related to the discipline in which you are studying) and what are often called *graduate attributes, competencies and behaviours that can be applied more broadly across a range of disciplines.

Each university has their own framework for developing graduate attributes which informs the design of the learning on your course. In many cases, learning objectives at a module level will be informed by these attributes so that you can clearly see how and where you will be developing each one. What do these attributes look like? Some are quite common, appearing across a number of institutions' frameworks. Examples include *communication*, in the sense of the ability to communicate clearly in a variety of ways. This might sound simple, but communicating complex information to different audiences, and through different means (i.e., in person via a presentation, in an email, or in a formal report) is not as easy as it sounds. Tutors therefore try to help you to develop the ability to adapt information and the way it is presented according to context by devising assessments based on different genres of writing. Other common attributes include: *time management, self-organisation, working in a team,* and *problem solving.* Some frameworks include attributes that are linked more closely to the workplace: *managing others,* for example, *working under pressure,* and, significantly, *making effective decisions.* (We'll meet decision making a number of times in this book; it's one of the defining features of *self-regulated learning.)

In addition to all of this, frameworks now emphasise certain attributes that reflect the ever-changing nature of the world in which we live. If you think about it, today's society is very different from society 10 or 20 years ago. The internet, for example, has fundamentally changed the way we engage with information as well as with each other, and this has inevitably impacted upon the workplace. The effects of the global pandemic in recent years have had a further impact on the way we work, with many people now based at home or working in a hybrid way. In short, these changes have meant that while attributes like those discussed above are still important, they've been overtaken by other, more in vogue attributes. *Creativity,* for example, in the sense of thinking innovatively in order to solve problems, features prominently among graduate attributes today, as does *adaptability* and *flexibility.* Universities are trying to prepare graduates for an uncertain future, where tomorrow's jobs are not yet properly defined (Barnett, 2012). Tutors are aware of this; it helps to shape the way learning is designed.

What does success in relation to personal development look like? It's not simply about developing stronger communication skills or feeling more confident about solving problems. It's more about recognising the value of the different aspects of studying in which you engage as you move through your course in relation to the development of these graduate attributes. What do you get out of these experiences? How does each one help you to become a graduate?

Let's look at an example. Here's part of Jess' reflection on a group task she worked on.

> *I felt frustrated while working on the presentation. This was because at least two members of the group weren't contributing properly. I wanted to get a good mark for the assessment, but they initially didn't seem that bothered about how well they did. As the project leader, I discussed with each of them which aspects of the project they would enjoy doing and how they might contribute effectively to the work. Having done this, we completed the presentation and delivered it reasonably well. We got a fairly decent mark, but I was disappointed with it. On reflection, when I think of the experience as a whole, I can see that it's given me valuable insights into how I might motivate others.*

In what ways do you think Jess' experience was valuable? She goes on to highlight the insights into leadership it offered. As the designated project leader, she had to motivate the two less engaged students by giving them each an area of responsibility. She had to think carefully about what to say and how to encourage their participation. In other words, how to work successfully with others. She also had to think about her communication skills, not just in terms of delivering the presentation, but in relation to how she got across her ideas when discussing the project with the other team members. Although the experience might've been frustrating for her, and the team didn't do as well as she would've liked, on a personal level, the experience was a success for Jess because she can see how it has helped her to develop stronger interpersonal skills, her ability to mediate with others, her communication skills, and her ability to lead others.

Task: Recognising the broader value of learning experiences

> Think back to a recent learning experience you've had on your course. Ideally, it should be an experience you didn't enjoy or that you found challenging. Think broadly: you could use an assessment, but what about something like a tutorial you took part in, or an in-class discussion or test? What was the broader value, related to your personal development, of that experience?
>
> You might like to look at your own university's graduate attributes framework to inform your answer. If you don't know where you can find it, ask your tutor or another member of staff. Look at it carefully: remember, it presents the personal qualities your university is trying to cultivate in you. Can you find any links between the framework and the experience you're reflecting on?

What is 'excelling'?

At a basic level, *excelling* is about doing really, really well. But what does this mean? We've seen that success in terms of academic performance is about the steps you take as you work towards mastery of your discipline: achieving the goals you set for yourself as you move through your course. Excelling is about exceeding expectations: achieving those goals and more. In other words, performing better than you had expected. In terms of personal development, whereas success lies in building an awareness of the broader value of the learning experiences on your course, excelling is about effecting tangible growth in relation to the competencies and behaviours involved – tangible in the sense that you can see your progress. Let's look at an example.

Jess, in the example above, excelled in her research task. Her goal had been to get a good understanding of databases to help her find a broader range of academic sources. She not only achieved this; she went beyond it. After finding more sources, she discovered an entirely new perspective on the topic which has only recently been published. This is excelling. Having achieved her goal, Jess' efforts yield a further success: finding this new perspective. She's achieved more than she set out to do. She's excelled in her task.

Jess' efforts not only impacted upon her academic performance. She also recognised the value of the experience in encouraging her to take greater control of her learning, make effective decisions, and use her initiative to improve her marks. The database workshop was an 'opt-in' event: she didn't need to go, but she decided to attend to develop her research skills. The success of the experience, and the fact that she would go to similar events in the future, provides tangible evidence of her growth as an individual.

Finding success and excelling at university is about three, inter-related factors: (i) your *mindset, (ii) your motivation, and (iii) the goals you set for yourself.

Your **mindset** is key. By mindset, we're referring to your attitude towards studying as a whole, including to the challenges you might face as you progress through your course. How do you conceive of studying? Does it represent, for you, a potentially transformative experience through which you might develop as an individual? Or does it simply represent a series of tests, your performance in which will ultimately be consistent with what you already know about your own capabilities? In addition, your mindset includes the way you conceive of yourself, your character, your capability, and your willingness to work hard in pursuit of your goals.

Linked to mindset is **motivation**. What pushes you to engage fully with your course? What sustains your effort? Why are you doing your course? What do you hope to get out of it? Understanding your motivation will help you to gain a better sense of yourself, as a learner, and how a change to your way of thinking might bring about an improvement in performance.

Goals emerge out of motivation, in that what motivates you determines what you are working towards. We've already met the idea of goal setting in our discussion of success. Here, it's important to stress the value of goals not only in academic achievement but also in personal development. Achieving goals helps to build confidence and confidence boosts your belief in your own capabilities and therefore your chances of excelling on your course.

Let's look more closely at each of these elements in turn.

Excelling as a mindset

If you're going to excel at university, you need to develop a mindset geared towards success. We mentioned above that mindset is about attitude; at a more refined level, it's also made up of the beliefs you hold about your own abilities and chances of finding success. It's shaped by experience. In the case of a degree programme, relevant experiences are all those things you do daily as you engage in the requirements of your degree programme, such as carrying out research using the library's *discovery service (what used to be called a 'library catalogue') or attending a tutorial. If you work hard on these tasks and perform well, you make a connection between the effort you put in and the positive result. This connection will then inform your approach to preparing for the next tutorial because you have reached an understanding that effort equals success. Mindset, as we've said, is key. Possess the right mindset and you'll have a much greater chance of excelling.

Research has highlighted two different types of mindset: fixed and growth (Yeager & Dweck, 2012). Let's look at examples of each one at work.

Tom joined university straight from school. He did well with his A-levels, achieving high grades, and managed to get on to a marketing degree at a prestigious university. Tom's A-level grades reaffirmed his beliefs about his own ability: he was always close to the top of his class at school and so it was inevitable that he would do well in those exams. He didn't really need to work that hard to get good grades, unlike some of his close friends. Tom carries these beliefs into his learning experience at university. For the first assessment on his course, Tom has to write a short critique of a journal article. He skims through the article, making two or three bullet points as he does so. He then writes what he thinks is a critique of the article using these notes. When he gets the mark back, he's shocked to discover that he's got a mark in the low 50s. Clearly, the tutor has got it wrong, he thinks. He ignores the feedback. Laughing about it with one of his friends on the course, he tells him that it was a stupid assessment and that the mark doesn't matter.

What do you make of Tom's mindset? The first thing to notice is that Tom's view of his own academic abilities is *fixed*: he did well on his A-levels and so he thinks that he'll do well on his degree programme – because he's pretty clever (in his view!). In other words, he doesn't link effort to performance. We can see this in his approach to that first assessment. He doesn't really try that hard because he thinks he's clever enough to do well. He isn't. But rather than looking at the feedback to find out why he didn't do as well as he thought he would or how he can do better next time, he laughs it off, blaming the tutor for not marking his work properly and dismissing the assessment as 'stupid'.

Now let's look at Saeideh, a student with a different mindset.

Saeideh worked really hard to get her A-levels. Her grades weren't quite good enough to get into her first-choice university, but she secured a place at another one to study a similar course on business management. Saeideh always did well at school, but that was because she listened to her teachers, tried her hardest, and asked for help when she needed to. For Saeideh, learning is about preparation, application and self-reflection; the only way you improve is by looking back at what you did to understand why things turned out that way. For her first assessment, Saeideh had to compare and contrast two different business management models. She does some basic research on each one to get a better understanding of them, creates a plan which includes similarities and differences, and then writes up her notes. She gets a mark in the high 50s, with which she's disappointed. However, recognising the value of the feedback provided, she reviews her work in light of the tutor's comments and immediately picks out improvements she can make next time round in relation to her writing style. She thinks to herself how useful the assessment was. She feels more confident now about getting higher marks in the 60s and 70s.

The principal difference between Saeideh's mindset and Tom's is that Saeideh recognises the learning potential of that first assessment. This is because Saeideh possesses a *growth* mindset. For her, intelligence is not fixed, as Tom thinks. It's something that develops naturally through hard work and application to task. Saeideh has learnt from experience: throughout her time at school, she's always had in mind the link between effort and success. You reap the rewards of what you put into a task. Assessment for Saeideh, therefore, represents opportunities for further development. Hence, she engages fully with the feedback. Why wouldn't you? The tutor is flagging up for you what you need to do to be more successful next time round. Through application and practice, you can work towards higher marks. Nothing is impossible; just try and try again.

Researchers who have looked into the links between mindset and success have often drawn examples from the world of elite sport. It might help here to use such an example to reinforce the point we're making. Football. And before some of you who don't like football switch off, bear with me. There are lots of young men and women who are really talented when it comes to football. But talent on its own is not enough to reach the very top of the sport. The best players in the world are there because of talent; but they're also there because of the amount of hours they've put in practising, listening to advice from coaches, reviewing their performance (often in minute detail), and by implementing new ways of doing things. In other words, they're at the top because they possess a growth mindset; they're always striving to be better. Young players who think they've 'made it' simply because they've got a professional contract, who don't work hard in training or who ignore any advice given to them, rarely make it to the very top. The same principle applies in education. Success is born out of having the right mindset: it's about effort, hard work, a willingness to listen to advice and guidance, and an awareness of the importance of learning through experience.

Task: What is your mindset?

> Now that we've taken a closer look at the fixed and growth mindsets, it's your turn to reflect on your own attitude towards learning. You can do this task on your own, but it might be better to work with someone else on it. Ask each other the following questions and make a note of your answers:
>
> - What degree classification/range of marks do you expect to get for the assessments on your course?
> - What link does this expectation have to the marks you received for assessed work you did at school or college?
> - What's the highest degree classification/range of marks you think you can achieve? Try to explain your answer.
> - What do you do/will you do with the feedback provided by your tutors on assessed pieces of work?
> - If you receive a lower mark than you expected for an assessed piece of work, how do you react? Does it demoralise you or does it push you to work harder?
>
> Review your answers to these questions. Whose mindset is closer to yours: Tom's or Saeideh's? If your mindset is similar Tom's, what do you need to do to start developing a growth mindset? What aspects of Saeideh's approach to studying are missing from your own?

Moving towards a growth mindset is about (i) being aware of the value to your own learning of the different experiences you meet on your course and (ii) putting into practice some of strategies used by Saeideh to bring about an improvement in performance. For example, making effective use of feedback, a simple yet fundamental element of successful academic practice, the importance of which your tutors will stress throughout your course. How will *you*, as the driving force behind your own personal development, develop a growth mindset?

Self-efficacy

Underpinning your mindset, as well as your motivation and the goals you set for yourself, is something that researchers call self-efficacy. Self-efficacy refers to your belief in your own capacity to work effectively in order to complete a task or achieve a specific goal (Bandura, 1977). It's about the confidence you have in your own ability to do the right things to get – for example – a higher mark on the next piece of assessed work. Belief is key: as we saw in the discussion of mindsets, if you believe that you're going to get a certain mark simply because you're clever enough to get that mark (as Tom did), you're unlikely to react well if the mark you receive is lower than the one expected. Similarly, if you have low self-efficacy, in that you think you're less capable of doing what's needed to complete that task, you're more likely to attribute your failure to a low ability level. This belief reinforces your low self-efficacy and you'll forever be trapped in a cycle of negativity which will work against you ever finding success or excelling. Students with high self-efficacy, on the other hand, see failure in terms of a lack of effort: falling short of expectations is the result of insufficient preparation or a lack of thought when it came to determining what strategies to use. To excel, in addition to developing a growth mindset, you need to build up your self-efficacy.

How do you build up self-efficacy? Research has suggested that self-efficacy can be developed in four main ways:

1 overcoming significant challenges through hard work;
2 seeing a friend find success through hard work;
3 listening to positive feedback from tutors and perhaps also friends and other students;
4 minimising the impact of stress and anxiety on your beliefs and the way you work (Bandura, 1994).

Overcoming significant challenges is usually seen as the most important of these methods. Finding success when tackling challenges – that is, something like an assessment, which has higher stakes than simply finding a particular book on the library's discovery service, for example – has the effect of boosting your confidence in your own ability to do the right things to overcome that challenge. It will, in turn, increase your motivation to succeed because you know what you're capable of doing. It's important to note here the link between self-efficacy and self-regulated learning, since a student with high self-efficacy is implicitly reflecting on what they did and assessing their own performance, both of which are key features of self-regulated learning.

Some researchers have emphasised the link between self-efficacy and the learning environment (Bandura, 2012). The most important ways of developing it, therefore, lie in the interactions you, as a student, have with that environment. For example, recognising how a friend has found success on the same task is useful because that friend provides an example to follow. Taking on board positive feedback helps to sustain belief in your own efficacy, while stopping yourself from being overwhelmed by anxiety effectively protects your confidence from negative thoughts.

Regardless of how you go about building up self-efficacy, it's clear that a student with high self-efficacy is much more likely to excel. That's because such a student feels more confident about achieving success and as a result will be better equipped to take on the challenges associated with successful academic performance. This student will also have a growth mindset, which, as we've seen, is vital to your chances of excelling, and so will embrace tasks and challenges as learning opportunities.

Task: Assessing your self-efficacy

> This is another task you can do either on your own or with a friend.
> How high is your self-efficacy? Think back to a significant challenge you've faced as part of your course, such as an assessment you've recently completed. Did you overcome that challenge? If so, what did you do to get a positive outcome? What was the most significant reason for your success? If you didn't overcome it, why not? What aspect of the challenge proved too much for you?
> Review your answers to these questions. What do they tell you about the level of your self-efficacy? If you didn't overcome the challenge, what might you do differently to get past the next one? In other words, what do you need to do to develop greater self-efficacy?

Understanding your motivation

Broadly speaking, our primary motivation when it comes to studying at university can be linked either to *performance*, in the sense of what marks you receive for assessments, or *learning*, as in the mastery of the discipline, as well as your broader personal development. Motivation is therefore essentially an extension of mindset: the way you conceive of learning determines what sustains all that effort you put into studying (Dweck, 2012).

Let's return to Tom and Saeideh again.

> *Tom is motivated by performance, in that he wants to get 'good' marks for his assessments. Furthermore, he thinks he should because he's pretty clever: he got good A-level grades and so it's logical that he should expect similar outcomes at university. It's important for him to perform well against other students on his course. His approach is shaped by his motivation: he carries out actions that are consistent with it. For example, he attends most of the lectures and tutorials, but he chooses not to go to extra sessions put*

on by the university's employability team because he can't see the relevance of them to any of his assessments. When faced with an assessment he feels less confident about, Tom puts it off until a few days before the submission deadline so that when he gets his mark, which he expects to be low, he can tell his friends it's because he didn't really try.

Saeideh, on the other hand, is motivated by learning. *She wants to gain as much knowledge and understanding about her discipline as she can. As a result, unlike Tom, she isn't selective about which bits of her course she engages with; she goes to everything, to get as much out of her course as possible, including extra-curricular sessions. When the employability team put on a workshop about writing CVs, Saeideh signs up immediately because she recognises what she might get out of it for her own personal development. When she's faced with an assessment she feels less confident about, she sees it as a challenge. She works as hard as she can on it and then considers the feedback carefully so that she can learn as much as possible.*

The first thing to notice about these examples is that motivation essentially reflects mindset. In Tom's case, his focus on performance is directly related to his fixed view of intelligence. It's all about how well he does, particularly when compared to other students, to the extent that he can't see the value of the extra-curricular activities on offer. Saeideh is the opposite. She sees value in all aspects of the course: each element represents an opportunity for learning and personal development, and in this sense the link between her motivation and her growth mindset is clear to see. It's interesting to note how the motivation of each student affects their approach to a challenging assessment. Tom's main concern is to not lose face among his friends, which is why he doesn't put much effort in. Saeideh, on the other hand, relishes the challenge and gives the assessment a good go. Who is more likely to take something positive away from the experience? Here's a clue: it isn't Tom.

What does this brief discussion tell us then about motivation? First, it's underpinned by your self-efficacy. If you feel less confident about your ability to engage successfully with the demands of your course, you're more likely to develop what we would call 'negative' motivation. We've met students, for example, who just want to 'do enough' to get by. It's unlikely that this type of motivation will bring you success; it certainly won't help you to excel. If, on the other hand, you feel more confident about your ability to engage with your course, your motivation will be 'positive'. Like Saeideh, you might see assessments, for example, as challenges that will ultimately help to improve your performance. With this type of motivation, you'll have a much greater chance of finding success and excelling.

Motivation isn't just made up of self-efficacy beliefs though; it's also about the value and relevance you place on an assessment or a learning task. As we saw with Tom, he effectively ignored the extra-curricular elements of his course because he couldn't see any value or relevance in them. As a result, he had minimal interest in them. Saeideh, on the other hand, signs up for the CV writing workshop because she can see its potential value. She knows that she'll be applying for jobs at some stage in the near future and so such a session will be really helpful to her personal development. By seeing its value, she was therefore more interested in it.

Task: Reflecting on your motivation

> What motivates you? Is your motivation similar to Tom's or Saeideh's – is it about performance or learning?
>
> Think about your next assessment: is your motivation to get 'good' marks or are you thinking about how the experience of completing the assessment will help your learning more generally?
>
> It might be a bit of both, in which case, which element is more important to you? Can you see a link between your motivation and your mindset?
>
> It might be helpful to discuss your findings with a friend.

Motivation, of course, is not static; it fluctuates as you respond to different experiences. A better than expected mark for an assessment might increase your motivation whereas a lower mark might demotivate you to some extent. It's important to have in place strategies for sustaining your motivation. A common one is positive self-talk: acknowledging when you've done something well (e.g., 'I did well to read through those journal articles today'). Another is to reward yourself when you've completed a task: I'm going to watch an episode of that programme on tv once I've finished writing this paragraph. But the most effective way of sustaining motivation is by setting achievable goals. The key word here is *achievable*. Setting smaller goals that are more easily attainable, even on a daily basis, is a really effective way of sustaining motivation because completing each one helps to build your confidence and therefore boost your sense of self-efficacy. It's to the setting of goals that we now turn.

Creating goals

Just as motivation serves as an extension of mindset, goals emerge out of motivation. Goals are vital in learning because they act as markers against which you, as a student and ideally a self-regulating learner, can measure your success (Zimmerman et al., 1992). Hence, when it comes to *excelling* at university, creating goals for yourself forms a key part.

Researchers have identified two types of goals. Different names have been given to these goals, but we're going to use *targeted* and *mastery* (Pintrich, 2005). Targeted goals are those which have a quite specific focus on, for example, a piece of assessment. 'In this assessment, I want to get a mark above 65%.' This statement represents a performance goal. Mastery goals, on the other hand, are less specific and more far-reaching. 'In this assessment, I aim to improve the quality of my formal writing so that I can communicate more effectively in professional contexts.' In this statement, there is a higher aspiration linked to forms of communication and the development of graduate attributes. By looking beyond the potential mark that might be awarded to the broader benefits of the experience of completing the assessment, it's more focused on personal development and mastery of the literacies involved.

The type of goal you're likely to set for yourself is determined by your motivation, which, in turn, is shaped by your mindset. Tom, for example, who is focused on performance, sets targeted goals linked to the marks he might get for assessments. Saeideh, who is more aware of the broader value of the learning experience, is more interested in the links between learning and personal development. Students like Tom, with fixed mindsets, who are motivated by performance, are more likely to set targeted goals, whereas students like Saeideh, who have a growth mindset, and who are motivated by learning and personal development, are much more likely to pursue mastery goals.

Clearly, working towards mastery goals will be more beneficial to you, since they're linked to behaviours that are more likely to lead to success and a better chance of excelling. Achieving such goals will boost your confidence, leading to a greater sense of self-efficacy. Such goals will give you a better chance of finding success and excelling. Targeted goals, on the other hand, are more likely to limit success and your chance of excelling because of their links to less efficient approaches to studying. Students who pursue targeted goals are in fact less likely to engage in the behaviours linked to success and excelling because to do so is to acknowledge that to some extent their abilities are deficient in some way.

Task: Defining your goals

> Think about any goals you might have set yourself for today or the coming weeks. Are they more related to performance, like Tom's goals, or mastery, like Saeideh's?

As we've seen, adopting mastery goals holds greater benefit for you because they'll give you a better chance of excelling. If your goals are more performance related, you can turn them into mastery goals by re-phrasing them. For example, you might want to read through three chapters of a book on digital marketing by the end of tomorrow. Why not express this goal in a more aspirational way as 'By the end of tomorrow, I want to have a deeper understanding of the different ways social media has influenced digital marketing'. In this form, the goal is more clearly linked to learning and mastery.

How would you re-phrase the following goals so that they better reflect mastery goals:

1   I want to know how to use databases to find sources.
2   I want to paraphrase this paragraph of text so that I'm not copying the original words.
3   I want to get a mark of 65% or higher for this assessment.

Here are some suggested alternatives:

1   I want to develop my research skills so that I can find a broader range of academic sources for my assessments.
2   I want to develop my understanding of this argument by explaining it in my own words.
3   I want to use this assessment as an opportunity to develop my ability to make critical use of academic sources; if I do this well, I hope to get an improved mark.

Summary

In this chapter, we've looked at what it means to be successful and, more than that, to excel at university. We've done this by looking more closely at elements of the psychology of effective studying: your mindset, what motivates you, and the types of goals you set for yourself. In the course of our discussion, we've tried to highlight for you the mindset, motivation, and goals that are more appropriate for you to develop if you want to find success or you want to excel.

Try to adopt a *growth* mindset, one which recognises the broader value of the learning experiences on your course as opportunities to develop the attributes associated with graduate identity. Coupled with a growth mindset is motivation geared towards *learning*. Look past the marks, for example, to the value of the experience of completing an assessment on your personal development. You're trying to become a graduate and so you're trying to develop the attributes associated with that identity. Finally, set ambitious goals aimed at mastery of the competencies associated with the learning on your course. Use these goals not only to sustain your motivation but to drive your engagement with learning.

References

Bandura, A. (1977). *Social learning theory.* General Learning Press.
Bandura, A. (1994). Self-efficacy. In V. S. Ramachaudran (Ed.), *Encyclopedia of human behavior* (Vol. 4, pp. 71–81). Academic Press.
Bandura, A. (2012). On the functional properties of perceived self-efficacy revisited. *Journal of Management, 38*(1), 9–44.
Barnett, R. (2012). Learning for an unknown future. *Higher Education Research & Development, 31*(1), 65–77.
Dweck, C. S. (2012). *Mindset: How you can fulfil your potential.* Robinson.
Lave, J., & Wenger, E. (1991). *Situated learning: Legitimate peripheral participation.* Cambridge University Press.
Pintrich, P. R. (2005). The role of goal orientation in self-regulated learning. In M. Boekaerts, P. R. Pintrich, & M. Zeidner (Eds.), *Handbook of self-regulation* (pp. 451–502). Academic Press.
Yeager, D. S., & Dweck, C. S. (2012). Mindsets that promote resilience: When students believe that personal characteristics can be developed. *Educational Psychologist, 47*(4), 302–314.
Yorke, M. (2006). *Employability in higher education: What it is – What it is not.* Higher Education Academy.
Zimmerman, B., Bandura, A., & Martinez-Pons, M. (1992). Self-motivation for academic attainment: The role of self-efficacy beliefs and personal goal setting. *American Educational Research Journal, 29*(3), 663–676.

Chapter 3

Defining 'learning' at university

What defines learning at university? In what ways is it different to learning you might have already experienced at school or college – or, perhaps, in the workplace? How do your tutors *conceive* of learning at university? How do they go about designing and delivering the learning and teaching on your course? What do they expect of you, as a learner, when it comes to your engagement with learning?

These are all very important questions. Your understanding of them, as well as your willingness to develop your approach towards the issues they raise, underpins your chances of *excelling* in your assessed work. For example, it's vital for you to appreciate what ideas inform and therefore shape the learning experience created by your tutors. Similarly, understanding *how* tutors expect you to engage in the learning experience is essential if you are to enhance your academic performance by making the most of the learning opportunities available.

In this chapter we take a closer look at the topics raised by these questions. By examining learning at this level in more detail, we start that process of opening up tutors' expectations. This chapter goes hand-in-hand with the next one, on self-regulated learning; it's also linked closely to the one on understanding assessment.

When reading through this chapter, don't forget to pay particular attention to the vocabulary we highlight. As we've just said, one of the aims of this book is to open up the practice of effective learning; making sure you're familiar with the language of learning at university forms a key part of this objective.

Learning Objectives

By the end of this chapter, you will have gained:

- a good understanding of what a discourse community is and how it shapes learning at university, including tutors' expectations of you, as a learner;
- an insight into the different academic literacies, as they are related to the discourse community;
- an appreciation of the nature of learning at university and the difference between surface and deep-level learning;
- an insight into learning design, as seen from the tutor's perspective;
- a greater awareness of how tutors expect you to engage in learning;
- an awareness of the structure and organisation of learning, including an understanding of its key elements.

Keywords

discourse; discourse community; constructing knowledge; sense-making; student-centred learning; constructivism; active learning; learning journey

Learning and the 'discourse community'

Learning at university takes place within what we call a *discourse community (Swales, 1990). The discourse community is an important concept for you to understand, for it neatly captures the essence of what distinguishes learning at university from learning in other contexts.

What do we mean by *discourse? Well, another word for discourse is debate or discussion. The development of *knowledge (we'll come back to this term shortly) in any given discipline (i.e., the subject area in which you are studying, such as marketing, English literature, social work, or fine art) is driven by the discussions that take place between academics working in the field. Knowledge is often contested, meaning that academics working within a discipline do not always share the same views on a particular issue. It is through the debate that accompanies the process of sharing and then discussing these views that deeper levels of insight and agreed understanding emerge.

Community, as it is used here, is an easier concept to understand. It simply refers to a group of people brought together by a shared interest in a discipline or topic area. As a student, this includes you, students already studying on your programme in the other year groups, postgraduates, some of whom will be doing research towards PhDs (doctoral study), and, of course, tutors and senior academic researchers. The collective goal of this community is to develop knowledge within the discipline by interacting with one another. This occurs at a variety of levels including undergraduate and postgraduate study, institutionally, nationally, and even internationally, and through a range of mediums – teaching, informal discussion, conferences, and via specialist publications, for example.

What does this mean for you, as a learner? As a student, on starting your programme of study, you are joining the discourse community related to your discipline. You might not feel, at first, that you are a part of this community, but by attending lectures, discussing relevant ideas or themes in greater detail in tutorials, and completing your assessed work – in other words, by immersing yourself in the study of the discipline – you are interacting with the community and engaging with other members of it.

It's useful to conceive of the community as a circle. As you can see in Figure 3.1, when you join the community at the start of your programme you are effectively sitting at the edge of it as a beginner. As a new student – new, at least, to the work of that community – you are less experienced at working within it. Therefore, at this moment, you are on its periphery. Your tutors, on the other hand, as more experienced members of it, are positioned at the centre. They are the experts, in that they are used to working within the community. As

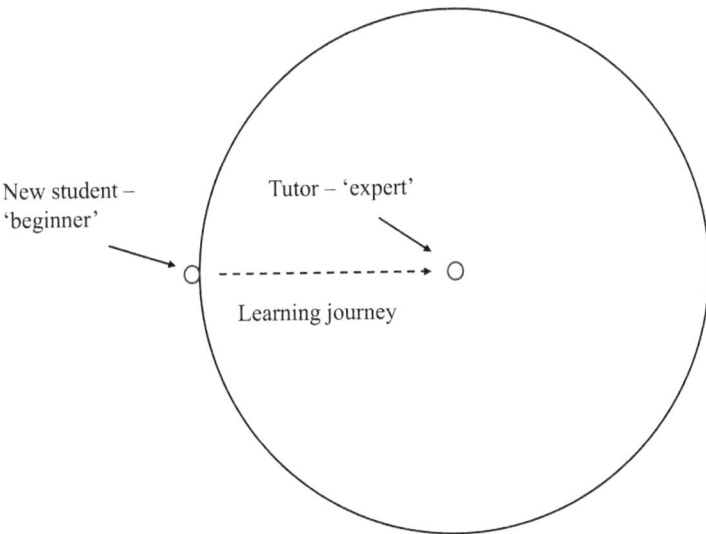

Figure 3.1 The discourse community and a student's learning journey.

you move through your programme of study, therefore, you effectively move from the periphery to the centre, from beginner to expert, as your expertise develops. Your learning experience can therefore be conceived as a journey on which you embark at the start of your programme: from the periphery to the centre of this community (Lave & Wenger, 1991).

What is 'knowledge'?

Knowledge is the outcome of the interactions within the discourse community. While data, facts, information, or evidence forms an important element of knowledge, it is also made up of the understanding and insights that emerge out of the debate that takes place within the community.

Knowledge is therefore better understood as *interpretations* of data, facts, information, or evidence found within a discourse community.

Some important points to note about 'knowledge':

- it is contested, since knowledge isn't fixed;
- since it isn't fixed, knowledge develops through debate within the discourse community;
- within this process of development, knowledge is constructed: academics make use of the work of other scholars in creating their own interpretations;
- interpretations are therefore linked to each other, and so debate can be traced as it develops, something that helps you, as a learner, to understand it.

Where, as a new student, do you find knowledge? It's found in academic sources; in particular, articles found in academic journals. Journal articles are often difficult for new students to engage with, since they assume that the reader already has a good level of understanding of the topic under discussion. But demonstrating that you have engaged with them in your assessed work is essential if you are to *excel*. There are other types of academic sources, such as books and edited collections of essays; but since journal articles are shorter than other source types, more are published, and so articles really sit at the cutting edge of the discourse.

Academic literacy and the discourse community

What, in the end, makes you an 'expert'? Well, the business of the community is to develop knowledge in the discipline through discourse.

Academics will publish research, for example, in academic journals, where they will critique the work of others and offer fresh interpretations of an issue. This research will then form the basis of further research. And so it goes on. As a learner, by submitting assessed work, you are essentially mimicking this process. In your case, particularly as an undergraduate, you are not usually offering 'new' interpretations; instead, you are demonstrating understanding by setting out established knowledge structures (e.g., contrasting views within the discourse). Regardless, in doing so, you are participating in the discourse of your discipline.

When your tutors are assessing your work, they are assessing your ability to contribute to the discourse in your discipline. Your assessed work represents the end product of a long process of research, beginning with identifying suitable sources, critiquing the content of those sources, structuring an argument or point of view in relation to a particular topic, synthesising evidence in support of this argument or point of view, and articulating (usually in writing) that argument or point of view. *This process is characterised by features, conventions, and expectations that are unique to each discipline.* Take the types of academic sources you might be using. A student working in marketing, for example, might be using advertisements in print media, market reports or articles in the Financial Times when completing an assessment, source types that a student working on an essay in English literature would have no need to use and little understanding of the relative value of each source type. Unfortunately, no one sets out these conventions for you in their entirety before you start the course. Instead, you have to figure them out, by reading scholarly work in the discipline, by engaging fully in the learning experience on offer on your course, and by submitting assessed work, reflecting on where you might have gone wrong, and learning through experience. Understanding this simple fact – that the process of creating knowledge varies from discipline to discipline – is key to excelling at university. Your ability to engage effectively with the business of the community is called *academic literacy (Wingate, 2018).

Academic literacy is therefore an umbrella term for all of the literacies discussed in this book which you need to develop as you go about working within your discipline. Each literacy involves a number of different activities. The literacy of research, for example, includes:

- devising a search strategy to identify appropriate academic sources;
- evaluating the relative value of each source;
- determining how you are going to engage with these sources so that you build your knowledge of a topic effectively.

And there are many more. The literacy of critical thought, which involves engaging with academic discourse, includes:

- locating an interpretation within the wider discourse;
- synthesising knowledge in order to create your own interpretation;
- articulating that interpretation in an appropriate way (i.e., in an essay, a poster presentation, a podcast or any other form of assessed work).

As you can see from these short lists, academic literacy is about more than simply acquiring what might be called 'study skills'; it's about *the way you do things*, your behaviour, in the context of working within a discourse community.

What is learning?

If academic literacy is about the way you work within a discourse community, what, then, is learning itself? Learning is essentially made up of two elements:

1. acquiring, understanding and being able to apply knowledge, as it is defined here as interpretations of facts, data, evidence, or information;
2. developing the academic literacy required in order to contribute to the work of the discourse community.

Learning therefore takes different forms and occurs in different ways. For example, it might refer to the process of memorising information that you can then apply in a tutorial or in an assessed piece of work. Similarly, it can refer to the practice of a particular behaviour, such as how to use the university library's discovery service or learning how to perform an experiment in laboratory conditions.

However, learning in higher education is also marked by more complex ideas. First, learning is linked to *sense-making, the notion that understanding is built by linking knowledge together or by connecting it to knowledge you already hold. Second, learning is also about change: the change in your perspective as you see the world differently by acquiring deeper levels of knowledge and understanding. What makes these ideas important is that they reflect the deeper levels of learning that teaching at university aims to nurture among learners. In pushing learning to these deeper levels, tutors ultimately aim to provoke personal transformation and development.

*Deep-level learning is learning based on the development of wider, interrelated understanding. In contrast, *surface-level learning is more often about learning something specific for the sake of knowing it. Tutors aim to develop deep-level learning when they design the learning on your programme of study.

For example, we could give you a factsheet explaining the anatomy of the heart. You could take away this factsheet and learn the names of its chambers and valves, and then reproduce this information if we asked you to. But you probably wouldn't be able to explain to us how the heart actually functioned. This is learning at a surface level. At a deep level, you might learn the names of the chambers and valves, but, in order to develop your understanding, you might explore what each one actually does, and how each one works in relation to the other. In this way, you will be able to demonstrate an understanding of how the heart functions and thus its role within the wider circulatory system.

What does this actually mean for you, as a learner? First, you've probably noticed that learning, as we've described it, is not about simply learning things 'by rote'. In other words, reading something, and then reading it again and again until you have memorised it. This is not the most effective way of learning, simply because you won't gain an understanding of whatever it is you are supposed to be learning. You'll be able to, at best, recite a list of facts, for example, but learning itself will only be at a surface level. Furthermore, learning in this way isn't an *active* process; sitting at a desk reciting information until it sticks is actually quite a passive experience.

Instead, learning is about engaging with knowledge at much deeper levels by sense-making. What does sense-making look like in practice? Sense-making rests on the principle that your knowledge and understanding is constructed. Rather than just memorising information by reciting, sense-making requires you to actively process that information by building knowledge structures. In other words, as you take in new knowledge, you think about it carefully, link it to other newly acquired knowledge and set it in the broader context of what you already know. It's by thinking critically about knowledge that you start to engage with the discourse and develop your own informed perspective on the topic you're researching.

Let's consider an example. Jess is doing some research for her next assessment task on the value of social media in the marketing strategy of clothing retailers. By reading textbooks on social media marketing, complemented by several of the tutor's lectures, she knows, for example, how important it is for companies to utilise the right social media platforms. From her own experiences, she knows that a lot of clothing retailers use Instagram. She then uses this connection between the issue of which social media platform to use and the popularity of Instagram among clothing retailers to inform her search strategy. Using her library's discovery service, she finds a number of journal articles, published in the last five years, on branding and Instagram. Reading through one in particular, she realises that the value of Instagram to clothing retailers lies in its use by influencers to promote and develop brand identity. This observation has the effect of highlighting several other topics she might like to look at as she builds her knowledge. In this way, there are deeper levels of learning going on here as a result of sense-making: linking new knowledge to what Jess already knows.

For some of you reading this, it might be helpful to set out a knowledge structure as you build it. Mind-maps, for example, are a well-known and, for some, very useful, way of depicting knowledge structures visually. Jess' might look like the one in Figure 3.2. Remember, she's extending the knowledge structure as she acquires new knowledge; she's also adding in some references so that she can see, at a glance, which sources relate to each point. It doesn't matter how you do it – which colours you use or whether you create a digital mind-map or a paper-based one. As long as it works for you then it'll be effective.

Building knowledge structures through sense-making encourages you to make use of knowledge you already hold (as seen in Jess' awareness of the use of Instagram by clothing retailers), as well as other learning experiences you might have engaged in, like lectures or tutorials. Connecting such experiences is an important part of learning. Degree courses are designed in such a way so that lectures, for example, feed into discussion topics in tutorials and cover topics used for assessment tasks. Equally important is the need to recognise the value to your learning of existing knowledge. This might be discipline-specific, gained, perhaps, as you studied A-levels or Access courses, or it might take the form of practical experience. Perhaps you had to work on coursework as part of your pre-university studies, a form of assessment which might have given you some insights into research. Tutors will expect you to draw on this knowledge and experience as you engage in the various elements of your course.

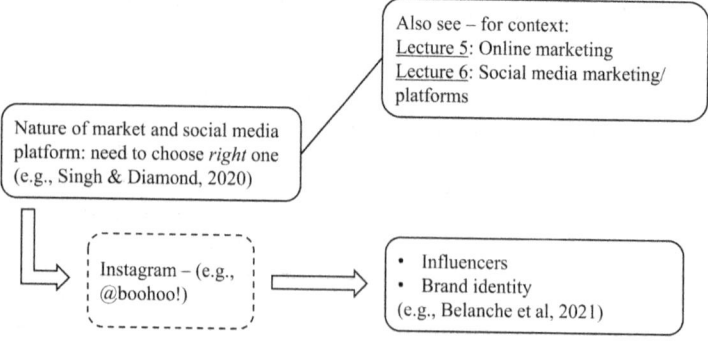

Figure 3.2 Jess' mind-map relating to the use of Instagram by clothing retailers.

How is learning designed?

If learning is more complex than simply memorising information – if it is about building knowledge structures through sense-making – then how do your tutors go about designing the learning in which you engage on your course?

Broadly speaking, learning is designed on the premise that students will actively engage with it. That is to say, students are expected to participate intentionally in the planned learning activities (e.g., lectures and tutorials) with a view to meeting the tutor's *intended learning outcomes, statements that reflect what you, as a student, will get out of each learning activity. 'Actively engage' is the key phrase here; what you're not expected to do is sit in lecture theatres or teaching rooms writing down (or recording) everything a tutor says to you. This type of learning is very passive. It will almost always give you only surface-level knowledge of a given topic; it rarely prompts the development of insights or deeper levels of understanding of that topic. This is why tutors utilise different learning activities when they design degree courses; they don't simply rely on lectures. Tutorials or seminars, for example, provide opportunities for deeper discussions of particular topics with smaller groups of students, facilitated by a tutor. Digital learning resources, used increasingly by tutors, can do the same: a bitesize video, for example, can explore an aspect of a topic in greater depth than might be possible in a lecture. Such a resource might be accompanied by set questions designed to test your understanding of the content. Tutors also use techniques that at first might appear odd to you. The flipped classroom, when you, as a student, are expected to lead a lecture, is an example of one such technique. Tutors aren't using these approaches because they're lazy; they're using them to move away from passive forms of learning to more active ones which promote deep-level learning.

Learning in higher education is designed to be *student-centred as opposed to *tutor-centred. For many years, learning was tutor-centred: its focus was on the tutor as an expert in the discipline and it was the tutor who decided what to learn, when and how. It is easy to associate such an approach with passive learning because it conceives of students almost as empty cups who are then filled up with knowledge by the tutor. Student-centred learning, on the other hand, is prevalent now. Here, the student is the driver of the learning, participating in it actively by engaging in tasks or activities that help develop deeper levels of learning and even, in some cases, making decisions over the pace of learning or the forms of assessment used. Rather than fulfilling the role of expert-teacher, the tutor, in this approach, acts as a facilitator of learning, empowering each individual student to take control over the direction of their personal development.

Many new students, on beginning their course, struggle to appreciate what might at first glance look like a 'hands off' approach on the part of their tutors. However, if you think of the tutor as a facilitator of learning rather than a teacher, as such, you'll better understand why they don't tell you what to do, as a teacher at school or college might have done. In higher education, tutors expect you to take control your own learning. In other words, they don't want to give you instructions; they want you to make your own decisions about your learning. That said, they are there to offer advice and guidance. But it's important that you demonstrate to them an ability to be proactive and to think for yourself.

Learning theory: How do tutors expect you to learn?

There are several learning theories that underpin tutors' decisions when it comes to learning design. Setting them out here will allow you to better understand tutors' expectations as to the way you engage with the learning on your course. It will also give you insights into ways you can develop deeper levels of understanding in your studies.

Constructivism

The most popular learning theory embraced by tutors in higher education is *constructivism. Constructivism is based on the principle that students need to participate actively in their learning in order to learn at deeper levels. Constructivist approaches emphasise the role of you, as a student, in learning; it is up to you to construct knowledge and develop understanding through the learning activities on your course, the interactions you have with your tutors and fellow students, and by reflecting on any relevant prior learning you might have done.

What does constructivism look like in practice, from a student point of view? Learning based on constructivism is characterised by activities: learning by doing. This approach helps to actively engage you, the learner, in the learning process.

For example, Jess attends a workshop on writing for assessment. Part of the workshop is focused on paragraph structure. The tutor sets out a model for arranging the sentences of a paragraph, so that the point being made is clear. The model sets out five sentence types, each one fulfilling a different purpose within the paragraph. An example is provided to show the students how the model might be applied in practice. Jess and the other students in the workshop are then given five different sentences reflecting each type within the model, but they're in the wrong order. Working in pairs, the students are asked to reorganise the sentences in the right order. Jess works with another student, Claire. They discuss each sentence to identify which type it is; having done this, they then put the paragraph back together in the right order. By engaging in the activity – the *doing* part – Jess figures out for herself, with a little bit of help from Claire, how the model works, and how important structure is in writing effectively.

Behaviourism

Constructivism emerged out of scholarly criticism of another learning theory called behaviourism. This theory is based on the principle that behaviour can be developed through teacher-led 'training': through repeated action, driven by clear output-focused outcomes, you, the student, can be trained to do something in a different way. Learning based on this theory tends to be highly structured and focused sharply on these outcomes. It is often associated with surface-level understanding: since its primary focus is on behaviour, it doesn't always allow much room for developing insights or in-depth understanding.

An example of learning based on behaviourism is a training session on how to use the library's discovery service. Here, the session is clearly based on behaviour. A specialist, usually an academic librarian, will demonstrate the most efficient way of searching for – for example – relevant journal articles. There will be a clear process: first, log in to the search engine; second, type your search words into the search box – and so on. At the end of the process, the results of your search – which will include relevant journal articles – will appear. As you can see, the approach is driven by very clear outcomes. In addition, as noted above, you can also see how it often leads to surface-level learning. The focus is on completing the process; much less attention is given to *why* you would look for journal articles ahead of other types of sources or the broader context in which the search sits.

Possessing an awareness of these approaches to learning will help you to appreciate the value of different learning activities. Behaviourist learning, as in the example of using the library's discovery service, will be process-driven and will have clear objectives. By the end of the session, you will be able to do something effectively – like using the library's discovery service. Constructivist learning is more about helping you to uncover meaning for yourself. It is less about process and more about practice. Each approach has its place within your broader learning experience.

The process of learning design

Learning theory underpins the decisions tutors make when it comes to designing your learning. The 'learning' in learning design can refer to the *curriculum, the degree programme on which you are enrolled, an individual module making up part of the programme, and a session in and of itself, whether that's a lecture, tutorial, seminar, or workshop. In what follows, we're going to look at the way a tutor designs a tutorial.

Where does a tutor begin? Oddly, the process of learning design begins at the end. The first thing a tutor does is identify the intended learning outcomes of the tutorial. If you remember, ILOs are statements that reflect what students will be able to demonstrate having completed the learning activity. They are often expressed using verbs, for example:

- By the end of this lesson you should be able to *describe* the process of osmosis through real-world examples in which it occurs.
- By the end of this module you should be able to *analyse* and *evaluate* the contributing factors that led to the disappearance of Buddhism from India.
- By the end of this online course you should be able to *design* and *code* a web-based calculator app using html, css, and javascript.

Verbs tend to be used because they help to communicate the *active* and participatory nature of the learning process. They are directive; as such, they indicate what sort of activities you might be expected to engage in as part of the learning process. You can see this in the examples of intended learning outcomes above; these are not the learning outcomes of a passive, lecture-hall learning experience!

For the tutor, learning outcomes are vital to the design process since they ultimately determine the approach, content, and organisation of the learning process. Once the learning outcomes are in place, tutors then work backwards to the start of the session, ensuring that the content is aligned properly with them. Alignment is key in successful learning design. The activities in which you engage, for example, should help you attain the learning outcomes associated with the session. The theory used by tutors for this part of the design process is termed 'constructive alignment' (Biggs et al., 2022). The alignment, as you can probably tell, is linked to constructivism; a design process based on this theory therefore promotes student-centred learning, in that it encourages you to build knowledge for yourself. All the decisions made by tutors based on this theory are made to support you as you drive your own learning forward.

Task: Reviewing learning outcomes

> Find the ILOs for a module you're currently studying. Where will you find them? Is there a module handbook available through a virtual learning environment like Moodle or Blackboard?

> When you find the outcomes, read through them carefully. Reflect on any learning activities you've already completed. Can you see how these activities are related to the ILOs? How will your new – or renewed – awareness of the ILOs affect the way you approach the remaining learning activities in the module? Does it help to make what you're expected to demonstrate in any assessment task any clearer?

Learning in practice: The *learning framework*

So far, we've discussed a lot of theory. Let's conclude this chapter by looking at how learning is actually structured.

There are a number of core elements to learning at university which we'll meet as we move through the topics in this book. These elements are interrelated, not least because they all form part of an overall scheme of learning aimed at helping you to meet the ILOs of your module(s) and then your programme. Together, they form a *learning framework. A bit of practical advice at this point: avoid seeing any of these elements in isolation. Just as an assessment provides an end point to which all the learning elements that have come before it have worked towards, so too is a lecture linked to the elements either side of it. In other words, the elements are linked together in a meaningful way. In order to get the most out of the whole learning experience on a particular module, it's important to take a broader view of the learning associated with each element.

As you can see in Figure 3.3, the first key element you'll meet as you begin a new module is the module handbook (or a similar document providing an overview of a module). It's vital to look carefully at the module handbook since it will provide you with all of the important information you need to complete the module successfully. In addition to setting out the learning outcomes, the module handbook will also likely include an overview of the structure of learning, including the dates and times of lectures and tutorials, details of the assessment, and, usually, recommended reading.

The module handbook might also include a breakdown of the formal elements of teaching: lectures and tutorials (or seminars), and, if relevant, laboratory or workshop sessions. Broadly speaking, lectures are used to communicate key ideas or theories related to the discipline. As we've noted above, lectures can be quite passive learning experiences; it's important for you, therefore, to have a clear understanding of what's going to be covered and how it might be related to your own learning goals, such as preparation for an assessment. Tutorials or seminars, and laboratory or workshop sessions, provide opportunities for you to explore an aspect of these key ideas or theories introduced in lectures. Tutorials or seminars often take the form

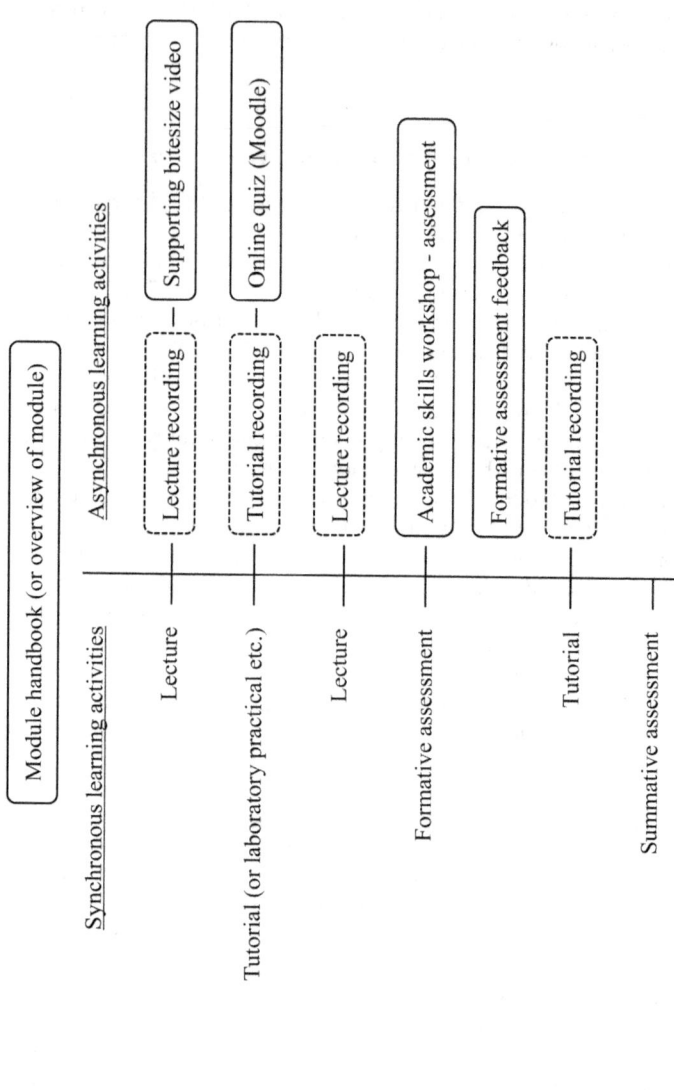

Figure 3.3 The learning framework (simplified version).

of structured discussion built around questions set by your tutor. Laboratory or workshop sessions might be more hands-on, in that tutors might expect you to practise a certain process using point-by-point instructions, with a demonstration offered at the start. The same principle with regards to lectures is relevant here: think about how the content of the session is going to contribute to the development of your learning.

Lectures, tutorials, and seminars are designed to be *synchronous learning experiences, meaning that you engage with it at the same time as the tutor and other students, in real time. This doesn't necessarily mean that you need to be physically present; a lecture, for example, might be streamed live via meeting software like Zoom or Microsoft Teams. In this case, it's still a synchronous learning experience. *Asynchronous learning experiences are the opposite, in that they don't occur in real time and you can engage with them whenever it is convenient. As reflected in Figure 3.3, lectures, tutorials, and seminars, while designed as 'live events', if streamed live at the same time, can often be viewed afterwards as recordings. This means that they also exist as asynchronous learning activities. However, often the recordings only exist to give you the opportunity to review content you've already seen; it's not meant to be a substitute for attending the live event.

Tutors include a variety of asynchronous learning activities in degree courses, ranging from video recordings of lectures, as noted above, to bitesize videos often accompanied by short Q&As to make sure you've engaged with it, e-lessons and so on. These activities are just as important as the lectures and tutorials. Often, they extend the content of a lecture or tutorial by looking at a topic in greater detail. Some cover contentious aspects of a topic. We've used activities like videos to provide general guidance or feedback on assessment tasks. Remember, it's all relevant; don't overlook a resource just because it looks less formal than a lecture.

Formal elements in the learning framework, like lectures and tutorials – elements that are timetabled and at which attendance is usually expected – are complemented by what we're going to call here '*add-on provision', such as workshops led by academic librarians on developing search strategies, IT training on specific software, or writing courses offered by academic skills teaching units or writing centres. This type of provision is extra-curricular, in that it sits next to the formal curriculum consisting of lectures and tutorials. It's also voluntary, in that attendance isn't compulsory; it's available to all students and is there to give you an opportunity to enhance the literacies you're already developing. Take advantage of such provision. Students we've met over the years have benefited greatly from it, and it might make the difference between doing quite well in your assessed work and excelling.

Within the learning framework, all elements build towards assessment. Most modules will include a *formative assessment task, a task designed to give both you and your tutor insights into your academic development. A formative assessment, which usually occurs midway through a module, is intended to prepare you for a *summative assessment task towards the end of the module. It's a trial run, to give you a chance to identify literacies or aspects of your practice you need to improve on if you're going to perform well in the summative task. By summative, we mean that it is designed to be the final assessment task on the module, the mark for which ultimately counts towards your overall degree mark. Lots of students played down the importance of formative assessment by not really trying when it comes to completing the task. We've never understood this. Engaging fully with the demands of a formative assessment task is vital if you're going to excel on your course because the feedback you get should inform the way you tackle the summative task which follows.

Task: Mapping your learning

> Now that we've identified the core elements of the learning framework, have a go at mapping out the learning for one of your modules.
>
> 1 Find the module handbook and plot each lecture, tutorial (or seminar) and practical session (if applicable) according to date on a calendar.
> 2 Note underneath each element the topic to be covered.
> 3 What key ideas are discussed in each lecture? How are these ideas related to the tutorials or seminars?
> 4 Using the learning outcomes set out in the module handbook, link each one to the relevant elements of learning. You might find that one tutorial addresses several of the learning outcomes. That's fine; the objective here is to gain an understanding of how each element contributes to the overall learning experience offered by the module.
> 5 Look at the recommended reading in the module handbook. Start to link items in this list to the relevant lecture or tutorial.
> 6 Read the assessment details. How are the elements of learning (lectures and tutorials) linked to the assessment? Are some of the elements more significant than others?
> 7 What add-on provision is available? Does any of it look useful to your learning on this module?
>
> Getting a good understanding of the structure and requirements of the module before it begins will provide your learning with a solid foundation.

Summary

In this chapter, we've looked at learning at university: what it is, how it's conceived, how it is designed by tutors, and how you, as a student, are expected to engage with it. Your learning takes place in a discourse community. It's really important, therefore, to start figuring out what conventions shape the way knowledge is created in your discipline as soon as possible. For example, which source types are commonly used in the discourse associated with your discipline? What types of assessment will you need to complete (i.e., will you have to write essays, or are you expected to complete reports or deliver presentations?)? What are the features of writing in your discipline? For example, will you be writing in the first person (i.e., 'I will argue that …')? 'Knowledge' not only refers to interpretations of data or evidence; it includes 'academic literacy', the behaviours or practices you need to engage with in order to excel on your programme. Searching for academic sources, for example, is far more than a 'study skill'; it's a complex practice that requires you to not only be familiar with how a library discovery service works, but also to be able to evaluate the sources it yields in any search. Learning is usually student-centred and active in nature: you learn by doing, and by engaging actively in the elements of learning. Tutors act as facilitators of learning; their role is to steer and support you on your learning journey. In this context, your success – and whether you excel in learning – is ultimately determined by you and the decisions you make about your learning. This is why it's vital that you take control of your own learning experience at university by proactively participating in the learning process and by practising self-regulation – a concept we'll come to shortly.

References

Belanche, D., Casaló, L., Flavián, M., & Ibáñez-Sánchez, S. (2021). Understanding influencer marketing: The role of congruence between influencers, products and consumers. *Journal of Business Research, 132*, 186–195.

Biggs, J., Tang, C., & Kennedy, G. (2022). *Teaching for quality learning at university* (5th ed.). Open University Press.

Lave, J., & Wenger, E. (1991). *Situated learning: Legitimate peripheral participation*. Cambridge University Press.

Singh, S., & Diamond, S. (2020). *Social media marketing for dummies* (4th ed.). For Dummies.

Swales, J. (1990). *Genre analysis: English in academic and research settings*. Cambridge University Press.

Wingate, U. (2018). Academic literacy across the curriculum: Towards a collaborative instructional approach. *Language Teaching, 51*(3), 349–364.

Chapter 4

Becoming a self-regulating learner

Now that we've set out the learning framework and given you some insight into learning design and how tutors expect you to engage in that learning, it's time to turn the focus back to you and your approach to learning. In defining what we mean by 'excelling' at university, we established the importance of mindset, goals, and motivation. All three are aspects of a broader concept, that of the self-regulating learner. When engaging in learning, tutors expect you not only to direct its course by taking control of it; they want you to monitor your own performance, to reflect on it, and then to put in place strategies to bring about an improvement. It's this process that we're going to look at here.

If you've come straight from a school or college environment, where learning is highly structured and teachers provide clear instructions over what you need to do and when, the idea of directing the course of your learning might seem alien. Making the leap from this environment to one in which you make the key decisions over your learning represents one of the most significant challenges you'll face as you transition into higher education. However, it's vital to your chances of excelling at university that you make this transformation into a self-regulating learner as quickly as possible.

Practising self-regulated learning, as you might have guessed, also holds an importance beyond the experience of learning at university. As a concept, it provides a framework for *lifelong learning*, the notion that learning is an ongoing process which continues in the workplace. As a graduate, you will be expected to engage in professional development processes driven by the core elements of self-regulated learning, such as reflective practice. We look at this in more detail towards the end of the chapter.

Here, in this chapter, we explore, through scenarios and reflective exercises, self-regulated learning. We define the concept before looking in more detail at its constituent elements. We also provide you with practical guidance on how to become a self-regulating learner. The ideas discussed in this chapter are important to the objectives of the whole book, and so it's

DOI: 10.4324/9781003217527-4

important to engage fully with the exercises it includes. You might also like to read this chapter in light of the preceding one, on learning at university, for the content offered here is meant to complement the information found there.

Learning Objectives

By the end of this chapter, you will have gained:

- a clear understanding of self-regulated learning, its significance in learning in higher education, and its value to excelling at university;
- an awareness of the importance of reflective practice in self-regulated learning;
- an understanding of the practical steps you might take to adopt self-regulated learning practices;
- an appreciation of the broader value of self-regulated learning to the process of becoming a graduate.

Keywords

self-regulated learning; reflective practice; mindset, motivation and goals; learning strategies; self-efficacy and efficacy beliefs.

What is self-regulated learning?

Let's begin by looking at what self-regulated learning isn't. Below is an account of how one student, Natalie, set about preparing for a tutorial on her Marketing undergraduate degree programme. Natalie's approach is fairly typical of lots of students. She isn't a self-regulating learner; her behaviour points to the core elements of self-regulated learning because she doesn't engage with them properly! Read through the account and consider: (i) what characterises Natalie's approach to this task and (ii) what do you think Natalie's example tells us about the core elements of self-regulated learning?

> Natalie has overslept again. She is told by one of her housemates that she has a tutorial that afternoon on digital marketing. Panicked, she asks her friend what she needs to do. 'It's all in the module handbook,' her friend replies. Looking at her watch, she realises that she has only four hours until the tutorial. 'Four hours should be long enough,' she tells herself, 'I only want to do enough to not look stupid; with any luck, I won't be asked any questions'.

Natalie's first task is to find a copy of the module handbook. Her friend has gone out and so she can't ask her. She can't remember ever being given one; it must be on Moodle. She gets out her laptop and tries to access Moodle, but she's forgotten her password. She tries several different passwords, but in the end she gets locked out. Not wanting to get any help from IT Support, she decides instead to get a copy of the marketing textbook her friend mentioned last week. She goes to the library and wanders up and down the aisles of books, but she can't find the textbook. She notices a PC at the end of one aisle with what looks like the library's discovery service on the screen. Using the discovery service, she looks for the book but can't find it in the results. She notices a fellow student from her course and asks her; she shows Natalie which book it is and where it is on the shelf. Natalie looks in the table of contents and finds the chapter on digital marketing. She turns to it in the book and flicks through the relevant pages. It's quite long; she doesn't have enough time to read it properly and so she decides to photocopy the chapter. Having done this, she sits down at a desk and tries to highlight relevant bits of the text. After twenty minutes, she's only looked at four pages, and much of the text is highlighted. She doesn't feel like she's learnt anything about the topic. Feeling hungry, and realising that there's only an hour and a half before the tutorial, she decides to go to the coffee shop for lunch. There she bumps into another friend who invites her to sit down. She spends the rest of the time before the tutorial discussing what they are going to do for another friend's birthday.

Natalie sits down in the tutorial. The tutor begins by asking some specific questions about the topic. Natalie doesn't understand the questions and recognises only one or two of the terms mentioned. She spends the next twenty minutes of the tutorial trying to follow the discussion; in the end, however, she gives up, because it's too difficult to follow. She leaves the tutorial confused and downbeat. The tutor offers to speak to anyone who might have any questions. Natalie leaves the room as quickly as possible without saying anything to the tutor. She puts the entire experience to the back of her mind, even though she feels disappointed by her performance.

i   What characterises Natalie's approach to the task?
    Natalie is very unprepared when it comes to the tutorial. For example, she didn't even realise she had a tutorial coming up until her friend told her about it. This forgetfulness sets the tone for the rest of her actions. Because she'd left so little time to prepare, she was forced to improvise, but she didn't do this very well. She made only a limited attempt to prepare, without even finding out exactly what the tutor wanted to cover in the tutorial. She at least did some preparatory

reading, but it was unguided, focusing broadly on the topic of digital marketing without considering any of its nuances. On the day of the tutorial she was caught out: although she'd done some reading, she wasn't able to answer any of the tutor's questions because she had little knowledge of them. As a result, she couldn't contribute to the discussion and felt lost and confused throughout. To make matters worse, she felt too anxious or embarrassed to ask the tutor for help. She left the tutorial without having gained anything from it – all because of her approach to learning – and there is little evidence that she learnt from her mistakes.

ii What does Natalie's experience tell us about the core elements of self-regulated learning?

Natalie clearly needs to be far more aware, not just of her commitments, such as the tutorial, but of the relatively ineffective actions she takes as she set out to complete the task. There is a sense that she is going through the motions, doing just enough to get by without having to exert any extra effort. This is not surprising when you consider her motivation (or lack of it), which is to avoid looking 'stupid' in the tutorial. The ineffectiveness of her actions stems from her limited motivation. It is this goal of not looking 'stupid' that essentially undermines any attempt she makes to prepare properly for the tutorial. For example, once she has got hold of a copy of the textbook, instead of making a greater effort to find out what questions the tutor has set, Natalie is content to just read something (anything) in an attempt to have some knowledge, however general, to hand. Even though she realises that the strategy she has employed of highlighting what she thinks are relevant parts of the text in her photocopy has failed, she makes no attempt to amend this strategy or to try something different to build her knowledge. She is inflexible. At the tutorial itself, she doesn't end up looking 'stupid' – the tutor doesn't ask her a question directly – but she certainly doesn't feel confident about the level of her knowledge. She feels so embarrassed that even though the tutor offers to speak to anyone who might have a question, she scurries away as quickly as possible. To make matters worse, rather than reflecting on why the experience was so distressing, she simply forgets it; there is no evidence that she has learnt anything from it.

Natalie's mistakes can therefore be grouped into three main areas:

- her lack of preparation;
- her inadequate performance as she prepared for the tutorial;
- and her inability to reflective meaningfully on the experience.

These three areas point to the core elements of self-regulated learning: (i) the need to prepare or plan before starting on a task; (ii) the behaviours used as the task is performed and the ability of the learner to monitor their effectiveness; and (iii) the importance of reflecting on an experience with a view to gaining a clearer understanding of how a task might be completed more effectively (Seli & Dembo, 2020; Zimmerman, 2002).

Let's take a look at how Jess, Natalie's housemate – who we've already met – prepares for the same tutorial. Jess is a self-regulating learner. Read through the account below and consider (i) what characterises her approach to this task and (ii) how does it differ to Natalie's, in light of what the account of Natalie's actions has told us about self-regulated learning?

Jess wakes up on the morning of the tutorial having already done a great deal of the background reading for it. This morning, she intends to read two journal articles flagged up by the tutor in a message on Moodle, before reviewing her notes in light of the questions set. She is determined to engage fully with this tutorial since the assessment due at the end of term is on the subject of digital marketing.

Jess has already downloaded the two articles as pdf documents, but she decides to go to the library to make the most of her time. She positions herself in a quiet corner where she won't be disturbed and opens the first of the two articles. Before she reads anything, she creates a new Word document and types out the title, author and all the details she needs to form a reference at the top of the page. With the questions for the tutorial next to her, she begins to read through the text. She makes a note of anything which she thinks is relevant to the questions. In a separate document, she makes a note of any terms or points she feels less confident about. Having read the article, she's able to link some of the points made by that author to information she's already found in her background reading. The second article, however, is more challenging to understand. She begins to read it but finds it difficult to relate the content to the set questions. She stops reading at the end of the introduction and turns to the abstract which provides her with a neat summary of the article's content and purpose. Realising how it relates to one of the questions in particular, she goes back to the article and finishes reading it. Once again, she's able to link some of the content to her background reading. Overall, without feeling overly confident, she's content that she will be able to answer the questions set to the best of her ability. She decides to go to the coffee shop before the tutorial where she meets Natalie and one of her other friends.

In the tutorial, she not only follows the discussion but is able to contribute to it at several points. The discussion broadens her understanding of several key points. Jess is really pleased because it has given her a much clearer idea of what she will include in her assessment later on in the term. When the tutor asks if anyone has any questions, she is able to raise several issues she made a note of while reading the journal articles. When reflecting on the experience, she realises that making those connections between the content of the articles and the background reading was crucial in her preparation. She decides to devote more time to that part of the process when she prepares for the next tutorial.

i What characterises Jess' approach to the task?
Jess is clearly prepared: the tutorial is not a surprise to her; she knows when it is taking place and she's already done some background reading beforehand. She also has a good understanding of the structure of her course, since she knows that the assessment task due to be submitted later on in the term is focused on the same topic. It is this that ultimately motivates her to prepare fully for the tutorial: she wants to deepen her understanding to make sure she has a good chance of doing well in the assessment. The strategies she uses as she prepares for the tutorial – the way she makes notes on the journal articles while also keeping a record of anything she doesn't fully understand – are largely effective. However, when she experiences difficulties when engaging with the second article, she changes her approach slightly, by reading the abstract carefully. She finds the tutorial itself a rewarding experience and takes advantage of the tutor's offer to answer any questions. She reflects on her performance by recognising the importance of linking information together. By doing so, she'll be able to get more out of the next tutorial as she looks to excel in her academic work.

ii How does Jess' approach differ from Natalie's?
Jess' approach to completing the task is almost the polar opposite of Natalie's. Whereas Natalie is unprepared, Jess has a much stronger grasp on what she's doing. She knows when the tutorials are and she's already read through the information about the assessment. More importantly, she's motivated to succeed. Rather than simply doing enough, she wants to deepen her knowledge and understanding so that she has a better chance of getting a good mark in the assessment. Motivation is key: whereas Natalie's lack of it works against her, for Jess, her positive motivation underpins the actions she takes when preparing for the tutorial, from deciding to make the most of her time by getting to the library early, to the decisions she takes about amending her approach to reading the journal articles. Since Jess's motivation is more aspirational, in that she is trying to develop her knowledge and understanding of the topic, she is more willing to be flexible when it comes to the strategies she uses to do so. In the tutorial itself, again,

due to the difference in their motivation, Natalie remains quiet (in part because she doesn't fully understand the questions being asked) while Jess follows the discussion and contributes to it when she can. Jess is actively trying to build her knowledge while Natalie is turning away from it in case her lack of knowledge is exposed. The same feelings prompt Jess to ask the tutor questions at the end while Natalie runs away. Jess then shows an ability to reflect meaningfully and constructively on the experience, whereas Natalie prefers to pretend that the tutorial didn't happen.

How, therefore, can we define self-regulated learning? Self-regulated learning is a process whereby a learner takes control of their learning by setting goals, monitors the behaviours used in pursuit of those goals, and evaluates academic performance through reflective practice.

Self-regulated learning as a process

Self-regulated learning is made up of three distinct phases:

i forethought (or planning, preparation, and goal setting);
ii behaviour (the strategies used in pursuit of those goals);
iii evaluation (self-reflection on academic performance in light of goals) (Zimmerman, 2002).

What does each phase involve?

i Forethought

Forethought refers to the preparatory phase of the process when you essentially plan out what you're going to do. Thus, it involves three, interlinked elements:

a analysing the task carefully;
b setting goals relating to its performance; and
c considering what strategies might be used.

Such activities are conditioned by two important factors: motivation and what psychologists have called efficacy beliefs, or your own belief in how capable you are of completing the task, both of which we've already met.

Analysing the task is about considering what you are expected to do and how you are to go about doing it. In the example above, the task facing both Natalie and Jess was to prepare for the tutorial on digital marketing. The fact that each student had a different motivation affected not only the goals they set but also the way in which in each student worked towards those goals. Natalie, motivated by a fear of looking inferior in front of her fellow students, and perhaps feeling less capable of contributing to the tutorial effectively, had a goal of doing just enough to get through the experience. She didn't recognise the value of the experience to the development of her knowledge and understanding, particularly with an assessment coming up in the next few weeks. Her planning was limited, in that she was thinking only in the short term. Jess, on the other hand, had the more ambitious goal of wanting to use the experience of preparing for the tutorial to deepen her knowledge and understanding with one eye on the assessment. Her planning was clearly more thorough because of this: she covered more material as she prepared and sought to fill any gaps in her knowledge by asking the tutor for further help.

Natalie's goal was related to her performance. She wanted to avoid looking inferior at the tutorial; she was motivated only to do just enough to demonstrate some knowledge of the topic. In contrast, Jess's goal reflected her desire to deepen her knowledge of the topic, or, more broadly, to achieve mastery over it. Setting a goal of this nature is typical of a self-regulating learner: such students engage in deeper levels of learning and are more concerned with self-development. Natalie's goal, on the other hand, is linked to surface-level learning: she wants to familiarise herself with essential facts without necessarily developing her understanding of the topic.

Motivation also underpins the selection of strategies used. Looking at the example of Jess again, given that she is motivated to deepen her understanding of the topic, and that her overriding goal is to make the most out of the tutorial, her strategies are geared towards the principle of building knowledge. For example, prior to engaging with the journal articles, she completed background reading on the topic using textbooks, which provided her with a foundation of knowledge that would help her to understand the content of the articles. Furthermore, she adopted an active approach to note-making, in which she not only recorded aspects of the content of the articles that related to the set questions; she also, at the same time, noted points she didn't fully understand, and she made an effort to link the knowledge she was finding in the articles to the knowledge she already had, principally from her background reading. Such strategies resonate with her motivation to deepen her knowledge and understanding.

ii Behaviour

By behaviour, we're referring to the performance of those strategies identified in the forethought stage. Jess, as we've seen, used several strategies to build knowledge. She enacted those strategies as she prepared for the tutorial, but something else characterised her approach to this preparatory work. As a self-regulating learner, she monitored her own performance. When she realised that she needed to amend her approach to maximise her performance, she adapted her strategy. This is an example of what sets apart self-regulating learners from students like Natalie who are less able – and even willing – to adapt their approach.

Task: Monitoring your behaviours and excelling in your academic work

> Here's an example from our own experiences as tutors of a student who was fairly successful but who might have *excelled* in their academic work if they had monitored their performance.
>
> Leon, who was studying an undergraduate degree in Business Management, had already received some high marks (in the 2:1 range) for his work before starting his dissertation. For his dissertation, he was determined to get the highest mark possible. When it came to writing up his research, his plan was to spend ten hours per day, six days of the week, writing. Soon after putting this strategy to work, he found that he spent most of the day staring at the screen or rewriting the same few sentences; he was making little progress. But since such intensive activity had worked before (on much shorter pieces of written work) he was convinced that it was the right approach and was therefore unwilling to use any other strategy. Perhaps through a lack of confidence, or a fear that it would all go disastrously wrong, he stuck to the strategy he knew. In the end, he didn't do badly; but he didn't *excel* as he had intended to do.
>
> - How willing are you to adapt the way you work if you think you're not meeting your goals?
> - Do you monitor your behaviours with your goals in mind?
> - Are you more like Leon or Jess?

iii Evaluation

The evaluation phase is about assessing the whole experience – the forethought and behaviour phases – in light of your goals. Did you achieve what you set out to do? If not, why not? What aspect of the process didn't quite work? If you could do it all again, what would you do differently? In essence, what did you learn from the experience and how is that information going to bring about an improvement in your performance? As these questions make clear, evaluation is about reflective practice: the action of looking back critically at past performances, including actions and decisions, with a view to bring about an improvement in performance through greater understanding of the self (i.e., you).

Reflective practice

Many of you will already be familiar with reflective practice; it's often used as a form of formative assessment on degree programmes, while on others it's an integral part of the learning experience (e.g., on some art and design courses, for which students are required to keep reflective journals). Here, as a key part of the process of self-regulated learning, we're encouraging you to reflect on your performance as much as possible. Development as a learner – and, ultimately, your development into a graduate – is driven by self-reflection.

There are lots of models or cycles available which can help to structure your reflective practice – just do a Google search and lots will come up. We suggest adopting a fairly simple one for this purpose: a three-stage model incorporating (i) an account of the experience ('describe'), (ii) an assessment of it ('reflect'), and (iii) an outcome stage ('take action'), in which you identify some actions to take based on the reflection to bring about an improvement in your performance (similar to those proposed by Driscoll (2007) and Jasper (2013)) (Figure 4.1). It's important to note, though, that for assessments based on reflective practice, you might be expected to use one of the more complex models, like Kolb's (1984) or Gibb's (1988).

In the (i) describe stage, you do just that: provide an account of the experience focused on what actually happened. Don't go further than that. You're not, at this stage, looking to explain why something happened or to highlight positive and negative aspects of your performance.

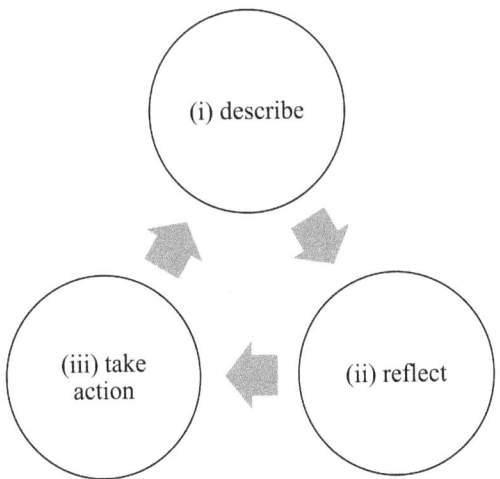

Figure 4.1 A three-stage reflective cycle.

Set out the experience so that you have a foundation on which to carry out the reflection. In the (ii) reflect stage, you need to go below the surface of the experience. You know what happened – you've already set it out. Now we're looking to explore why the experience panned out as it did. You need to flag up any aspect of your performance which you think went well. It's important to look at the positives first, even if they're overshadowed by the negatives. No piece of reflection should be entirely positive or negative. Lots of students tend to be overly critical when reflecting by focusing on the negatives. If you begin with the positives, you set a more balanced tone. Also try to reflect on the reasons why something went well; equally, consider why your performance fell short of your expectations. Overall, as you reflect, you're looking to uncover the meaning in your actions. Try to think as deeply as you can about your performance. In the final stage, (iii) 'take action', you need to turn some of your reflective comments into actions, practical steps intended to bring about an improvement in performance. This stage is often neglected by students, but if the experience of reflecting is going to hold any value for you, as a learner, it's important to engage fully with this final stage.

Jess, our self-regulating learner, put this model into practice when she reflected on the experience of preparing for and taking part in a tutorial, which we described above. First, she (i) described the experience by setting it out clearly in her notebook. She then (ii) reflected on the experience in a structured way by answering a series of questions she came up with:

- What went well?
- What didn't go as planned?
- Why did certain aspects of the experience go well?
- Why did others not go as planned?

The answers to these questions had the effect of opening up the experience for her and drawing out not only the positives and negatives of it but also the underlying reasons for why the experience panned out as it did. This structured reflection, therefore, afforded her valuable insights into her own performance. Having recognised the importance of linking new knowledge to what she already knows, in the final stage, (iii) 'take action', Jess decides to develop this aspect of her performance. For the next tutorial, she'll use a mind map to illustrate the various links she identifies as she prepares for it.

The evaluation phase of self-regulated learning as a whole holds particular value in relation to *becoming a graduate*. In professional contexts, the ability to reflect constructively on performance is vital to continuing professional development (CPD). We should all be *lifelong learners, in that we should continually look to engage in personal and professional development. Reflective practice sits at the heart of this process and so it's vital that you get into the habit of engaging with it while you're studying at university.

Becoming a self-regulating learner

It's one thing to make you aware of self-regulated learning, but it's another thing entirely for you to actually become a self-regulating learner. This might be a really difficult thing for you to do since it can involve adopting an entirely different approach to learning – one that feels very alien to you. We think that the biggest challenge facing new or less experienced students is making that transition from learning at school or college and the expectations on you, as a learner, that go with it, to learning in higher education. It also represents a challenge to international students for whom self-regulated learning might be a world away from what they're expecting from the learning experience at a UK university. To help you make that transition, we think it's important for you to focus on five broad areas. In what follows, we're going to draw on some of what we set out in Chapter 2 on excelling.

1 Reflect on your motivation: is it mastery or performance which concerns you? Can you identify any aspects of your approach to academic work which reflect your motivation?
2 Set goals: consider what your goal is in relation to a task on which you're working. What are the smaller goals you need to achieve in the course of working towards this larger one? Setting out these smaller goals and then achieving them is a great way of building confidence. Ensure that all goals are realistic and achievable.
3 Devise strategies relevant to the task and to the goals you've set. What approach is going to help you achieve these goals?
4 Monitor your performance by considering the effectiveness of the strategies you've put in place. Are they working? If not, why not? What alternative strategies are available?
5 Evaluate your performance through reflective practice against the goals you've set. Think carefully and critically about the experience. Identify what didn't go to plan, but also examine what did work by considering why it worked. Remember to turn that reflection into practical steps to help with your personal development.

Task: Becoming a self-regulating learner: Practical steps

Let's try to put into practice the guidance set out above so that you can start working towards becoming a self-regulating learner.

Reflecting on current practice

To begin, reflect on how you currently do things. Think of a recent task you've completed. It might be preparation for a tutorial or seminar, as in the examples we used in this chapter relating to the experiences of Natalie and Jess, or you might prefer to look at a recent experience of completing an assessment. It can be anything related to academic work.

- What goal(s) did you set for yourself?
- What strategies did you use to work towards those goals?
- Did you monitor your performance as you were completing the task? If so, how? Furthermore, did you amend your strategies at any point?
- On completing the task, did you evaluate your performance? If so, how did you do it? Did you use a model of reflective practice to structure your evaluation? Did any actions emerge out of your reflection to help bring about an improvement in your performance?

Your answers to these questions will give you some idea of the extent to which you currently regulate your learning. If you don't think you do any of these things at the moment, don't worry; this exercise is designed to help you identify how you can amend your current practice so that you can begin to self-regulate. Most likely, you'll do some, but not all, of these things already.

Identifying your motivation

Are you looking to deepen your knowledge and understanding in your discipline area – to *master* it, like Jess? Or are you more concerned with your performance – getting higher marks than the other students (or, as in Natalie's case, doing just enough to get by)? To *excel* in your academic work, motivation like Jess' is needed: deepening your knowledge and understanding will inevitably impact positively on your results.

Picking a task

Is there a task you're currently working on which you can use for the purpose of this exercise? Do you have an assessment to prepare for, or a tutorial to attend? Pick a task to use here to practise the self-regulated learning approach. It can be anything related to academic work.

Setting goals

Once you've picked a task, set your goals. If you've chosen to use assessment preparation as your task, your overall goal, in light of your motivation, might be – for example – to complete a draft of an essay. You might then identify several sub goals, such as (a) understanding the assessment question, (b) identifying five key sources to use, (c) making notes on those sources, (d) creating a plan – and so on.

Strategising

Having set your goals, you now need to come up with strategies to use to achieve them. For (b) in the above example, you might decide to use the recommended reading section of your module handbook to identify the sources. Alternatively – and with a bit more ambition! – you might turn to the library's discovery service and use keywords taken from the assessment question to find the sources. It might be that you have to modify the latter strategy by using limiters to narrow down the range of results (e.g., applying a date range to get the most recent sources). The key point here is to remember to monitor your performance. If one strategy isn't working effectively, amend it; choose another that you think might be more effective.

Evaluating your performance

Having completed the task and hopefully achieved your goals, it's time to reflect on the experience. Using the simple model of reflection highlighted above, do just that: reflect on your performance. Set out exactly what you did, perhaps in a notebook, as Jess did. When reflecting, consider both the good and bad aspects of the experience, what went well and what went less well. What did you learn about yourself and your approach to learning from the experience? How might you bring about an improvement the next time you're faced with a similar task? Try to turn the reflective comments into actions – practical steps that can help you to bring about an improvement in performance.

Summary

In this chapter, we've explored self-regulated learning. We've built on elements of the discussion about excelling in Chapter 2: mindset, motivation, and goal setting are all key to self-regulated learning and it's important to consider each one carefully if you're going to become a self-regulating learner.

Practising self-regulated learning is key to excelling in your academic work. Those students who excel are self-regulating learners: there's a direct correlation here. Motivation is also key: if you think like Natalie and only want to 'get by', your chances of excelling are limited. Try to align yourself with Jess' motivation: if your objective is to master a topic or discipline, you're much more likely to engage in deeper levels of learning and, as a result, to achieve higher marks. Set goals as you complete tasks: an overriding goal, together with smaller or 'sub' goals. Achieving each sub goal as you work towards completing a task will incrementally build up your self-efficacy, your belief in your own abilities. Reflective practice forms a key part of self-regulated learning: engage in it meaningfully if you want to develop as a learner and to excel in your academic work. Remember that self-regulated learning underpins lifelong learning: becoming a self-regulating learner is also about becoming a highly employable graduate.

References

Driscoll, J. (2007). *Practising clinical supervision*. Elsevier.
Gibbs, G. (1988). *Learning by doing: A guide to teaching and learning methods*. FEU, Oxford Polytechnic.
Jasper, M. (2013). *Beginning reflective practice*. Cengage.
Kolb, D. (1984). *Experiential learning: Experience as the source of learning and development*. Prentice Hall.
Seli, H., & Dembo, M. (2020). *Motivation and learning strategies for college success: A focus on self-regulated learning* (6th ed.). Routledge.
Zimmerman, B. (2002). Becoming a self-regulated learner: An overview. *Theory into Practice, 42*(2), 64–70.

Chapter 5

Understanding assessment

In the previous three chapters, we've set the scene: we've looked at what 'excelling' at university might look like to you, we've set out the learning framework to give you a better sense of what the learning experience looks like in practice, and we've explained self-regulated learning and stressed its importance to your chances of finding success on your course and to excelling. Now it's time to look at the literacies that make up the broader idea of 'academic literacy', your ability to contribute to the work of the discourse community you've joined, in more detail. We begin with assessment and feedback. This chapter, on assessment, is complemented by the following one, on feedback. The main reason for starting here is fairly obvious: the marks you get for assessed work ultimately determine the level of your success on your degree programme; as such, they also reflect your progress on the journey of becoming a graduate. However, there is another important reason for our decision to begin with assessment and feedback. Assessment and feedback also provide a lens through which we can view the other literacies (such as research and writing) discussed in this book. In order for you to understand why a particular literacy is important to the idea of excelling, you need to explore it in the context of assessment. Doing so will also help to bring tutors' expectations in relation to that literacy into sharper focus.

When many of you read the word 'assessment', you'll be thinking 'test'. The stressful experience of taking exams at the end of several years of study might come to mind or the pressure of completing a coursework project on time. It's easy to see these types of assessment as obstacles which you need to overcome if you're going to get a high mark. In higher education, however, assessment – and its counterpart, feedback – holds a broader significance as a learning tool. Yes, it's important that you do as well as you can on assessed work since success is measured by the mark you receive. Yet assessment is designed into learning by tutors so that it might act as a driver of learning; your experiences of completing assessments are meant to support your personal development and your transition into a graduate. We'll be looking at assessment and feedback from this perspective.

DOI: 10.4324/9781003217527-5

In this chapter, therefore, we open up the literacy of assessment. We consider what assessment looks like in higher education and how it differs from assessment you might have already done at school or college – or in the workplace. In doing this, we consider its purpose and how it is designed by tutors. We also look at how tutors assess the work you submit. In Chapter 6, we emphasise the importance of engaging with the feedback you receive along with your mark. The importance of understanding assessment only becomes fully clear when it is set in the context of self-regulated learning.

Learning Objectives

By the end of this chapter, you will have gained:

- a broad understanding of assessment in higher education: the way it is conceived by tutors, its purpose, and the different forms it takes;
- an appreciation of the importance of assessment in (i) the learning associated with your programme and (ii) your own personal development;
- an understanding of the differences between formative and summative assessment, and the unique value of formative assessment;
- an understanding of how assessment is designed and its links to intended learning outcomes (ILOs);
- an understanding of marking criteria and the importance of engaging with it in order to excel in your academic work.

Keywords

formative assessment; summative assessment; marking criteria; assessment genre; authentic assessment; student-centred assessment; self and peer assessment

Putting assessment into perspective

What do we mean by 'assessment' in the context of learning in higher education? As we alluded to in the introduction, lots of students tend to think of assessment in formal terms as 'tests' in which you need to perform well in order to get a good degree classification by the time you've completed your course. Exams, for example, essays, and perhaps even presentations. This is, of course, true: assessments do act as tests; the marks you get for many pieces of assessment do count towards your final degree classification; and lots of assessment in higher education does take the form of exams, essays and presentations. However, it's important for you to take a broader view of assessment while studying at university, for it isn't always formal and doesn't always take these forms. Any task set by a tutor which tests something – usually your knowledge and understanding, but perhaps also your competency regarding a particular literacy (e.g., a research task in which you might be expected to find a journal article on a specific topic using the library's discovery service) – should be classed as an assessment. For example, lots of tutors include quizzes in their lectures. The results of such quizzes might not be recorded, but your answers might help the tutor to get a general impression of the level of understanding among the cohort (all of the students on your course) and, on a personal level, will undoubtedly give you some insight into the level of your own understanding and where you might need to do some more work. We routinely add three or four multiple-choice questions to resources like videos we post onto Moodle, so that (i) we know the students have engaged with the resource and (ii) to give each student the confidence that comes with knowing that they have understood the points being made. Assessment – and, to some extent, feedback, even if it's only acquired through self-reflection – is all around you in higher education. It's not just about more formal elements like essays and exams.

Why is it everywhere? Why do tutors incorporate quizzes into lectures, questions into tutorials, multiple-choice questions into online learning resources? This is down to the way tutors conceive of assessment. Tutors are as invested in making sure that you do as well as you can on your degree course as you are. Put simply, it reflects well on them if marks within the cohort are high! Assessment, in whatever form it might take, is invaluable in this context because it gives them insights into aspects of the learning experience which students might be finding a challenge. Tutors can then focus on these problem areas in their teaching. Quizzes in lectures represent a quick and easy way of doing this. Formative assessment tasks – which we'll come to shortly – afford a more detailed perspective of an individual student's performance. Take, for example, a short essay used as formative assessment. In their feedback to you, as an individual student, a tutor might highlight a problem with a specific point you've made; they might also point to problems with the structure of your writing and faults with the format of your references. All of which is useful to you when it comes to preparing for the next piece of assessment. At the level of the cohort (all students on the course), based on the experience of marking the work of 30 of 40 students, the tutor might have realised that referencing is a problem. They can then address that by creating a resource setting out the expected standard. Assessment, from the tutor's perspective, is *for learning* (Sambell et al., 2012); it acts as a tool allowing them to assess the level of understanding across the cohort, to measure the personal development of individual students, and to enhance the overall quality of the learning experience by flagging up problem areas (Brown & Race, 2021).

From your perspective, as a student, assessment also functions as an important learning tool. Just as a tutor might use assessment to measure your progress, the experience of completing an assessment, when considered next to the mark you received and the tutor's feedback on your performance, helps to sustain a self-regulated approach to learning (Nicol & Macfarlane-Dick, 2006). By reflecting on the experience and engaging with the tutor's feedback, you can better understand why you got the mark awarded and how you might go about improving that mark in the next assessment. This process of reflection underpins self-regulated learning. Try, therefore, to look upon assessment as a learning tool that will help you to excel; it's not a barrier to finding success.

Formative and summative assessment

We've already met formative and summative assessment in the chapter on learning. To remind you, formative assessment, as its name suggests, is designed to help you 'form' or develop your learning. It's informal, in that although it's assessment, the mark you get doesn't contribute towards your final mark for the module (i.e., the mark that counts towards your final degree classification). It's often 'low-stakes', meaning that the task itself is less complex and it might not take as long to complete. For example, one such formative assessment task we've worked on recently for new students on an undergraduate human resource management course involved summarising the content of a journal article on a specific issue within the discipline. Students were required to find a suitable article first using the library's discovery service before summarising the interpretation offered in the article. The word limit was 1,000 words. Summative assessment, on the other hand, is formal, since the mark you get will count towards your final module mark and therefore your overall degree classification. In this sense, it's 'high stakes'; the task is more demanding and therefore takes longer to complete. The same students, for example, later on in the term, might be expected to work on a group presentation in which they explain, through examples drawn from their own learning experiences, self-regulated learning and how they might go about changing their practice to become self-regulating learners. The presentation itself, which requires an accompanying slide presentation, might be 20 minutes in length.

Lots of students think that formative assessment is less important than summative assessed tasks because formative ones don't count towards your final mark. This is a mistake. Formative assessment plays a very important role in helping you to develop as a learner, since it provides you with an opportunity to measure your performance against assessment criteria and therefore to see where you need to improve before tackling

Understanding Assessment

any summative assessment. The tutor's feedback will help you to identify areas for improvement, but you can do this for yourself by reviewing your work against the marking criteria used by the tutor to mark your work. As long as you are receptive to the tutor's feedback and that you reflect carefully on your performance, you'll be able to learn from the experience. In this sense, formative assessment is a vital learning tool. Summative assessment is clearly important because it's your performance in this type of task that determines the mark you receive. If you want to excel in summative assessment, you must engage fully with the formative assessment task(s) which come before it.

Let's have a look at the contrasting approaches of Natalie and Jess to a formative assessment task on a compulsory PDP (personal development planning) module which forms part of the first year of their course. The task involves reflecting on a recent learning experience on the course, such as a tutorial, and then writing up that reflection using a simple, three-step reflective cycle to structure it. Here's what Natalie did first:

> *Natalie has heard her friends talk about an assessment due in next week, but she hasn't thought about it too much because they all said it didn't count towards her marks. 'Just get it done,' Mike had said. With only three days to go until its submission date, Natalie opens the module handbook on her laptop, flicks to the page with the assessment details on, and begins to read. She doesn't really understand the purpose of the assessment – she attended the tutorial, made a few notes and left; why does she need to go over it again in so much detail? Anyway, it's only 1,000 words (no more than!), so it doesn't really matter. She begins to write down what happened. She does it quickly without thinking too much about style or structure. She quickly reaches 500 words. Looking at the 'cycle' she's supposed to use, she realises that she needs to add a conclusion. She writes down that it didn't go very well because she needs to read more in future. That'll do.*

Natalie's approach is best expressed by the final words of this account: 'That'll do'. The fact that she doesn't understand why she's doing it is a worry. It points to a lack of engagement with her course which will work against her in all the other pieces of assessment she'll be expected to complete as part of her programme.

Let's look at how Jess approaches the task. Jess, as we've already established, is a self-regulating learner.

> *Lots of Jess' friends have had a bit of a laugh about the formative assessment due in on Monday. 'What's the point?' 'It doesn't count.' 'Do as little as possible.' Jess, however, recognises that the experience of*

completing the task offers a chance to develop not just her writing skills but her ability to think critically and constructively. By focusing on her own performance, the reflective part of the task, if done well, will also provide her with insights into her own performance and the possibility of finding more effective ways of doing things. She looks carefully at the three-step cycle. With a 1,000 word limit, she realises that she should probably write no more than 300 words per step. Having thought carefully about the learning experience, she makes some notes for each step. She then writes up these notes and spends a bit more time analysing her actions in the tutorial. To conclude, she tries to turn her observations into actions. In doing so, she realises that reading more than what's recommended by the tutor will deepen her knowledge of the topic and allow her to make more valuable contributions to the discussion.

Needless to say, Jess' approach to completing the task is far more effective than Natalie's. She sees the task in the same way we do: as a 'free hit', an opportunity to further develop her academic literacy (specifically, her writing and her ability to think critically). She's engaged, not just in the task, but in her course, and this allows her to recognise the broader value of the task. She plans what she's going to do, thinks about it, and then puts effort into producing her response. She's quick to link it to her own development, as any good self-regulating learner will do. She uses her reflection to create an action plan designed to bring about an improvement in her performance. All in all, she gets a lot more out of the task than Natalie – even though it doesn't 'count'.

How might Jess use this experience to bring about an improvement in her performance in the summative task that follows? She noted in her reflection that it's important to read more than what has been recommended by the tutor. The feedback from her tutor has highlighted other aspects of her practice that she needs to think about. First, although the tutor praised her reflective writing, they did highlight some sentences where the meaning of what she was trying to say was less clear. Second, he suggested that the structure of her writing might be improved by adding more paragraphs. Jess reviews her work in light of these comments by the tutor. She identifies examples of each and can see why tutor made these points. In relation to the first piece of feedback, she takes two sentences where the expression is less clear and tries to write them out again. This gives her some useful practice which she can develop further when tackling the summative assessment.

One final point about the importance of engaging fully with formative assessment is that if you do well in such a task it will boost your confidence before taking on any summative assessment. It might also motivate you to try even harder in an effort to excel.

Forms of assessment

Assessment – whether formative or summative – can take a variety of different forms. When designing assessment, tutors ensure that it is relevant, in the sense that it resonates with the ILOs of the module, as well as its discipline-specific content. In the example of Natalie and Jess' experiences above, the reflective nature of the assessment task was entirely suitable for a PDP module which is focused on the practice of learning in the context of personal development. It would have been much less appropriate if it had been used on their digital marketing module. Tutors also aim to create assessment that is authentic. An authentic piece of assessment for marketing students, for example, might be to re-create a boardroom scenario where students are expected to pitch their ideas in front of a mock board made up of members of staff or invited guests with industry experience. Education students might be expected to create a lesson plan which might be used in the classroom. Or they might be asked to write a policy document on safeguarding. We've even come across an example of education students being assessed on their interactions within a virtual school, a school environment which replicates the real-world experience of teaching but which sits entirely within the Moodle virtual learning environment (Smith & Hewston, 2020). Such tasks, when done well, not only help to develop the learning experience on the degree course; they speak to the experience students can expect to find in the workplace as graduates. Of course, authentic learning is not appropriate for every discipline. You wouldn't, for example, arm a group of undergraduate history students with swords and shields and then get them to fight each other to convey a sense of the experience of battle in the Middle Ages! But you might ask archaeology students to write a description of an object uncovered on a dig suitable for a museum handbook. Tutors are encouraged to think imaginatively about assessment tasks; don't be surprised if you meet what might at first appear to be unusual assessment tasks.

As a result, you're likely to meet a range of assessment genres on your course. It's difficult to tell you exactly which genres you'll meet because much depends on the discipline in which you're studying. The point to note here is that tutors won't necessarily stick to traditional genres, like essays, when designing assessment. Their aim is to create innovative assessment tasks to engage you fully in the learning experience. Nor should you assume that all assessment is about writing. As we noted above, briefly, assessment can also test your ability to communicate complex information orally, as you would be expected to do in a job interview as a graduate. You might also be asked to use technology. We've asked students in the past to create video presentations using their mobile phones; even video diaries are possible instead of a written reflective journal. Our advice is to review the details of any assessment you might be facing with an open mind. If you're unsure of how to approach an assessment genre which might be new to you, ask your tutor for guidance.

One traditional form of assessment many of you will meet towards the end of your undergraduate course is the dissertation. This is an extended piece of research of approximately 10,000 words. The dissertation draws on all of the literacies discussed in this book but on a grander scale. For example, in terms of research, you'll be expected to engage with a broader range of academic sources than you might have done for other assessment tasks. The dissertation represents the ultimate test of your competencies in relation to these literacies. Given the length of the work and the amount of time needed to do it properly, it's important for you to adopt an organised approach towards it. At some institutions, the task of completing it is broken down into smaller pieces of assessment; for example, we've helped students to write up dissertation proposals, a task often placed in the second year of study. For postgraduates, at master's level, the dissertation is similar in terms of tutors' expectations, which are focused on your competencies in relation to the literacies, just as they are at undergraduate level. The quality of the work will need to be higher at this level though; for example, your engagement with the relevant discourse will need to be deeper if you're going to excel. At master's level, the dissertation is also usually longer, at, perhaps, 20,000 words. This might seem a lot, but a PhD thesis – the next step in an academic journey after a master's degree – is usually about 75,000 words.

The fact that tutors make use of a variety of assessment genres – deliberately so – means that you need to be agile enough to recognise the differences in expectations between these genres. These differences can be quite nuanced. For example, it's fair to say that all assessment genres test your ability to communicate. Yet your communication will be qualitatively different when writing a critique of a journal article, for example, than it would be if you were participating in an assessed marketing pitch. In other words, be alive to these differences and look carefully at assessment criteria to identify them.

A final point concerns self and peer assessment. We've already mentioned how, when designing learning, tutors look to ensure that it is student-centred. One way of doing this in relation to assessment is to use self and peer assessment tasks. Many new or less experienced students find participating in such assessment tasks challenging, simply because they haven't done anything like it before. But these are valid and potentially very valuable forms of assessment that can really help your personal development. In self-assessment, you're required to apply the marking criteria to your own work. This isn't about the tutors being lazy; they're not passing off their responsibilities on to you! Rather, the process of reviewing your own work in light of the marking criteria, when done conscientiously, can provide invaluable insights into your own performance while, at the same time, enhancing your understanding of what tutors are looking for in assessed work, as reflected in the marking criteria. Put simply, you can learn a lot through self-assessment. Peer assessment is similar, in that your work is passed to another student who then applies the marking criteria. Alternatively, for assessed presentations, for example, students might be asked to assess each presentation in turn. Peer assessment is often used informally by tutors as a way of promoting greater understanding of the marking criteria. When it's used more formally, the marks awarded by other students usually only contribute a small proportion of the final mark. In other words, the mark you get for a peer-assessed piece of work won't simply reflect what your friends think of it. Self and peer assessment is used by tutors to enhance the learning experience and give you a better chance of excelling. It's important to engage in it properly, just as you would do with other genres of assessment.

How do tutors assess your work?

Understanding the role of assessment within the learning designed by your tutors represents only part of what you need to know in order to become assessment literate. It's also important that you understand what tutors are looking for in assessed work and to do this you need to be able to interpret *marking criteria.

Marking criteria are the measures used by tutors to determine what mark should be given to your work. Each criterion is normally separated into levels, with a range of marks attached to each one, next to descriptors setting out the features of the work at each level. The criteria will reflect different literacies, which make it easier for your tutor to get an overview of your academic performance and to flag up areas for improvement in their feedback.

We've included a simplified example of the marking criteria used for an assessment at Level 4 (first-year undergraduate study) below. For the purposes of this chapter, we've reduced the number of criteria it includes to three: knowledge and understanding; communication; and critical evaluation. We've simplified these criteria further by including only one descriptor within each area. In the marking criteria used in your modules, you'll find several descriptors for each.

If we take 'knowledge and understanding', you'll notice that the descriptor changes slightly for each range of marks. At 70–79%, knowledge and understanding will be 'developed'. This is different to work in the 60–69% range which will be 'detailed' rather than 'developed'. At 50–59%, there will only be 'some' knowledge and understanding, while at 40–49% it will be 'basic'. Below 40%, it will be 'limited'. As you can see, the mark ranges correspond to different levels of quality in the work.

The same pattern can be seen in the other areas: at 70–79%, work will be much more developed in relation to that area than in the lower mark ranges.

When marking your work, tutors will first determine which level it sits at within each criterion. Once they've done this, they'll use its position within each criterion to determine an overall mark. For example, the knowledge and understanding in your work might be 'developed', placing it in the 70–79% mark range. However, communication might only be 'clear' (60–69%), while there might only be 'some engagement with academic sources' for critical evaluation (again, 60–69%). With one mark in each of the three highest levels, the work will sit in the 60–69% level. Depending on the relative quality of the knowledge and understanding on the one hand, and the critical evaluation on the other, the tutor will likely award a mark either just above or just below 65.

Task: Applying assessment criteria

Below, you'll find a student's response to the following question on public health:

How far does radon gas pose a risk to the health of occupiers of domestic buildings in the United Kingdom?

This is a formative assessment task given to first-year students at the start of their programme. Its purpose is to introduce them to research and writing critically about the interpretations and evidence they find. The response needs to be between 750 and 1,000 words. They need to demonstrate knowledge and understanding, an ability to communicate effectively, and an ability to engage with the academic sources they find in a critical way.

Apply the marking criteria in Table 5.1 to the extract below. How well does this student perform in relation to each of the criteria? I would suggest determining the level for each criterion first before considering the mark.

It should be noted that you don't need to know anything about radon gas or public health to do this task. Just look at the writing objectively and consider the quality of the work next to the three criteria highlighted above.

1   *Radon gas is a radioactive gas that doesn't smell or have any colour. It occurs naturally in the ground as a result of the decay of radioactive uranium which is found in all rocks and soil in very small quantities. Concentrated amounts can be found in small spaces, such as domestic buildings, but because it doesn't smell or have any colour, it can be very hard to detect. As a result of the decaying process, radon gas has been shown to have a potentially serious risk to the health of those living in domestic buildings in the United Kingdom. Research has established*

a strong link between the effects of radon gas inhalation and the development of lung cancer. As seen in the UK Health Security Agency's recently published 'action plan', UK Government's response to the health risks it poses is based on the principle of building awareness of exposure to radon gas (Public Health England, 2018). In the United Kingdom, the UK Health Protection Agency (Miles et al., 2007) produces maps on the location of radon gas areas. An area of noticeably high concentration is south-west England, particularly in Devon and Cornwall. The effectiveness of this response is open to question, but the health risks of radon are undoubtedly better known among the general public in the United Kingdom than ever before.

2   In terms of health risks, radon is most commonly associated with lung cancer. A number of studies since the 1980s have established a strong link between it and the disease, with miners in particular susceptible to respiratory disease, including lung cancer. The inhalation of radon and its decay products has the effect of damaging lung tissue and increasing the chance of developing cancer. A number of important studies have analysed large amounts of data drawn from a range of geographical locations (e.g., Lubin et al., 2004; Krewski et al., 2005; Darby et al., 2006), with each one confirming not only the heightened risk of developing lung cancer through exposure to radon, but even providing estimates of the level of risk involved. In domestic dwellings where there are high levels of radon gas, research has shown that the risk of developing lung cancer is greater among smokers due to the combined exposure to tobacco smoke and radon (Corrales et al., 2020). Furthermore, more generally, the World Health Organization (2009) has estimated that radon may cause between 3% and 14% of all lung cancers. In light of these facts, it is clear that radon presents significant health risks to those living in domestic dwellings in the United Kingdom.

3   The links between radon and other forms of cancer are less clear. Palmer et al. (2023) have proposed a link between radon exposure and a higher incidence of brain tumours, based on research conducted in the United States. However, similar studies relating to different types of cancer, such as those by Monastero et al. (2020) on radon and brain and spinal cord cancer, and Mozzoni et al. (2021) on radon and leukaemia, brain, skin, stomach, kidney and breast cancers, have played down the significance of radon as a risk factor. But this research is not conclusive. Monastero et al. (2020), for example, note that the possibility of a link cannot be entirely refuted. Therefore, with more research, it may be shown that radon poses a much greater health risk than we currently think.

4   UK Government has chosen to tackle these health risks by building awareness of the presence of radon gas and the potential health risks it poses. In 2018, Public Health England published the UK National Radon Action Plan which emphasised the importance of building up knowledge of radon exposure in domestic dwellings to help members of the public decide whether to buy a home in an area where there are high levels of radon. For this purpose, a map became freely available, illustrating the concentrations of radon across England and Wales (Miles et al., 2007). UK Government also implemented a communication plan, which included media communications and training for health officials and building surveyors. Building standards, based on the Housing Act (2004) which identified the potential health risks of radon, are also in place to ensure that domestic dwellings are adequately protected against its effects. The result of this work is that the general public are better informed than ever before about radon and so the risks to the health of those living in domestic dwellings is as low as might be expected.

How well do you think this student did? Let's take a closer look at their performance next to the assessment criteria set out above.

Knowledge and understanding

Is there knowledge and understanding here? Yes – broadly speaking, there is. The student demonstrates a good understanding of the topic itself: there is a clear awareness of what radon gas actually is, where it can be found in the United Kingdom, the health risks it poses, and the UK Government's response to the issue. The handling of research, particularly in paragraph (3), points to fairly in-depth understanding of the health implications of radon exposure, as does the less developed discussion of the UK Government's response in (4). However, is it 'developed', as required in the 70–79 level? We would argue that it isn't. The main reason for this is (4), where the government response is set out, but there's little sense of its effectiveness. We would suggest it is 'detailed' (60-69).

Communication

The communication is quite good: the writing is confident and the expressions used are generally clear. The author successfully uses what we would call 'academic language'. Phrases such as 'played down' are used instead of verbs like 'said', which help to get across an awareness of the lack of certainty in the conclusions

> of the research discussed. Along a similar line, 'better', 'more' and 'greater' are used to indicate the relative value of something. Rarely in academic writing will you treat something as entirely right or wrong. There is also a formality to the language used which is typical of academic writing: for example, in (2), the sentence beginning, 'Furthermore, more generally …'. But above all, the student is able to say more or less exactly what they mean: (3) 'The links between radon and other forms of cancer are less clear', and (4) 'UK Government has chosen to tackle these health risks by building awareness of the presence of radon gas and the potential health risks it poses'. All of this is impressive, but is the communication 'sophisticated'? Overall, it probably sits just inside the 70–79 level.
>
> *Critical evaluation*
>
> As indicated by the in-text references, there is at the very least here 'engagement with academic sources'. The discussion of the health risks in (2) is particularly rich with references to the literature and there does appear to be a good grasp of what's been written in this area. There's also some good engagement with publications by the UK Government and its agencies, an important source type for students in public health to make use of. Given the nature of the assessment – a first-year undergraduate formative assessment task, early on in the programme – we think there's evidence of 'developed engagement with academic sources', though perhaps, once again, it would fall into the lower 70s.
>
> *Overall*
>
> With two criteria in the 70–79 level and one in the 60–69, a mark in the low 70s (perhaps 72) would be appropriate.

This task gives you an insight into how tutors actually go about assessing your work. If you thought that all the tutor did was put a tick, cross or wavy line next to or under bits of your work, think again. Assessing student work is actually quite difficult. In many respects you're looking between the lines – at what isn't explicit, rather than what's in front of you. This points to a key bit of advice we've got about your approach to assessment: remember that you are demonstrating your proficiency in a particular literacy or aspect of academic practice and to do that you need to provide evidence of it. Let's consider 'critical evaluation' in the above task. You might have looked at 30 different academic sources for a particular piece of assessment, but if you only cite three

Table 5.1 Simplified marking criteria used for assessment at Level 4

	70–79%	60–69%	50–59%	40–49%	Below 40%
Knowledge and understanding	Developed knowledge and understanding	Detailed knowledge and understanding	Some knowledge and understanding	Basic knowledge and understanding	Limited knowledge and understanding
Communication	Sophisticated level of communication	Clear communication with some precision	Some clarity in communication	Basic level of communication	Communication lacks clarity
Critical evaluation	Developed engagement with academic sources	Engagement with academic sources	Some engagement with academic sources	Basic engagement with academic sources	Limited engagement with academic sources.

of these sources you won't have successfully demonstrated broad engagement with what's been written about a topic. Similarly, for 'knowledge and understanding', you might know a great deal about the topic you're writing about, but if you don't add that detail into your work it won't be recognised by the tutor. Linked to this point, never assume that your understanding is clear to the tutor reading your work. Work hard at making understanding stand out: add in an explanation, for example, if you think that will help to make it clearer. The tutor can't read your mind; it's up to you to demonstrate which level your work sits at in relation to each of the assessment criteria.

Task: Peer Assessment in practice

> Using a piece of recently submitted assessed work and working with a friend on your course, review each other's work using the relevant marking criteria. Assess the work without looking at any of the tutor's comments (if it's already been marked). Justify your decisions about which level you award for each criterion. What evidence is there to support your judgements? Can you identify any areas for improvement based on your assessment of the work? If you have the time, write out some feedback for your friend summarising your thoughts. In discussion with your friend, what does the task reveal about marking criteria and tutors' expectations?

Summary

Understanding the role of assessment in learning and what tutors are looking for in assessed work, as seen in marking criteria, is vital if you're going to excel. We recommend reviewing marking criteria before you start work on an assessment, so that you have the tutor's expectations in mind as you work. Make use of the opportunities afforded by formative assessment to inform your approach to summative assessment tasks. Formative assessment is designed by tutors to form an important part of the learning experience. Don't play down its importance as Natalie did just because 'it doesn't count'. Try to be flexible when it comes to assessment. Different assessment genres require slightly different approaches; it's important to be alive to these differences, as we said above, which are often quite subtle or nuanced. We also urge you to reflect on the experience of completing an assessment. It's this reflection and the conclusions you draw out of it, together with the feedback on your work provided by your tutors, that will underpin your personal development as you move through your programme of study.

References

Brown, S., & Race, P. (2021). Using effective assessment and feedback to promote learning. In L. Hunt & D. Chalmers (Eds.), *University teaching in focus* (pp. 135–162). Routledge.

Corrales, L., Rosell, R., Cardona, A., Martín, C., Zatarain-Barrón, Z., & Arrieta, O. (2020). Lung cancer in never smokers: The role of different risk factors other than tobacco smoking. *Critical Reviews in Hematology, 148*, Article 102895.

Darby, S., Hill, D., Deo, H., Auvinen, A., Barros-Dios, J., Baysson, H., Bochicchio, F., Falk, R., Farachi, S., Figueiras, A., Hakama, M., Heid, I., Hunter, N., Kreienbrock, L., Kreuzer, M., Lagarde, F., Mäkeläinen, I., Muirhead, C., Oberaigner, W., ... Doll, R. (2006). Residential radon and lung cancer – Detailed results of a collaborative analysis of individual data on 7148 persons with lung cancer and 14,208 persons without lung cancer from 13 epidemiologic studies in Europe. *Scandinavian Journal of Work, Environment & Health, 32*(Supplement 1), 1–83.

Housing Act 2004, c. 34. https://www.legislation.gov.uk/ukpga/2004/34/contents.

Krewski, D., Lubin, J., Zielinski, J., Alavanja, M., Catalan, V., Field, R., Klotz, J., Létourneau, E., Lynch, C., Lyon, J., Sandler, D., Schoenberg, J., Steck, D., Stolwijk, J., Weinberg, C., & Wilcox, H. (2005). Residential radon and risk of lung cancer: A combined analysis of 7 North American case-control studies. *Epidemiology, 16*(2), 137–145.

Lubin, J., Wang, Z., Boice Jr, J., Xu, Z., Blot, W., De Wang, L., & Kleinerman, R. (2004). Risk of lung cancer and residential radon in China: Pooled results of two studies. *International Journal of Cancer, 109*(1), 132–137.

Miles, J., Appleton, J., Rees, D., Green, B., Adlam, K., & Myers, A. (2007). *Indicative atlas of radon in England and Wales.* Health Protection Agency and British Geological Survey.

Monastero, R., & Meliker, J. (2020). Incidence of brain and spinal cord cancer and county-level radon levels in New Jersey, Wisconsin, Minnesota, Pennsylvania, and Iowa, USA. *Environmental Geochemistry and Health, 42*, 389–395.

Mozzini, P., Pinelli, S., Corradi, M., Ranzieri, S., Cavallo, D., & Poli, D. (2021). Environmental/occupational exposure to radon and non-pulmonary neoplasm risk: A review of epidemiologic evidence. *International Journal of Environmental Research and Public Health, 18*, Article 10466.

Nicol, D., & Macfarlane-Dick, D. (2006). Formative assessment and self-regulated learning: A model and seven principles of good feedback practice. *Studies in Higher Education, 31*(2), 199–218.

Palmer, J., Prasad, R., Cioffi, G., Kruchtko, C., Zaorsky, N., Trifiletti, D., Gondi, V., Brown, P., Perlow, H., Mishra, M., Chakravarti, A., Barnholtz-Sloan, J., & Ostrom, Q. (2023). Exposure to radon and heavy particulate pollution and incidence of brain tumours. *Neuro-Oncology, 25*(2), 407–417.

Public Health England (2018). *UK National Radon Action Plan.* Crown.

Sambell, K., McDowell, L., & Montgomery, C. (2012). *Assessment for learning in higher education.* Routledge.

Smith, S., & Hewston, R. (2020). Opening the door to the virtual school: Enhancing student engagement through online learning communities. In C. Dennis, S. Abbott, R. Matheson, & S. Tangney (Eds.), *Flexibility and pedagogy in higher education* (pp. 109–121). Brill.

World Health Organization (2009) *WHO handbook on indoor radon: A public health perspective.* World Health Organization.

Chapter 6

Making effective use of feedback

The counterpart to assessment is feedback, the comments you receive from a tutor on your performance, together with the mark. It's this feedback, which explains why you got the mark you received and how you might be able to improve it in the next assessment task, – and more importantly what you do with it – that ultimately drives forward your personal development.

Feedback is an integral element of learning in higher education. Tutors know this, which is why they spend so much time encouraging you to read it carefully. However, despite all the efforts of tutors, research has shown that students are, in general, less willing to utilise feedback as a tool for improving performance. There is a paradox here: lots of students clearly recognise the importance of feedback to their learning, are quick to bemoan what they consider to be inadequate feedback, but then make little attempt to engage with it once it's been received. The bottom line is that most students are concerned about their mark and little else – they don't engage effectively with the feedback provided, even if they appreciate its potential value to their learning. Feedback is there to be acted upon: self-regulating students look at the mark and then spend more time unpicking the feedback as a means of bringing about an improved performance. Such a student will also use it to pinpoint attributes or aspects of their character to develop as a way of growing into their graduate identity.

The purpose of this chapter therefore is to persuade you of the critical importance of feedback and the process of engaging with it effectively to excelling in your studies and to your personal development more broadly.

Learning Objectives

By the end of this chapter, you will have gained:

- a clearer understanding of what feedback is and its key role as a learning tool in higher education;
- the formal and less formal nature of feedback (it's not just used in relation to assessment);
- greater awareness of the importance of engaging with feedback and then making use of it as a means of improving academic performance;
- an appreciation of the role of feedback in helping to drive personal development;
- a better understanding of the relationship between your mindset and your approach to feedback;
- an appreciation of the value of feedback within self-regulated learning.

Keywords

feedback; feedback dialogue; corrective and diagnostic feedback; feedback cycle; action plan; self-regulated learning

What is feedback?

Feedback can be broadly defined as comments on or insights into your academic performance, usually but not exclusively provided by your tutor. It's most commonly associated with assessment: eventually, once the work you've submitted has been looked at by your tutor, you'll get a mark back, together with relevant feedback, which explains why you were given the mark you received, what you did well, and which areas need improvement if you're going to get a higher mark on the next assessment. Assessment doesn't provide the only context in which you might expect to receive feedback. In fact, feedback can be found across the learning experience, at different points, in formal and less formal settings. Interactions in lectures and tutorials, for example, not only with tutors, but also with other students, can provide valuable snippets of feedback on your knowledge and understanding, as well as on aspects of your approach to studying. One of our colleagues values conversations he has with his students when queuing up in the coffee shop. Such informal exchanges can often provide more impactful feedback than comments offered through more formal channels, such as through the return of marked assessment. It's therefore important to keep an open mind when it comes to receiving feedback. You'll find it in lots of different places. The learning challenge for you, on a personal level, is to make sure that you don't just *hear* feedback, but that you actually *listen* to it, think about it, and then use it positively to bring about a change in your approach to academic work.

What sort of comments do tutors usually make in feedback? This is a tricky question to answer, since expectations vary according to discipline, as do the demands of assessment and the practices associated with them. It should also be noted that no two tutors are the same: one tutor might be very quick to pick up on faults with referencing and other academic integrity issues, whereas another, even working in the same discipline, might prioritise comments on the structure of writing, for example. However, tutors should align their comments – however positive or negative – with the marking criteria and, more importantly, the language it uses.

Let's consider some feedback one of our students, Jess, received for a recently submitted piece of assessment. She was asked to write a critical review of a journal article that looked at the effectiveness of social media advertising as part of a digital marketing strategy. She received a mark of 64%, one of the highest marks in her tutorial group. The tutor provided the following feedback:

> *This is a well-organised and well-researched piece of work. You've clearly engaged with the article itself and you've made a good attempt at critiquing its content in light of what else you know about the role of Facebook in digital marketing. Your writing is also clear and easy to follow and there is careful referencing throughout. However, I think there was room to be more critical, particularly in relation to where the views of this author sit within the wider debate on the role of social media in digital marketing. You concentrate on Facebook, as the author of this article does, but Facebook is just one social media platform with its own strengths and limitations. How is the case study offered in the article related to the broader themes in the literature associated with social media? Similarly, some of your comments were a little too tentative. If you disagree, disagree! But remember to include an explanation of why you disagree. By doing so, you'll be taking the critical element of the work to a deeper level.*

Look at the language in this short extract: it echoes the sort of words you'll find in marking criteria. In terms of the overall impression of the work, the tutor describes it as 'well-organised' and 'well-researched'. To take the former phrase first, by 'well-organised' the tutor is referring principally to its structure and the way Jess has ordered her points to convey her argument. 'Well-researched' alludes to the range and variety of academic sources she's used in her answer. Research, in the sense of your ability to identify suitable academic sources, forms a key element of what tutors look for in assessed work. Here, Jess is praised for the research she's done. However, further on in the feedback, the tutor suggests that she might have gone further by exploring some of the broader themes in the literature associated with the use of social media in digital marketing. In other words, she needs to think more broadly about how this article fits into the wider discourse related to the topic. Two more positive features are identified: the clarity of her writing ('your writing is clear and easy to follow') and the accuracy of her references ('careful referencing'), both of which are key in marking criteria. The positive feedback here would suggest that Jess has already set for herself fairly high standards in relation to both criteria. In fact, the only real 'criticism' (for want of a better word) is the comment about engaging at a deeper level with the literature or, to put it another way, to *be more critical*. This is a phrase often used by tutors to encourage students to offer sharper critiques of the work they use. In Jess' case, the tutor thinks she is being too tentative in her analyses; while she disagrees, she isn't pressing her point of view as firmly as she should. The tutor suggests that she thinks more about why she disagrees. This is useful advice, for, as the tutor goes on to say, it is by providing a fuller explanation of her view that she will sharpen the edge of her critical insight.

What sort of issues do tutors highlight in feedback?

Based on our own experience of giving feedback – as well as many discussions with academic staff about this very topic – issues that recur across disciplines include:

Range of academic sources used

Lots of less experienced students engage with only a limited number of academic sources. While there is no right answer about how many sources you need to use for any particular piece of work (e.g., we are often asked by students how many items should be in the references list), to get higher marks, you clearly need to engage broadly with the relevant literature. Engaging broadly and more effectively with relevant academic sources will allow you to demonstrate greater depths of knowledge and understanding and this, in turn, should help you to engage more critically with these sources.

Critical engagement with academic sources

As we've said, it's really common for tutors to stress to students at all levels of study the importance of engaging with academic sources critically. 'Being critical' is about making use of academic sources as you construct your argument. It's not enough simply to present information. Such an approach is too passive. You need to *use* what you find in the sources selectively and constructively as you express the points you're trying to make. You can always be more critical in your approach; don't be disappointed if you see the words 'be more critical' in your feedback. It doesn't necessarily mean you're not being critical; you just need to work on taking your critical comments to deeper levels.

Writing conventions

Writing for assessment is shaped by the conventions associated with writing within your discipline. Sentence structure often comes up. Lots of students, in an effort to elevate their writing to what they think is a more 'academic' level, write long and complex sentences which, if anything, only serve to obscure the meaning of their writing. If you've done this, tutors will flag it up in feedback.

Structure and organisation

Linked to the point above about writing conventions, tutors might also comment upon the organisation and structure of your work. In general, it's not difficult to spot when a student hasn't properly planned a piece of written assessment. Such writing tends to be characterised by repetition, muddled paragraphs, contradictions (on occasion), and even confusion. Tutors might then add something into the feedback about the lack of clarity in the argument, the need for greater consideration of structure and planning, or even the importance of thinking carefully about the work prior to the act of writing itself.

Referencing and academic integrity issues

If there are faults with your referencing – perhaps inconsistencies or errors in the format of references – then your tutor will flag it up in feedback. You might also find comments about your use (or lack of use) of paraphrasing in your writing. Software like Turnitin will check the work you submit for similarities against other work available in its database. A high similarity score often indicates where your words have been too close to those in the source. This means that you need to develop your ability to paraphrase or to express what you read in other sources in your own words.

There are more, but these are the issues that we come across more than any others in our own teaching and assessment, and in discussion with other academics. If you look back at this section once you've read the entire chapter, you'll notice, of course, that each issue is directly related to marking criteria, as set out below. That's not a coincidence: feedback is very closely linked to these criteria.

Diagnostic feedback

What does the example of Jess' feedback tell us about its purpose? Feedback is corrective, in that it tells you where or how you might have gone wrong (assuming you got a mark you're disappointed with); but it's perhaps more appropriate to see feedback as being diagnostic. Using the word diagnostic to describe its purpose is important because it points to the definition of feedback as a process, a dialogue, even, between you, as a learner, and your tutor: positive and negative aspects of the work are highlighted in order to help you gain deeper insights into your performance and greater understanding of tutors' expectations. These comments can therefore act as the starting-point for a conversation – or dialogue – between you and your tutor about how you can improve your performance so that you can get a higher mark. In Jess' case, for example, she could use the feedback given to her to begin a dialogue with her tutor about how to be more critical in her handling of the academic sources. That sort of conversation can help you to clarify and deepen your understanding of what the tutor expects to see. It's therefore important to use feedback to start a dialogue with your tutor if you're not sure that you fully understand what point they're trying to make (Brown & Race, 2021). Our other student, Natalie, would almost certainly ignore any constructive feedback provided by the tutor; doing so means that it's highly unlikely she'll be able to improve on her performance as Jess will undoubtedly do.

On the flip side, feedback provides an opportunity for a tutor to open up a dialogue with you and in doing so to support your learning. On a more abstract level, feedback offers a tutor the chance to inspire, encourage, and motivate students.

Forms of feedback

Feedback on assessment is often written – in days gone by, submitted work would be annotated by a tutor by hand, with written comments appearing on the hard copy of the work itself (which weren't always easy to read!), and summary comments added at the end or on a separate proforma or cover sheet. Things are a little different now, but feedback on assessment is usually still provided in a written form, only now it's added to the digital version you submit via Moodle or another VLE. Tutors are encouraged to think creatively about how feedback is presented. Some, for example, now offer audio or video feedback, which is often quicker for the tutors to put together. If you do get audio or video feedback, it doesn't mean that it's worth less than traditional, written feedback. In fact, you might find that a tutor provides more detailed comments through these media. Whatever form the feedback takes, make the effort to engage with it fully.

How do you make effective use of feedback?

Feedback is intended to feed *forward*, in the sense that it is provided in order to help bring about an improvement in your academic performance. While the tutor will inevitably critique what you've done in that particular assessment, their comments will provide a foundation of understanding about the positive and negative features of your work which will then allow you to focus on those areas requiring an improvement (Hattie & Timperley, 2007). Thus, in commenting upon the past, in the shape of the work you've submitted, it looks to the future, or the work you're yet to submit.

The challenge to you, as a learner, lies in (i) interpreting the feedback provided and (ii) using that interpretation to inform the creation of an action plan, a series of positive, tangible steps you can take to bring about that improvement. Creating the action plan can be more difficult than interpreting the feedback. The real value of feedback to you lies in actualising the insights you've been able to draw out of the tutor's comments.

How much effort you put into engaging with feedback and what aspects of your performance or features of your work you choose to focus upon will be determined by your mindset, which we looked at in an earlier chapter. If you remember, there are two types of mindset: fixed and growth (Yeager & Dweck, 2012). A student with a fixed mindset might be inclined to either ignore feedback entirely or take only a superficial look at the comments explaining the positive and negative features of the work. Either way, engagement with the feedback will be limited and there'll be little attempt to make use of it constructively in the context of personal development. For a student with a growth mindset, feedback provides vital information needed to drive that growth. This student will diligently review the feedback and reflect on their performance. They will also look to the future by carefully considering how these comments can help to bring about an improved performance in the next assessment.

The feedback cycle

To engage effectively with feedback, we recommend you use something we call the 'feedback cycle' (Figure 6.1). This cycle is inspired by lots of research into how to help students to develop their feedback literacy, in particular by Carless and Boud (2018). The cycle is made up of four stages:

1 Review (read through the feedback provided)
2 Interpret (review work in light of feedback; identify strengths and weaknesses)
3 Articulate (turn the strengths and weaknesses into an action plan)
4 Apply (implementing those actions identified at the Articulate stage)

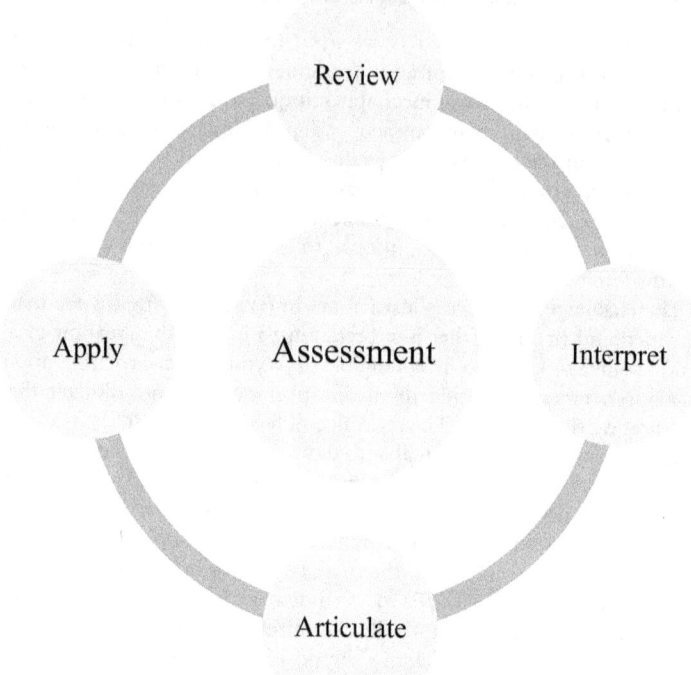

Figure 6.1 The feedback cycle.

At the 'Review' stage (1), you'll read through the feedback provided, take it in, and form some initial thoughts about it. Questions that might come into your mind include: is it reasonable? Does any of it surprise you? Is anything missing? Do you understand all of the comments? The purpose of this stage is to gain an overall impression of the feedback – to familiarise yourself with it in the context of the work.

At the 'Interpret' stage (2), you take a closer look at the feedback comments and review the work with them in mind, as well as the marking criteria to which they refer. What do we mean by 'interpret'? In order to understand the full significance of each of the tutor's comments, you need to see them in the context of your work. Interpreting feedback begins therefore with the task of breaking it down into positive and negative comments. Once you've done this, consider how these comments relate to the marking criteria. Usually, as noted above, the tutor's comments echo the language of the marking criteria, so that it's fairly easy to see which criterion each comment refers to. (It's also possible that each comment refers to more than one criterion.) With the breakdown of the feedback and an understanding of how each comment is related to the marking criteria, you can then start to review your work in light of the feedback. This will entail reading it through carefully and noting where each comment relates to your work, something that is usually made easier when tutors have annotated it. The purpose of this part of the cycle is to give you a deeper understanding of where your work needs further development by using the feedback to flag up these areas. This is why it's important to spend as much time as you can on this part of the process.

Articulating your interpretation of the feedback (3) is about using the feedback to shape an action plan designed to bring about an improvement in your performance. We'll look at this stage in more detail below. Applying (4) these actions means just that: implementing each one to facilitate an improvement in that particular aspect of your performance.

As an example, let's look at the feedback given on the Radon Gas exemplar we looked at in the previous chapter. To begin with, we recommend reading through the annotated version of the text below, as well as reminding yourself of the marking criteria. Next, read the summary feedback comments provided at the end of the exemplar.

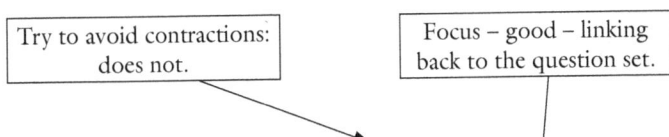

| Try to avoid contractions: does not. | Focus – good – linking back to the question set. |

(1) Radon gas is a radioactive gas that doesn't smell or have any colour. It occurs naturally in the ground as a result of the decay of radioactive uranium which is found in all rocks and soil in very small quantities. Concentrated amounts can be found in small spaces, such as domestic buildings, but because it doesn't smell or have any colour, it can be very hard to detect. As a result of the decaying process, radon gas has been shown to have a potentially serious risk to the health of those living in domestic buildings in the United Kingdom. Research has established a strong link between the effects of radon gas inhalation and the development of lung cancer. As seen in the UK Health Security Agency's recently published 'action plan', UK Government's response to the health risks it poses is based on the principle of building awareness of exposure to radon gas (Public Health England, 2018). In the United Kingdom, the UK Health Protection Agency (Miles et al., 2007) produces maps on the location of radon gas areas. An area of noticeably high concentration is south-west England, particularly in Devon and Cornwall. The effectiveness of this response is open to question, but the health

risks of radon are undoubtedly better known among the general public in the United Kingdom than ever before.

> An interesting introduction with some critique of UK Government's approach – trying to critique/evaluate

(2) In terms of health risks, radon is most commonly associated with lung cancer. A number of studies since the 1980s have established a strong link between it and the disease, with miners in particular susceptible to respiratory disease, including lung cancer. The inhalation of radon and its decay products has the effect of damaging lung tissue and increasing the chance of developing cancer. A number of important studies have analysed large amounts of data drawn from a range of geographical locations (e.g., Krewski et al., 2005; Lubin et al., 2004; Darby et al., 2006), with each one confirming not only the heightened risk of developing lung cancer through exposure to radon, but even providing estimates of the level of risk involved. In domestic dwellings where there are high levels of radon gas, research has shown that the risk of developing lung cancer is greater among smokers due to the combined exposure to tobacco smoke and radon (Corrales et al., 2020). Furthermore, more generally, the World Health Organization (2009) has estimated that radon may cause between 3% and 14% of all lung cancers. In light of these facts, it is clear that radon presents significant health risks to those living in domestic dwellings in the United Kingdom.

> Arguably, you might have gone into a bit more detail about one of these pieces of work (the most significant?). But there is good engagement with the literature here. Structure is sound.

> Again, structure is good here – very clearly organised.

(3) The links between radon and other forms of cancer are less clear. Palmer et al. (2023) have proposed a link between radon exposure and a higher incidence of brain tumours, based on research conducted in the United States. However, similar studies relating to different types of cancer, such as those by Monastero et al. (2020) on radon and brain and spinal cord cancer, and Mozzoni et al. (2021) on radon and leukaemia, brain, skin, stomach, kidney, and breast cancers, have played down the significance of radon as a risk factor. But this research is not conclusive. Monastero et al. (2020), for example, note that the possibility of a link cannot be entirely refuted. Therefore, with more research,

it may be shown that radon poses a much greater health risk than we currently think.

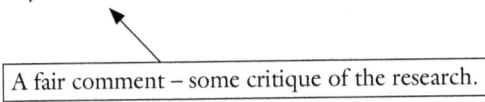

A fair comment – some critique of the research.

(4) UK Government has chosen to tackle these health risks by building awareness of the presence of radon gas and the potential health risks it poses. In 2018, Public Health England published the UK National Radon Action Plan which emphasised the importance of building up knowledge of radon exposure in domestic dwellings to help members of the public decide whether to buy a home in an area where there are high levels of radon. For this purpose, a map became freely available, illustrating the concentrations of radon across England and Wales (Miles et al., 2007). UK Government also implemented a communication plan, which included media communications and training for health officials and building surveyors. Building standards, based on the Housing Act (2004) which identified the potential health risks of radon, are also in place to ensure that domestic dwellings are adequately protected against its effects. The result of this work is that the general public are better informed than ever before about radon and so the risks to the health of those living in domestic dwellings is as low as might be expected.

This may be true, but I think you might have used more detailed knowledge to support it.

The tutor added the following summary comments:

This is a good piece of work characterised by clear communication (helped by strong organisation and structure) and effective engagement with academic sources. In addition, there is some detailed knowledge and understanding. I particularly liked the way you handled the relevant literature: there is a clear sense of your understanding of the limitations of some of this research, notably in relation to other types of cancer which may (or may not) be linked to radon gas exposure. Given that you have demonstrated that awareness, I think you might have gone further in your critique of this literature. You noted, for example, that there is little conclusive evidence of its links to leukaemia but that Monastero et al. had not ruled out a connection entirely. What led them to this point of view? I think you might have gone deeper into this particular aspect of the research. Similarly, I think you might have offered further critique of the UK Government's approach to the radon gas issue. I don't disagree with your conclusion that the public are better informed, but is there any evidence out there to support this point? What is the government doing now about radon gas? Has its approach changed? There's clear engagement with academic sources here, as I've said; the challenge in the next piece of work is to have the confidence to really open up the arguments of these authors and then assess them at a deeper level.

In the assessment chapter, we simplified the marking criteria used in this exercise. It concentrates on only three areas: knowledge and understanding, communication, and critical evaluation (Table 6.1).

How might the feedback cycle be used to make sense of this feedback?

1 Review

After reading the tutor's summary feedback and the annotations on the piece of work itself, are the comments clear? Do any of the comments surprise you? Is there anything you don't fully understand? If there is, we suggest looking again at the marking criteria to see if that helps to clarify the comment. If there is an annotation you don't understand, read through the text it applies to carefully, including the text which precedes and follows it. Does that make it any clearer?

2 Interpret

This is a trickier and more involved stage. As we've said above, interpreting the feedback can be broken down into three distinct stages. The first is (i) to unpick it by distinguishing what you consider to be the positive comments from the negative. To do this, you need to take a holistic view of the feedback – in other words, look at the annotations as well as the summary comments as a whole. There might be some repetition here, but that's okay. You can simply omit any comments that crop up twice. We've set out the positive and negative comments in a table, with one column for each (Table 6.2). (ii) How does each comment relate to the marking criteria? Let's look at the positive comments first, as set out in Table 6.3.

As these links suggest, the student's ability to communicate clearly is high. The response is focused sharply on the question, which points to the clarity of the argument (in other words, what the student is trying to say), while the writing as a whole is underpinned by a strong and effective structure. Each paragraph, for example, considers a separate point, and the arrangement of the paragraphs means that each one builds on the one before it – there is a logic and flow to the points being made. Again, this feature of the work points to the clarity of the communication: it's easy to read and so is reflective of the student's ability to communicate clearly. The student has also demonstrated an ability to engage with academic sources. This is key: a deficiency here would seriously undermine the student's chances of excelling. Taken together, these comments are really encouraging. The student has done very well in relation to two key marking criteria.

Table 6.1 Simplified marking criteria used for assessment at Level 4

	70–79%	60–69%	50–59%	40–49%	Below 40%
Knowledge and understanding	Developed knowledge and understanding	Detailed knowledge and understanding	Some knowledge and understanding	Basic knowledge and understanding	Limited knowledge and understanding
Communication	Sophisticated level of communication	Clear communication with some precision	Some clarity in communication	Basic level of communication	Communication lacks clarity
Critical evaluation	Developed engagement with academic sources	Engagement with academic sources	Some engagement with academic sources	Basic engagement with academic sources	Limited engagement with academic sources

Table 6.2 Positive and negative comments identified in tutor's feedback

Positive	Negative
Clear focus on the question	Contractions [=Punctuation] – need to avoid
Strong and effective structure	More critical handling of academic sources
Good engagement with academic sources	Supporting evidence needs to be more detailed

How do the negative comments relate to the marking criteria? We've summarised these links in Table 6.4.

Although we've described these comments as 'negative', this isn't to say that the student hasn't done very well overall. The comments summarised here should be seen as highlighting aspects of the work where an improvement might push the overall mark into the higher mark range (70%+). The point about contractions, which may be taken as a broader point about punctuation, is related to communication, but it is only a minor issue that is easily corrected. Generally speaking, as you might already know, when it comes to traditional academic writing (i.e., the more formal writing style associated with assessment genres like essays), there is often an expectation to avoid contractions (abbreviated versions of words like 'do not' or 'would not') by writing out these words in full. Thus, 'is not', 'does not', or 'would not'. The

Table 6.3 Links between positive comments and marking criteria

Clear focus on the question	Communication: [at least] clear communication with some precision (60–69%)
Strong and effective structure	Communication: [at least] clear communication with some precision (60–69%)
Good engagement with academic sources	Critical evaluation: [at least] engagement with academic sources (60–69%)

Table 6.4 Links between negative comments and marking criteria

Contractions [= Punctuation] – need to avoid	Communication: albeit a fairly minor point
More critical handling of academic sources	Critical evaluation: [at least] engagement with academic sources (60–69%)
Supporting evidence needs to be more detailed	Knowledge and understanding: detailed knowledge and understanding (60–69%)

point about the need to 'be more critical' when it comes to handling academic sources needs to be seen in context. We've already established that the handling of the academic sources is pretty good. This comment should be interpreted in light of the positive feedback. In essence, the tutor is saying 'you've done well, but if you want to do even better, you need to be a bit more critical in the way you approach academic sources'. This comment will make more sense in the next stage, when we review the work with the feedback in mind. In relation to supporting evidence, the tutor isn't trying to tell the student that the knowledge and understanding is lacking in the work. It's just that on occasion the argument could be strengthened – in the sense that a mark in a higher mark range might have been awarded – at times by more detailed knowledge to support the point being made.

Next, you need to (iii) explore these comments further by reviewing the work itself. In doing this, the annotations provided by the tutor will be very useful. Most, if not all, of the comments identified will be flagged up in these annotations. On reading the work through again, it's easy to see why the tutor has praised its structure and the clarity of the communication. If it wasn't obvious to begin with, it certainly is on a second reading. As noted above, the work is easy to follow, and the points are conveyed effectively through the use of paragraphs. The final positive point, relating to the way the student has engaged with the academic sources, is also clearer on a second reading. Note the in-text references (or citations) which clearly flag up where the student is using these sources. The variety of academic sources and the frequency with which references to them appear in the work help to make clear the extent of this engagement. Moving beneath the surface, we can see evidence of *synthesis in the way that the student 'controls' the academic sources included. For example, in the grasp of the literature revealed in such comments as 'A number of important studies have analysed large amounts of data drawn from a range of geographical locations …' (Paragraph 2) and 'However, similar studies relating to different types of cancer, such as those by Monastero et al. (2020) …' (Paragraph 3). Looking at the student's comments about this latter source, by Monastero et al., there is an attempt at critiquing its conclusion in the comment 'But this research is not conclusive …' (Paragraph 3). But it represents a light touch; more might've been said.

In relation to the negative comments, the process of reviewing the work in light of the feedback helps to bring each one into sharper focus. Let's not spend too long on the contractions. You can see via the annotation where this has occurred; there's a second example just below the one highlighted. As we said above, this is easily corrected. In relation to the 'be more critical' comment, again, you can see, via the annotations, where the tutor thinks this comment applies. He's highlighted the sentence ending 'but even providing estimates of the levels of risk involved' (Paragraph 2). Reading this sentence again, you can see what is meant. There is good awareness of the debate itself, but the sentence might have had greater impact if – as the tutor has pointed out – the student had provided a more detailed explanation of one of the academic sources cited. The supporting evidence point can be found in the final annotation, on UK Government's approach to the issue of radon gas awareness. The student makes a fair but inadequately supported statement about the success of this approach. Clearly, this point would have been strengthened with a reference to data supporting it.

Reviewing your work as part of the interpretation of feedback is therefore vital to maximising the value of the tutor's comments. Reading through your work again having already analysed the feedback has the effect of opening up the tutor's comments. You can see the work in a different light and this in itself may help to bring into sharper focus both the positive and negative comments you've identified. Reviewing your work effectively allows you to contextualise the feedback. As a result, it makes more sense. Don't skip this part of the process; spend as much time as you need on it so that you can squeeze the feedback for all its worth.

3 Articulate

Interpreting feedback takes a lot of time, energy, and concentration. Creating an action plan, however, arguably represents a greater challenge. How do you turn the insights you've gained into your academic performance into meaningful, purposive, practical outcomes that will help to bring about a clear improvement in your performance?

If we look at the negative comments first, the best thing to do at the outset is to rank them according to how difficult you think it will be to address each one. With the comments we've been looking at, the point about contractions/punctuation will clearly be the easiest of the three to put right. But how do you address it? What practical step can you take to put it right? It might be possible, for example, to find out more about contractions in an English grammar handbook, the sort of text that your library will hold. Alternatively, you could find some information about punctuation more quickly in a guide provided by your university's academic skills specialists, or even by looking for resources (from suitable sources, like another university or the British Council) through Google. Whichever action you choose, putting this right will be fairly straightforward.

Addressing the remaining comments constitutes more of a challenge. In relation to being more critical, this isn't about drastically rethinking your approach to the use of academic sources in your work. It's actually about enhancing it: making more of the sources you use; having the confidence to challenge the views you find with greater conviction; recognising the value of exploring the sources you find in greater depth as a way of getting across to your tutor the high level of your understanding. How do you achieve this? How do you build your confidence when it comes to handling academic sources? A practical step you could take here might involve asking your tutor directly for advice or asking for guidance from an academic skills specialist or librarian. Any one of these people might suggest looking at a suitable handbook on critical thinking, for example. But you might not need to spend time doing that. Ultimately, in order to handle academic sources with greater confidence, you need to have a more developed understanding of their content. This can be acquired by reading more and more, building up your knowledge of the topic in a structured way, so that you feel more confident about discussing the content of academic sources or contextualising it within the relevant discourse associated with that topic. Read, read, read – it's a mantra we often repeat to students. Other practical steps touch on what you do when you engage with these sources. Most students will make notes on – for example – a journal article; but how do you compile these notes? Do you simply list relevant points, in bullet form, under the heading of the work? Or do you take a more active approach to the creation of these notes? A really positive step to take for all students – not just the author of the radon gas exemplar who needs to be more critical – is to challenge yourself by writing a summary of the article as part of your notes. By articulating the argument in the work in your own words, you'll develop your understanding – and in doing so will feel more confident when it comes to writing about that particular source. You might also include in your notes your reflections on how this source relates to what else you've read on the topic. For example, if you find a section which contradicts something you've recently read in another source, make a note of it. Such notes help to build up a picture of the structure and contours of the discourse relating to that topic, its themes and points of contention, for example. Overall, such steps work towards expanding your capacity for critical thought – and this, in turn, will help you to be more critical in your writing.

The final comment to address is about knowledge and understanding. More specifically, it's about making better use of knowledge and understanding as supporting evidence for the points you make. What practical steps can you take to effect a change here? It's important to note that this student almost certainly has the knowledge needed to support the statement in the final paragraph which attracted the tutor's eye. It's therefore more appropriate for the action to focus on the need to recognise when such supporting evidence is needed. A practical exercise to help address this problem might be to review this piece of work – and any other in progress or recently submitted – and highlight any points which might have been strengthened through the use of more supporting evidence. In addition, it might be helpful to do the same when reading published work: look to see how the authors use evidence to support their arguments. All in all, this bit of feedback is about building greater awareness of how and when to use supporting evidence.

It can be difficult to translate your interpretation of feedback into practical steps intended to bring about an improvement. That's why it's important to seek out further advice, in the first place from the tutor who compiled the feedback, or, if needed, another member of staff, like an academic skills specialist or librarian; you might also find it useful to discuss your feedback with a friend. Getting someone else's perspective on how you can effect meaningful change in your performance might be just what you need if you're struggling to figure out how to make good use of your feedback.

4 Apply

Once you've identified the actions you then need to put them into practice. It's important here that you monitor your progress, as any good self-regulating student will do. If you find it difficult to implement a particular action or that action doesn't have the desired effect, do you need to identify an alternative action to use? Keep an open mind when it comes to reflecting on your progress. Don't be afraid of making changes to what you're doing or even taking further action if it's needed.

Task: Thinking about feedback

With the 'feedback cycle' in mind, it's time to look back at a piece of feedback you've recently received. If you haven't yet had any feedback, you can always revisit this task once you've got some.

We're going to apply the cycle by reflecting carefully on this piece of feedback. To do this, you'll need copies of the feedback itself, the work you submitted (preferably a version annotated by the tutor), and the marking criteria used by the tutor.

Remember, the feedback cycle is made up of four stages:

1 Review
2 Interpret
3 Articulate
4 Apply

Begin by reviewing the feedback as whole (1); consider, in particular, whether you fully understand all of it or if you need to ask your tutor for further clarification. Once you've done that, move on to the interpretation stage (2). This can be broken down into three steps:

> i unpicking the feedback so that you can distinguish between positive and negative comments;
> ii linking each comment to the relevant marking criteria;
> iii reviewing the work submitted in light of the breakdown of feedback and its links to marking criteria.
>
> Go through each step, using the discussion above to guide you if necessary.
>
> Now that you've interpreted the feedback, you need to think carefully about how you're going to use it (3). This involves creating an action plan. We recommend setting out the positive and negative comments in one or two tables. Once you've done this, try to respond to each one by coming up with an appropriate action. If you find this bit tricky, use the examples above to prompt some deeper thought. Once you've identified the actions, you've got your action plan. It's up to you then to apply each action to your practice (4). Remember to monitor the impact of your actions on your performance; if you have to change things by using a different or complementary action, then do it. Your goal is, of course, to bring about an improvement in your performance.

Summary

Engaging with feedback (by employing the feedback cycle) is vital if you're going to excel in your academic work. Feedback performs an essential role in learning in higher education by offering insights into your academic performance and, in doing so, the expectations of tutors. It's important to be open-minded about feedback. It comes in a variety of forms, both formal and informal, and the most useful bits of feedback often come from casual conversations you might have with your tutor or even with other students. In order to engage effectively with feedback, consider each stage of the feedback cycle. Feedback needs to be interpreted first; that interpretation is then used to create an action plan. Ultimately, the value of feedback lies in the way you use it; if you choose not to act upon it, it won't have any meaningful impact upon your performance.

References

Brown, S., & Race, P. (2021). Using effective assessment and feedback to promote learning. In L. Hunt & D. Chalmers (Eds.), *University teaching in focus* (pp. 135–162). Routledge.

Carless, D., & Boud, D. (2018). The development of student feedback literacy: Enabling uptake of feedback. *Assessment & Evaluation in Higher Education*, *43*(8), 1315–1325.

Corrales, L., Rosell, R., Cardona, A., Martín, C., Zatarain-Barrón, Z., & Arrieta, O. (2020). Lung cancer in never smokers: The role of different risk factors other than tobacco smoking. *Critical Reviews in Hematology*, *148*, Article 102895.

Darby, S., Hill, D., Deo, H., Auvinen, A., Barros-Dios, J., Baysson, H., Bochicchio, F., Falk, R., Farachi, S., Figueiras, A., Hakama, M., Heid, I., Hunter, N., Kreienbrock, L., Kreuzer, M., Lagarde, F., Mäkeläinen, I., Muirhead, C., Oberaigner, W., ... Doll, R. (2006). Residential radon and lung cancer – Detailed results of a collaborative analysis of individual data on 7148 persons with lung cancer and 14,208 persons without lung cancer from 13 epidemiologic studies in Europe. *Scandinavian Journal of Work, Environment & Health*, *32*(Supplement 1), 1–83.

Hattie, J., & Timperley, H. (2007). The power of feedback. *Review of Educational Research*, *77*(1), 81–112.

Housing Act 2004, c. 34. https://www.legislation.gov.uk/ukpga/2004/34/contents.

Krewski, D., Lubin, J., Zielinski, J., Alavanja, M., Catalan, V., Field, R., Klotz, J., Létourneau, E., Lynch, C., Lyon, J., Sandler, D., Schoenberg, J., Steck, D., Stolwijk, J., Weinberg, C., & Wilcox, H. (2005). Residential radon and risk of lung cancer: A combined analysis of 7 North American case-control studies. *Epidemiology*, *16*(2), 137–145.

Lubin, J., Wang, Z., Boice Jr, J., Xu, Z., Blot, W., De Wang, L., & Kleinerman, R. (2004). Risk of lung cancer and residential radon in China: Pooled results of two studies. *International Journal of Cancer*, *109*(1), 132–137.

Miles, J., Appleton, J., Rees, D., Green, B., Adlam, K., & Myers, A. (2007). *Indicative atlas of radon in England and Wales*. Health Protection Agency and British Geological Survey.

Monastero, R., & Meliker, J. (2020). Incidence of brain and spinal cord cancer and county-level radon levels in New Jersey, Wisconsin, Minnesota, Pennsylvania, and Iowa, USA. *Environmental Geochemistry and Health*, *42*, 389–395.

Mozzini, P., Pinelli, S., Corradi, M., Ranzieri, S., Cavallo, D., & Poli, D. (2021). Environmental/occupational exposure to radon and non-pulmonary neoplasm risk: A review of epidemiologic evidence. *International Journal of Environmental Research and Public Health*, *18*, Article 10466.

Palmer, J., Prasad, R., Cioffi, G., Kruchtko, C., Zaorsky, N., Trifiletti, D., Gondi, V., Brown, P., Perlow, H., Mishra, M., Chakravarti, A., Barnholtz-Sloan, J., & Ostrom, Q. (2023). Exposure to radon and heavy particulate pollution and incidence of brain tumours. *Neuro-Oncology*, *25*(2), 407–417.

Public Health England (2018). *UK National Radon Action Plan*. Crown.

World Health Organization (2009) *WHO handbook on indoor radon: A public health perspective*. World Health Organization.

Yeager, D. S., & Dweck, C. S. (2012). Mindsets that promote resilience: When students believe that personal characteristics can be developed. *Educational Psychologist*, *47*(4), 302–314.

Chapter 7

Research

Developing effective search strategies

Research is arguably the most important of all academic literacies. It's therefore vital for you to get to grips with the practice of searching, with all of its nuances, as quickly as possible if you're going to excel in your academic work.

Why is it so important? We only need to think back to the way we conceived of learning as the journey you take through a discourse community from the position of being a novice (i.e. a new member of this community) to that of an expert (i.e. an experienced contributor to the work of this community). Movement on this journey is driven by your engagement in the work of this community, and this work revolves around its discourse. We've mentioned discourse already; it refers to the debate and discussions – the creation of knowledge – that takes place within that community. This discourse is published in academic journals and books, as well as in lots of other different genres of academic sources. It is in identifying these sources and then beginning to work with them that searching takes centre stage.

In this chapter, we'll take a closer look at the practice of effective searching. Searching is very much about behaviour and so our guidance will be focused on shaping the approach you take by explaining the principles that underpin effective searching. It's also important to recognise the complexities of searching, particularly as academic sources in digital format are so easily available now through your university library's discovery service and more widely via the internet. If anything, the landscape of research today has heightened the importance of mastering the literacy of searching if you're going to excel. So much is published and so much is available – not all of which is necessarily useful or of sufficient academic rigour – that getting your *search strategy right has taken on a new significance.

DOI: 10.4324/9781003217527-7

Learning Objectives

By the end of this chapter, you will have gained:

- a clear understanding of what we mean by research;
- an understanding of the principles that underpin effective searching;
- an appreciation of the value of developing a search strategy;
- an understanding of the value of keywords in shaping search results;
- an awareness of the need to evaluate the sources in your results;
- an awareness of the tools available for extending your search – or for advanced searching.

Keywords

searching; search strategy; keywords; synonyms; limiters; source type; evaluative criteria; extending searches; databases; Google extensions

What do we mean by 'searching'?

At the heart of research is the practice of searching. At a basic level, searching can be defined simply as 'looking for information'. It's something we all do, every day, as we engage with the world around us. You might wake up in the morning and 'search' for the opening times of your local supermarket. You might be chasing trivia: when did Abraham Lincoln become president? Who is that actor you've just seen on television married to? How many goals did Cristiano Ronaldo score for Real Madrid? To answer each of these questions, you need to 'search' for the answer. In almost all cases, you'll pick up your phone (or, perhaps, a tablet), type in your question (or, if you're a more experienced researcher like us, you might use *keywords, which we'll come to shortly) into Google, and see what comes up (or, for us, what results are returned). With the supermarket, Google will likely provide you with the answer. For the trivia, you'll probably get a response that incorporates (or takes you to) the relevant page from the Wikipedia. Either way, the answer is there, in front of you, immediately.

Searching in the context of higher education is different. It's driven by many of the same principles, but it's more complex – more of a *science*, as we like to tell students. Searching in higher education is exploratory; you won't find an exact answer, as you would do when searching for trivia. It's also laborious, in that it requires a lot of effort and thought, because there isn't always a precise answer to the search query you might have. Effective searching is therefore based on a strategy, in the sense of a plan or structure to help guide your searching and improve your chances of finding the right sources. Search strategy is iterative, which means that it's repetitive: you'll do a search, reflect on the results, amend the parameters of the search, and then search again. The idea is that as you complete each round of searches, you'll narrow down the range of sources you find. Clearly, effective searching requires time; it can't be done the night before an assessment is due to be handed in.

With all of this in mind, how do we define searching in an academic context? It's clearly about more than 'finding information', although, at a basic level, that is what's going on. Searching in an academic context is about: (i) identifying academic sources relevant to the discourse in your discipline and, specifically, to the topic you are studying; (ii) engaging critically with those sources as you sift them, prioritise what you need to read, and reflect on what gaps there are in your knowledge and understanding.

Searching is a complex practice that involves application, thought, decision-making and reflection, as well as many other things. In this sense, searching provides an acid test of your ability to act as a self-regulating learner.

Effective searching: Identifying key principles

In order to identify the key principles of effective searching, let's look at a couple of examples of student behaviour.

We'll begin with Natalie. Natalie, as you will remember, is not a very proactive student. She's quite disorganised and tends to leave things to the last minute. In this example, she's about to start her research for the next assessment. What does Natalie's example tell us about the principles of effective searching?

> *'What's the essay question?', Natalie asks her friend, Jess. She knows there's only a couple of weeks before the deadline, which gives her just enough time to get that 2,000 word essay finished. Jess replies, 'It's on marketing: How effective is social media as a marketing tool for small businesses?' Natalie asks Jess to text it to her. Later that day, once she's back at home, Natalie opens-up her laptop and types out the essay question into a blank Word document. Where to begin? Natalie knows that the tutor included a reading list in the module handbook. She downloaded a copy from Moodle and so she opens it up. Sure enough, in the reading list is a book she thinks will be useful: Dave Chaffey's* Digital marketing. *Natalie remembers the tutor joking that they would need to have it with them at all times. So that's one source. Nasser, another friend, told her that you only need to use five sources. Four more to go, then. She opens-up the library's discovery service on her browser. First, she*

decides to check whether Chaffey's book is available online; she'd much rather work at home than in the library. It is, and so she downloads the chapter on 'Digital marketing strategy', which is all she's allowed to download. She then types in 'social media marketing' in the discovery service. Nearly 200,000 results are returned. She starts to scroll down the list but all the items she finds look the same. She picks one – on social media marketing (they all have similar titles), published in 2008 – which is available online. She notices that lots of the others are only available on the shelf in the library. She keeps scrolling and eventually comes across a journal article, in Business Horizons, on social media, marketing and human needs, published in 2015. She downloads it. She skips through the next couple of pages, but nothing really jumps out at her. She closes the tab with the library discovery service open on it and turns to Google. She copies the essay question from her Word doc and pastes it into the search box before hitting return. Scrolling down the page, she clicks on a guide to social media for small businesses, available at www.businessnewsdaily.com. It looks interesting and so copies the URL into her Word doc. Realising that much of what Google has returned looks less 'academic-y', she remembers something Nasser once told her. If you click on 'Books' along the top, lots of proper books will come up. On the second page, she finds a link to a book published in 2018 on tips for using social media in marketing. It looks relevant, so she takes a look. Parts of the book are available, but in one chapter, on the drawbacks of using social media, every other page is missing. It looks 'academic-y' though, so she makes a note of the URL. Finally, she remembers that she's borrowed a book on marketing from the library, by an American author, published in 2003. That'll do – that's the five sources Nasser mentioned.

There's a lot to unpack here. Natalie clearly has some idea about how to go about searching, but she doesn't do it very effectively, in part because she's not self-regulating (in particular, the environment in which she decides to work, which restricts the approach she can take).

In the first place, she isn't helped by her disorganised approach to studying. She doesn't know what the title of the assessment is, which immediately puts her at a disadvantage because she has little understanding of the topic area that provides the context for the search. In addition, she's given herself only two weeks to complete the assessment. Leaving sufficient time to search for sources properly is vital if the search is going to be effective. She is right to turn first to the *reading list provided in the module handbook though. This reading list will be indicative rather than comprehensive, meaning it will highlight what the tutor thinks are key texts rather than giving you a list of everything the tutor wants you to read. It's there that she finds Chaffey's book, which will certainly be useful to her. Her first big mistake is in listening to the advice of her friend, Nasser, who tells her that she only needs to use five sources. We often get asked by students how many sources to include in an essay. In truth, there is no correct number of sources to use; much depends on *how* you use the sources, rather than how many you look at. This is one of two factors that essentially restrict her search by limiting its effectiveness. Having, rightly, decided to use the library discovery service, she then undermines this decision by choosing to use sources only available online. This is because she wants to work at home. However, this decision further restricts her search. She fails to regulate the environment in which she is studying. She also finds it difficult to discern the relative value of the sources she finds, even at a surface level. She seems to pick items almost at random. For example, she chooses one online title simply because she'll be able to look at it at home; there is little awareness of the potential problems she might encounter using a source published long ago in 2008! But the same lack of discernment impacts upon her use of Google Books. Her decision to use Google is not necessarily a bad one. However, particularly for undergraduates, we present Google to students as a tool for extending your search rather than for conducting initial inquiries. Using the essay question for her search term isn't a great idea: a more thoughtful approach is needed. She is then rather undiscriminating in her selection of sources. The website she finds is of questionable relevance given that it appears to be a business news outlet. Realising that she's not finding what she expects to see, she then turns to Google Books, an extension of the Google search engine. Again, this is a tool that in normal circumstances you would use to extend your search. Natalie doesn't know this and so she searches it using her essay question. She picks a book on the second page, again without much thought about its relevance. She also doesn't realise that Google Books will often only give you a preview of the book. She saves the link, but she can only access a few pages. All in all, whatever Natalie might think, her search has been fairly unsuccessful.

How does Jess go about the search? Jess, if you remember, is a self-regulating learner. She is organised and proactive; she plans her work carefully and is mindful of the time available. What does her example tell us about the principles of effective searching?

> *Jess has had the essay question – How effective is social media as a marketing tool for small businesses? – in mind since the start of the module, when she first made a note of it after reviewing the module handbook. With the question in mind, she has prepared for the lectures and tutorials that make up the module in advance, paying particular attention to those that looked more relevant to the question's topic area. She, too, is aware of Chaffey's textbook on* Digital Marketing; *she's used it several*

times already and knows that there are sections in it relevant to social media marketing and small businesses. Having marked these sections, she reviews her level of knowledge of the topic. Ideally, she thinks, given that she already has a good understanding of the principles that underpin the use of social media for marketing – and that these principles are discussed in several textbooks – it would be more useful for her to find case studies of the use of social media marketing by small businesses. She realises that she might find these in textbooks, but she's more likely to find them in journal articles. Taking out a piece of paper, she starts to note down what she thinks might be useful keywords to use in the search. She decides to begin with 'social media' and 'marketing'. She opens-up the browser on her laptop, goes to the library's discovery service and types in those keywords. Scrolling through the results in the first couple of pages, she realises that most of the items returned are textbooks; they've all got the same title: 'Social media marketing'! As a result, she makes the decision to use one of the limiters on the right-hand side of the screen. She selects, under 'Source type', 'journals'. This has the effect of reducing the number of results by only returning journal articles. Some of the articles she finds are more than ten years old, which she considers to be less relevant, and so she selects another limiter, 'Date range', and narrows the publication date to the last five years. This produces an even smaller number of results. She finds a couple of case studies within them, but they're not related to small businesses. Having made a note of them – just in case she decides to look at them at a later date – she starts a new search, this time adding 'small business' to the search terms. She repeats the steps she took with the first search, eventually adding both limiters. As a result, she finds two case studies which she thinks will really enhance the quality of her essay. As a final task, to be sure that she hasn't missed anything that might be useful, she uses Google Scholar. Using the same search terms, Google Scholar returns a list of journal articles, one of which did not appear in the results from the library discovery service. She makes a note of it, completes her own library's online request form for an 'Inter-library loan' and receives a digital copy of the article after a couple of days.

Jess' approach, as you can tell, is far more structured. She knows what she's looking for, even the type of source she'll need. She plans carefully, the first stage of which is to reflect on the level of her knowledge and understanding before undertaking any searches. This allows her to target her searches on gaps in her knowledge. She's right to think that the principles that underpin the use of social media in marketing are fairly easy to find – just look at how many social media marketing textbooks she finds in her first search. There's little point, therefore, in spending lots of time looking at general information in textbooks. She needs to find research focused on case studies, to draw out the nuances associated with the practice of using social media in marketing. This is an intelligent decision which makes the most of the time available, but it is only possible for her to do this because of her organised approach and the planning she has undertaken. Before she starts searching, she also thinks carefully about the keywords she will use in the search. Unlike Natalie, she avoids using the essay title as a search term; instead, she realises the importance of breaking down the question into its constituent elements. She therefore uses 'social media' and 'marketing' to begin with, but on reviewing the results she realises that she needs to do something to narrow them down. Since she knows how the library's discovery service works – she's probably engaged in a library induction; we doubt Natalie did – she applies a *limiter, in this case to pick out journal articles, the genre of source she's most interested in. When she finds that the results are still a little too broad, she applies a second limiter related to currency. By applying a date range, she's able to identify the most recently published journal articles – which will contain the most up to date research – easily. As expected, however, the case studies she finds, while useful, are not really related to small business. She therefore undertakes a second cycle of searching by adding 'small businesses' to the search terms. Repeating the steps she took with the first search, she eventually identifies two case studies relevant to the topic. She then uses Google Scholar – another of Google's own extensions to its search tool – to see if she can find anything that isn't held in or subscribed to by her library. In other words, she extends her search by using Google. She does find something which she is able to request through her own library. All in all, Jess' search has been successful: through effective searching practice, she's found exactly what she was looking for.

The efficiency of Jess' approach is clear to see. You should also be able to see the links between her approach and the features of self-regulated learning. Self-regulating learners do things the right way! That's why they're much more likely to excel.

If we break down what we've taken from these examples, we can identify the different stages of effective searching practice:

1. Plan carefully. This includes reviewing what you already know so that you can target aspects of a topic to focus on when searching. This means that you're more likely to make effective use of the time available.
2. Identify keywords to drive your searches. Spend some time – as Jess did – thinking about what keywords you're going to use. This is important, in that the keywords you use need to generate an appropriate range of results.

3 Understand how to use your library discovery service. What limiters are available in the service you're using? How might you use these limiters to narrow down the search results.
4 Evaluate the different sources you find. Try to be discerning when it comes to selecting which sources to use.
5 Extend your search. There are various tools available to do this, not just Google; find out what databases, for example, are relevant to your discipline. We look at databases in more detail below.

In the following sections, we'll consider these stages in more detail. We'll also offer some practical guidance on how you can adapt the way you currently search for academic sources into a more efficient and effective approach.

Task: What approach do you take to searching?

> Think back to a recent lecture or tutorial you prepared for, or an assessment you were working on. How did you go about searching?
> Try to break down your approach into stages.
> Here are some questions to help structure your reflection:
>
> - Did it begin with planning? If so, how much planning did you do?
> - What sort of sources or information were you looking for? In other words, what were the objectives of your search?
> - What keywords did you use? How easy was it to identify these keywords?
> - Did you use your library's discovery service? If so, did you make use of the limiters to narrow down the search results?
> - What type of sources did you find? How easy was it to distinguish between the different source types? Did you perform multiple searches?
>
> When you compare your approach to the stages of effective searching we've identified above, which ones are missing? Which stages do you need to work on to make your current searching practice more effective?

Planning your search

As we've seen with Jess' example, effective searching begins with careful and considered planning. There are reasons for this, not least that on a practical level, you don't have the time to waste on searches that might only provide tangential information or knowledge you can glean from background reading (i.e. reading you've already done preparing for lecture or tutorial). More than this, however, planning is needed to ensure that your searches are targeted. Jess' example above is a good one: she spent some time reviewing what she already knew about the topic – reflecting on the level of her own knowledge and understanding – so that she could identify gaps in her knowledge which she could then target in her searches. She even identified source types – journal articles – which she thought were more likely to provide her with the relevant type of information she needed. As a result, when it came to searching, she could identify keywords relevant to these gaps and she could use the limiters in the discovery service to narrow down her results. Her approach was effective because it was efficient.

Having reflected on what we might call your existing knowledge and understanding, the next step is to use that reflection to set the objectives of your search. In the end, Jess was looking for case studies focused on the use of social media in marketing by small businesses. You might have a similarly specific objective, but to begin with your goal might be simply to find information about the advantages and disadvantages of using social media in marketing for a business of any size. This will be beneficial, since it will help to inform your discussion of how a small business might see the role of social media in marketing. There might be several other aspects of the topic you'd like to look into to plug those gaps in your knowledge. That's fine: you would form an objective related to each one. At this stage, you might also consider what type of source you might be looking for. For example, as Jess did, you might want to look for journal articles. Similarly, think about the date of publication of any sources you want to look at. Given that social media use has evolved over the years, with the popularity of platforms changing, it would be better to look for sources published more recently, perhaps in the last three to five years. Such questions help to flesh out your plan. More experienced researchers would also consider what search engines or tools they were going to use for their search at this stage. However, if you're an undergraduate, particularly if you're new to higher education, we recommend sticking to your library's discovery service to begin with. We'll talk more about extending your search towards the end of this chapter.

Identifying keywords

You've identified gaps in your knowledge and set appropriate objectives for your search. Now you need to identify the keywords you're going to use in your search.

Keywords – those words or short phrases you use when searching – act as the drivers of the searches you do. They usually come from the context in which you're searching: if you're working on an assessment, for example, the keywords will be related to the assessment task or question; if you're preparing for a tutorial, the keywords will reflect the topic of that tutorial and the questions set by the tutor. In some cases, such as a dissertation, you might have to identify the keywords for yourself, without any help from assessment questions or material created by the tutor.

What makes keywords difficult to identify is that they need to be specific to be useful. In other words, if you're searching for information related to the use of social media within marketing, using 'marketing' as a keyword isn't going to help you to narrow down the search results. It's too broad. However, combining it with another keyword, such as 'strategy', will produce a more manageable set of results. Adding a third keyword, such as 'digital', will narrow down the results even further. Identifying keywords is therefore not always straightforward. You'll have to test the keywords you come up with; if you can't find what you're looking for, start again using different keywords. Searching, as we've said, is iterative: you'll do repeated searches until you get useful results.

Librarians will also encourage you to think about *synonyms for your keywords. A synonym is a word that essentially means the same as another word: for example, a synonym for 'car' is 'automobile'. It's almost certain that the keywords you use will have synonyms. A good example is provided by a research workshop we did for undergraduates studying social work. We used the word 'teenager', which has several synonyms. When we asked the students what synonyms came to mind, we were given several, including 'adolescent' and 'youth'. Sure enough, when you look at the relevant discourse, these words are used interchangeably. Even in the indexes to several different books on the topic we were looking at, we found different words for 'teenager'. What impact can this have on your searches? If you're not aware of the synonyms used in relation to the topic, you might find that you overlook key sources. In the 'teenager' example above, the use of so many different synonyms across a range of sources means that it would be a good idea to perform separate searches using each synonym. It's up to you in the end, but you might improve your chances of finding relevant sources if you do. This example highlights the importance of becoming familiar with discipline-specific vocabulary. To students of social work, 'teenager' carries greater significance than it would to students of economics. Try to be aware of such vocabulary.

Using your library discovery service

Once you've identified the keywords you're going to use, it's time to put them to use in your library's discovery service. We've already stressed the importance for less experienced students to use the library's discovery service before using any other searching tool. Using it will give you a more manageable set of search results, since you'll be searching within the resources your university has access to (i.e. those requested by your tutors!).

Searching here follows similar principles to the everyday searching you might do on Google. You enter the keywords, hit return, and review what results are returned. The skill in using any search engine lies in how you interpret the results. Before we get to that stage though, let's just pause to consider the features of a typical library discovery service. Discovery services might look different to one another, but they share a number of common features.

The centrepiece of the discovery service is the search box where you enter your keywords. That much is obvious. Usually, the landing page on which you'll find the search box is fairly simple. You might find a link to the advanced search, which allows you to set certain criteria for your search. You may, in time, find this useful, as you gain more experience of searching. Elsewhere, you might have the option of searching for a database or looking for a journal title from an alphabetical list. All are designed to make it easier for you either to find the information you're looking for as quickly as possible or to access the search tool you're looking for.

Task: Searching in practice: Using Boolean logic

1 Go to your library discovery service.
2 Enter the following keywords: 'marketing' and 'social media'. Enter the keywords in this way: 'marketing AND social media'.

The AND is what librarians call a 'Boolean operator'.

Boolean operators provide a way of telling the discovery service either to narrow down or broaden the results. In this case, AND combines the keywords; the discovery service will look for results which included marketing *and* social media. Other Boolean operators include:

NOT

This one also narrows down search results by excluding a specified keyword from your results: 'marketing NOT strategy' will identify all those sources that contain marketing but not strategy.

OR

To broaden out the results, you can use OR: 'marketing OR strategy' will search for sources including either marketing or strategy.

" "

Quotation marks can be used to look for a particular phrase with words in that exact order. Thus, "marketing strategy" will search for sources containing just that phrase, as it appears here.

( )

Parentheses are used to prioritise particular keywords: '(marketing OR strategy) AND digital' will look for sources including marketing or strategy, as well as digital.

*

The asterisk can be used to look for different forms of word: 'market*', for example, would search for all words beginning with market, such as marketisation, marketing and many more. It is sometimes called 'truncation' or 'wildcard' searches.

Try each one using the keywords suggested here. What impact does it have on the search results?

Once you've hit that return key, the discovery service will return the search results. Using our library's discovery service, a search for 'marketing AND social media' returns over 180,000 results – far too many to wade through looking for relevant material. The results are sorted according to relevance. However, you can change this to 'date', for example, or 'title'. Among our first ten results, we've only got books, and not all of them are in English. We need to find a way of narrowing down the results to get to the most relevant items.

Limiters are used for this very purpose. As Jess demonstrated above, selecting a particular source type, such as journals, removes all items not of that source type from the returns. Doing something similar here removes almost 80,000 results. Other limiters are available, depending on the objectives of your search. These include:

Date:
In some disciplines where information can go out of date very quickly (as in social media marketing), a source's date of publication is very important. You can use this limiter to narrow down the date of publication to a specific date range; for example, the last five years. Your tutors will be quick to tell you what they consider to be an 'old' source.

Subject:
Most library discovery services will now allow you to refine results according to subject. In our discovery service, for example, we actually have a subject called 'marketing strategy', which includes nearly 80,000 results. If you want to filter out sources that aren't focused on this subject term, just select it. Remember, though, that you're relying on the discovery service's categorisation of sources; you might like to have a look through the results before you apply it.

Availability:
Whether the source is available online or only as a physical copy in the library itself. Natalie should've used this one to find sources she could access from her bedroom.

There are more. We suggest checking which ones are available in your library's discovery service and applying each one to see what impact it has on the results of your search.

Task: Searching in practice (continued)

3 Apply the source (or resource) type limiter to filter out all source types other than journal articles.
4 Apply the date range limiter to include only those sources published in the last five years.
5 Apply the subject limiter to include only those relevant to 'marketing' and 'social media'.
6 Apply the language limiter so that the results only include sources published in English.

We've now got just over 2,000 results left. Still too many, but it's better than 180,000! How many results are in your list?

> The discovery service is still sorting results according to relevance. Let's change that by sorting them according to the date of publication. We've selected here 'Date-Newest' to get the most recently published articles at the top of the list.
>
> What's at the top of your list? We've got an article on 'influencer marketing' published this year in the *Journal of Business Research*. On page 2 of the results, we've got a recent article on social media marketing in microbusinesses, a study Jess might have found useful.
>
> If you're still not satisfied with the range of results produced, amend the search by adding another keyword or changing an existing one. Alternatively, you could start an entirely new search. Often, adding another keyword has a significant impact on the results. If we add 'AND sme' ('sme' means 'small and medium-sized enterprises'), the results come down 1,000. It's all in the keywords. Get those right – however many searches it takes – and you'll find the results you're looking for.

Evaluating sources

Natalie, if you remember, wasn't too worried about which sources she used as she prepared for her assessment. If it looked relevant, she added it to her list of five. She wasn't very discerning when it came to selecting sources. Jess, on the other hand, was, since she knew what source type was more appropriate to the objectives of her search and she could also confidently use the limiters on the discovery service to narrow down her results. She applied evaluative criteria when sifting through the results in order to find what she was looking for.

If your searches are going to be efficient then you have to do the same. But what criteria should you use? It largely depends on the objectives of your searches, but there are certain core criteria that you will likely use to evaluate the sources in your results. The first and most important is to be aware of what to expect from different source types. Our library's discovery service produces results that include the following source types:

- journal articles
- books
- newspaper articles
- conference proceedings
- theses or dissertations
- book chapters
- reviews

Do you know what sort of information you might find in each source type? Which are what we might call 'research heavy'? Which, on the other hand, are more accessible?

Of the source types in the short list, articles, conference proceedings and theses or dissertations will have a sharper focus and are more likely to contain cutting edge research. Book chapters, too, will likely be similar. Books will include 'textbooks' which provide overviews and summaries of topics that are informed by research but, at the same time, are meant to be accessible to undergraduates. Reviews offer critiques of books; often, they include concise summaries of the content of the book being reviewed and some indication of where it sits next to related studies. Reviews can be very useful if you are trying to get an overview of what has been written on a particular topic. Newspaper articles are just that. Not all disciplines will require you to use newspaper articles; if they do, they are easily found through you library's discovery service.

Having an awareness of what to expect in each source type will inevitably impact upon how you engage with the sources. This will also be determined by the objectives of your searches. If, for example, you're trying to find out more about the models that underpin digital marketing strategy, you're more likely to find this information in a textbook. Thus, you might use the resource type limiter to filter out all source types other than books. If, like Jess, you're looking for case studies related to the way a small business might make use of social media in their marketing, you should probably use the same limiter to search for journal articles.

Other criteria to use include *currency* (i.e. the date of publication). Generally, in most disciplines, it's advisable to use the most recently published source first. However, that might not apply in a discipline like history which is less date sensitive. *Authority*, too, is important: who has written the source? If it's a name you recognise, an author who has published widely in the discipline, it's probably going to be valuable. Perhaps the most important criterion, however, is *relevance*. Not in terms of its relevance to the topic you're working on; rather, its relevance to your reflections on your own knowledge and understanding. How will the source help you to build up your knowledge in relation to the topic? How will it add to or enhance your existing knowledge? How do you think its content will link to the other sources you've looked at? How is the source related to the context in which you are searching? In other words, what is its significance next to the assessment task or tutorial questions? These questions reflect the principle of building knowledge: adding to what you already know in a structured and organised way. It's this principle that should be at the forefront of your mind as you go about evaluating the sources in your results.

Extending your search

The importance of building knowledge brings us on to the final stage of effective searching: extending your search, if it is appropriate. Not all searches need to be extended, but if you're working on a dissertation as a final year undergraduate student or a master's student, or a thesis as a PhD student, it's likely that you will search outside the library's discovery service.

Several tools are available to you if you want to extend your search. Librarians will point you first and foremost to *databases. Databases are essentially collections of references that have been indexed or classified using their authors, titles, content, year of publication – and so on. As a result, they allow you to do broader, more comprehensive searches; your searches will go deeper into the discourse than the ones you do using the library's discovery service and, at the same time, they can be more precise. Many are usually focused on a particular discipline or subject area, but some are multi-disciplinary. Searches in databases don't favour academic sources that are available immediately, either on the shelf or via the click of a button, which your library discovery service will focus on. In other words, they look beyond what your own library pays for. Databases are particularly important for performing more complex searches, as might be needed for *systematic reviews, for example. Searching within databases broadly follows the same principles we've already discussed in relation to your library's discovery service.

Task: Exploring relevant databases

> Your library will have access to lots of databases, but not all of them will be relevant to your discipline. We suggest making an appointment to speak to one of your librarians to find out which databases are related to your discipline. Once you've identified some, have a go at using them; consider how each database works and how similar it is to the university library's discovery service; also consider how using databases has enhanced your searches.

Extending search strategies by using Google

Two of the most popular tools for extending searches are those provided by Google: Google Books and Google Scholar. These are extensions offered by Google which are available by clicking on the 'dots' icon at the top of the Google homepage.

These apps are particularly useful in *citation searching. Citation searching refers to the process of looking for citations (i.e. references; where a source has been used by other authors) to a specific journal article or book in other academic sources. This can expand your search significantly but in a controlled way; the citations will quite logically be found in sources that are related to the topic you are researching. You can then look for these sources in your own library's discovery service to see if your institution has them.

Google Books allows you to search for keywords or phrases within the full texts of the books made available online by Google. As a research tool, it has a broader, more fundamental role in helping you establish what has been written about a specific topic. It often, for example, highlights recently published books that your library is only in the process of buying.

It's easy to use; just follow the principles we've already discussed in relation to your university library discovery service.

1 Visit books.google.co.uk;
2 in the search box, enter the keywords you're interested in;
3 hit return to get the results.

Running across the top of the results screen, you'll see a series of fairly basic limiters: type of book (i.e. a preview or a Google ebook), document type (e.g. book or newspaper), date of publication (by century!), and relevance. Further limiters are available via the advanced search in 'Settings'.

Using Google Books does, however, have its problems:

- usually, only a preview of a book is available;
- it doesn't just search academic sources; as the document type limiter suggests, it also searches media, like newspapers and magazines;
- it only searches books provided by its partners; although these partners include well-known publishers and some very well stocked university libraries, it does, as a result, have its limits.

You're more likely to use Google Scholar as you try to broaden out your reading. Google Scholar is a really useful tool, particularly for citation searching because its searches are focused on academic sources – source types like journal articles, dissertations or theses, books and abstracts, provided by publishers, professional organisations, online repositories and the repositories of university libraries.

Like Google Books, Google Scholar allows you get a broader sense of what has been published on the topic; you can even use a limiter to restrict the search to a certain date range, allowing you to see what has been published more recently, for example.

It's most useful for citation searching. This is because Google Scholar is a search engine that searches within the full texts (i.e. an entire journal article) of sources and the data associated with them (i.e. author's name; titles; keywords, known as subject headings). This means it can easily flag up for you other sources that refer to, for example, a particular journal article you find useful: clicking on 'cited by' after doing a search will bring up another list of sources that include citations (or references) to that source.

Before using any of these extension tools, it's really important to figure out whether you really do need to use them. Students like Natalie often turn to Google in the first place when they're looking for sources, but they have little control over the results that come back. The same problems apply to Google Books and Google Scholar. To less experienced students, these tools might actually undermine their efforts to search effectively. If you find what you're looking for using the library's discovery service, stop there. It's not compulsory to use Google or its extensions.

Summary

Effective searching is a science: it's complex and based on the development of a structured approach which we've called a 'search strategy'. Although it uses the principles of everyday searches you might do, it's not the same as looking up trivia on Google; it's more involved, requiring careful planning, critical thought and persistence. There are no shortcuts to effective searching, particularly for less experienced students. Always use your library's discovery service first; it will give you a much higher chance of finding the *right* sources than Google would. Planning your searches is key: reflect on what you already know before starting, so that you can add to existing knowledge. Use the discovery service's limiters to refine the results produced by your searches; make use of those limiters which reflect your search objectives. Search strategy is iterative: amend searches by adding or changing keywords. Try to be discerning when it comes to choosing which academic sources to engage with; evaluate each one with the principle of building knowledge in mind. Finally, make use of research tools like Google Scholar to enhance or add to the searches you've done. In this way, you can be more certain that you are engaging as broadly as possible with the relevant discourse.

Chapter 8

Critical thought and developing a critical edge in writing

If you're going to engage effectively with the relevant discourse, you need to be able to find the right sources. This is what we looked at in the previous chapter: the literacy of searching. Once you've found these sources, you need to able to make effective use of them in an assessment context. It's here where we come to one of the most challenging literacies discussed in this book, the ability to think critically about the discourse and then to communicate that critical thought, clearly and effectively, usually in writing.

The literacy of *criticality is the one we get asked about by students more than any other. This is because tutors from across the disciplines encourage students in formal and informal feedback to 'be more critical'. In the past, we've had students ask us what this means. Well, it refers to the way you make *use* of the academic sources you find, the extent to which you engage critically with their content as you go about creating your own interpretation of the issue at hand.

In this chapter, we take a closer look at 'critical thought' as a key literacy within academic practice. The chapter is divided into two parts. In the first part, after we've defined what we mean by 'critical thought' within the broader context of learning in higher education, we look at how you build-in critical thought into your work at the research and planning stages. We also consider some of the key skills or techniques involved in how you engage critically with the different interpretations you find, such as analysis and evaluation. In addition, we look in more detail at the importance of journal articles and how you can make effective use of them in your work. In the second part, we consider what 'being critical' looks like in writing, as well as some of the techniques you can use to develop what we call 'a critical edge' in your writing. Although assessment takes different forms, not all of which require you to communicate in writing, it's in writing that you'll most likely be expected to articulate your critical thought.

DOI: 10.4324/9781003217527-8

Learning Objectives

By the end of this chapter, you will have gained:

- a sound understanding of what we mean by 'critical thought' and its significance within learning at university;
- clearer insights into the way critical thought is developed through research and the planning of assessed work;
- an appreciation of the value of journal articles in engaging critically with academic discourse and an understanding of how to make effective use of them;
- an appreciation of what 'being critical' looks like in writing;
- insights into the techniques available for developing a 'critical edge' in your writing.

Keywords

discourse; critical thought; being critical; active and passive engagement with academic sources; language of criticality; critical edge; analysis; evaluation; synthesis; judgement

Defining 'critical thought'

Taken at a glance, 'critical thought' is fairly easy to define: it's about all of those 'critical thinking skills', such as analysis and evaluation, which you've already met as you worked on the qualifications that got you onto your degree course. Critical thought *is* about these skills. We're not about to pull the rug from under your feet by telling you that you've got it all wrong! However, critical thought in higher education is about much more than developing skills.

Guidance on critical thinking – whether found in handbooks devoted to the topic or delivered via well-intentioned workshops by professional services staff – is often focused on the skills involved. Such guidance might highlight the importance of analysis, for example, or the need to look critically at academic sources by comparing different viewpoints; it might even encourage you to improve your own understanding of a particular topic by summarising a journal article or book chapter. Provision of this nature can be helpful, but it's not without its problems and limitations. First, it can have a reductive effect. It might suggest to some students that critical thought is all about applying three or four different skills and that once you can do this you can essentially 'think critically'. Second, linked to this point, it might also suggest that critical thought can be learnt, in the same way as you might learn how to use the library's discovery service. Third, for some students, this provision might suggest that critical thought can, and even should, be something that you switch on when you tackle a piece of assessed work and then switch off once you've completed it. Needless to say, none of these points do justice to the importance of critical thought in learning at university.

'Being critical' – to use a slightly different phrase to 'critical thought' or 'critical thinking skills' – is a mindset, a way of thinking and acting that is characteristic of the approach of a successful, self-regulating student to learning. Reflecting on your learning experiences in order to bring about an improvement in your own performance, which lies at the heart of self-regulated learning, is simply an extension of the way you engage critically with academic sources, since it involves very similar skills. As a literacy, therefore, it is important to recognise that it is about more than the skills involved; if you're going to excel, 'being critical' needs to form an integral part of the broader approach you take to learning.

We can illustrate this by taking a closer look at marking criteria. Doing so helps to bring some clarity to what is meant by 'being critical', since the criteria reflect what tutors are looking for in your work.

Generic marking criteria can be broken down into five main areas. Generally speaking, in assessed work, you'll be asked to demonstrate:

1 disciplinary knowledge together with good understanding of it;
2 clear, precise, and effective communication (which often means writing);
3 an ability to analyse and discuss the outcomes of research; locating these outcomes within disciplinary discourse;
4 broad engagement with relevant academic discourse;
5 an ability to develop a clear, convincing and well-supported argument; to challenge assumptions and demonstrate an awareness of the complexities of academic discourse.

By 'discourse', remember, we're referring to the academic debate which you will find in the different sources you use, whether that's books, edited collections, or journal articles. It's particularly associated with the latter: since journal articles sit at the cutting edge of research, it's here where you're likely to find more detailed discussion of the academic debate.

Critical thought is needed if you're going to engage fully with each of these criteria. 'Good understanding' of disciplinary knowledge (1), for example, is acquired through the application of critical thought to what you are reading and learning, as are the abilities to handle the outcomes of research and to develop a clear and effective argument (3, 5). Critical thought is inherent within the research involved in the process of engaging broadly with academic discourse (4), while the ability to communicate clearly and precisely (2), as we see in the second part of this chapter, is about articulating critical thought in writing. Critical thought is therefore not something you flick on when you start an assessment. 'Being critical' underpins your ability to meet marking criteria. It's a mindset, as we said, a way to approach all aspects of academic practice; if you're going to excel, you need to develop it as quickly as you can.

Consider this example of a first-year student, John. John is using his library's discovery service to identify suitable academic sources to use for an essay assessment on creativity and primary school education. The essay title is: 'With reference to your own subject area, how might teachers develop children's creativity in primary education?' John's subject area is music.

> *John types his search terms into the search box at the top of the screen. He notices that when he types 'creativity', the first search term he identified, the discovery service suggests searching for 'creativity in primary education'. He clicks on it and finds that 4,330 results have been returned. There are lots of books on 'creativity', but most don't look relevant to education; they're too broad in scope. Using the 'Subject' filter, he selects 'education' and immediately the number of results is reduced to 1,149. At the top of the list is a textbook on creativity in primary education which might be useful in providing an overview of the topic. This book, however, was published in 2014. Looking further down the list, he finds another textbook with a similar title for which there is second edition published in 2015. He makes a note of it. Next, he wants to see if there are any case studies available. He chooses 'articles' under the 'Resource type' filter (the results are reduced again, this time to 704), but then he uses another filter – 'Date' – to find the most recent articles. He notices several that look at the topic in wider, European contexts, before finding another article which looks at creativity and children's emotions. On reading the abstract, he thinks that this article provides an important perspective on the issue and so makes a note of that as well.*

This is only a snapshot of John's initial research activity as he prepares his essay. He's searching for sources; is it possible to say that he is 'being critical'? The answer, of course, is 'yes'. John is thinking critically, first and foremost, notably when he is identifying search terms to use, but also as he picks out which sources to engage with. By reading the abstract of one article, he is preparing to make an informed judgement about its potential utility. He reviews the results his searches produce and then uses filters – having thought about which ones to use – to get closer to what he's looking for by narrowing down the results. And, ultimately, he is making informed decisions about which sources to use; this decision-making process is driven by a critical mindset.

Think back to that marking criteria: the need to demonstrate disciplinary knowledge and understanding; to engage broadly with the discourse; to create an argument; to discuss the outcomes of research. All of this requires critical thought and that critical thought can be traced back to the decisions John is making here. The approach he takes in this early stage of research effectively determines how likely it is that he will successfully demonstrate those things tutors are looking for. 'Being critical' is not switched on further down the line. It's used here, at the very start, and it will continue to play an important part in all that John goes on to do as he prepares his essay.

Thinking critically about academic sources

As the example of John's initial research cited above makes clear, critical thought is a fundamental part not only of the research you do for your response, but also its planning. It's at these stages when you develop your argument and establish where it sits within the discourse related to the topic. Writing is then about articulating this critical thought clearly, so that your tutor can see how and in what ways you're engaging with the discourse.

When beginning your research, therefore, your goal should be to open up the relevant discourse. What is its scope? In other words, what has been written about it and when? What topics within the broader subject area have been looked at? What are the key works? Who are the most influential authors? What themes are highlighted within it? What aspects of the subject area are currently being debated? What are the contentious areas? Questions like these will help to direct your research. By answering them, you'll be mapping the discourse, in your mind, and, quite literally, digitally (on a Word document or note-making app) or on paper.

In addition to the sort of questions we've just highlighted, your approach to opening up the discourse will be governed by the principle of 'building knowledge' – the idea that your knowledge and understanding is built progressively and logically. When exploring these questions, it's important first of all to reflect on the extent of your knowledge of the topic area. How much do you know? Where are the gaps in your knowledge? Once you've done that, you can more confidently begin to add to your knowledge and understanding of the subject area and its discourse. To begin with, you therefore need to look for source types that are more likely to give you what we can call foundational knowledge. Textbooks, for example, can be very useful in highlighting what aspects of the subject area have been studied. While keeping the principle of 'building knowledge' in mind, it's also important to think about the broader topic area when mapping the discourse, particularly as you identify search terms to use. You might, for example, be looking at the role of Instagram in marketing strategy, but you wouldn't attempt to map the relevant discourse by performing a narrow search on Instagram. You'd look for discourse relevant to the broader topic of social media and marketing strategy. What you find will then inform the way you engage with the discourse focused more specifically on the use of Instagram.

Opening up the discourse in practice

Let's take a closer look at how John attempts to open up the discourse related to his assessment topic: developing children's creativity in primary education with reference to his discipline, which is music.

As a less experienced learner, and with the principle of 'building knowledge' in mind, John begins by looking at the textbook he found, *Creativity in Primary Education*, edited by Anthony Wilson (3rd ed., 2015). Looking at the table of contents, John notices that one chapter, by Sarah Hennessy, is about creativity in the music curriculum, precisely what the assessment is focused upon. However, before he looks at this one, he moves to the first chapter, on the context of creativity in education. Reading through it, he realises that this chapter gives him a very useful overview of the impact upon creativity of the different 'waves' of policy since the 1960s. Much of this is contextual; he isn't going to cite policy from the 1960s in his essay. But it provides a really useful backdrop to his research, foundational knowledge, as well as some idea about the challenges facing primary schools and teachers wishing to stimulate creativity.

He then moves on to another chapter which he thinks might be useful in building up this foundational knowledge. 'Creative teachers and creative teaching', by Teresa Cremin, provides John with an overview of creative teaching practice, focusing in particular on the personal attributes associated with 'creative teachers'. In doing this, Cremin includes a lot of references to case studies and research relevant to this aspect of the topic (relevant, but dating to 2015 or earlier). Given that this chapter is focused upon 'creative teachers' and it includes a number of references to related studies on the characteristics of creative teachers, it's highly likely that John has uncovered here a key part of the relevant discourse.

Together, these two chapters give John a level of understanding he needs in order to engage more fully with the chapter on music in the curriculum by Hennessy. In this chapter, John identifies several important aspects of the topic which he might use to direct the next stage of research. The first of these concerns the different ways teachers conceive of 'creativity'. This inevitably has an impact on how they attempt to develop it in the classroom. The second one points to the role of imagination in fostering the development of creativity. And the third highlights the importance for teachers of using a structured approach to classroom teaching with the aim of developing the creativity of children. All three represent *themes* within the discourse; doing more research on each one will really help John to further open it up. The chapter also highlights important work and key authors John might like to look at, notably the studies by Anna Craft, whom he identifies as an influential author.

John then extends the foundational knowledge he has started to acquire through this initial stage of research by looking in more depth at the themes he's identified in Hennessy's chapter. He takes, for example, the issue of imagination and creativity. Using the search terms 'imagination AND creativity' and then applying the subject filter 'Education', John finds a number of academic sources, including books, book chapters, and research articles. He quickly realises that there are different ways of exploring imagination. Higgins (2008), for example, noted the broader importance of creativity to the development of imagination, while others, such as Trivedi (2017), have looked at it in relation to a child's cognitive development. These different interpretations of imagination, which reflect the research interests of each author, highlight the contentious nature of the term. As such, noting this in his essay will help to demonstrate John's critical engagement with the discourse.

Analysing an interpretation

In order to appreciate the difference between the ways Higgins and Trivedi have looked at imagination, John needs to analyse each interpretation. *Analysis refers to the breaking down or opening up of an interpretation, a body of evidence, or a data set through close examination. In other words, rather than simply describing the car and its colour, you lift the bonnet and consider how it works. Analysis requires you to look below the surface. What is Higgins arguing? What are the elements of this argument? Why is he making this argument? How does it fit within the discourse as it was in 2008 and as it is now?

This source, by Higgins, is a chapter in an edited book. The first thing John notices about the chapter, once he has found a copy, is its title: 'Modest beginnings of a radical revision of the concept of imagination'. The words 'radical revision' provide important clues as to how the work might have contributed to the discourse in 2008. He then reads the introductory paragraphs, which provide some idea of Higgins' intention to set out 'a realist conception of imagination'. Note that these paragraphs explain for John how Higgins' work sits within the existing discourse. As he reads through the rest of the paragraphs, he traces the development of Higgins' argument by noting down key points. These are usually found in the first sentence of each paragraph. He pays particular attention to the discussion sections towards the end. By doing this, he builds up a clearer understanding of what Higgins is arguing and how it contributes to the broader discourse. He recognises its value in seeing imagination 'as a core component of our ideals of the educated person' (Higgins, 2008, p. 46).

By reading through the chapter in this way, John engages more deeply with Higgins' work. He is analysing it, breaking it down, trying to understanding where it fits into what he already knows and the broader discourse itself. It's only by doing this that John can then contrast Higgins' approach to that of Trivedi. It's hard work, but by analysing Higgins' work, and then Trivedi's, John is able to engage critically with both.

On reflection, John realises that imagination can play an important role in fostering children's creativity. However, much depends on how imagination is perceived by teachers and what imagination refers to in music education. Yet, in terms of developing creativity, it occurs to John that it is more important to understand teachers' perception of creativity itself before we can look in more detail at imagination. This, of course, was another of the themes he identified in the Hennessy chapter. John's critical thought has led him to connect these two themes. By emphasising the greater importance of teachers' conception of 'creativity', John is effectively evaluating both factors in the context of the question. This is an example of 'being critical'; John has achieved this at the planning stage by thinking carefully about the discourse and its themes.

Evaluating interpretations

*Evaluation refers to the practice of assessing the *relative* value (i.e., importance or significance) of a factor (such as teachers' conception of creativity) against that of other factors (i.e., a range of alternative factors, including, in this example, the conception of imagination).

Some assessment questions are explicitly evaluative. Questions beginning with 'To what extent...' require you to assess the relative value of a named factor against that of others. For example:

To what extent does business size determine the usefulness of social media within marketing strategy?

In this question, 'business size' is the named factor which is often addressed first in answers to a 'To what extent' question. In the paragraphs that follow, you will assess the role of other factors in determining the usefulness of social media, such as the nature of that business, the resources it has available, and so on.

Another explicitly evaluative question steer is 'How far ...', which can replace 'To what extent'.

Even if a question steer isn't explicitly evaluative, if you're going to engage critically with the discourse, you'll need to be evaluative at times. Some essay questions we've encountered over the years begin with steers like 'Assess ...'. Such steers are not, on face of it, as clear in what is expected as those like 'To what extent', but evaluation provides one way in which you can 'assess' whatever factor the question is focused upon.

Evaluation is closely linked to 'judgement'. We consider this in more detail in the second part of this chapter.

Engaging with journal articles

John's research has gone well so far. By using a methodical approach to research, based on the principle of 'building knowledge', John has identified several themes in the discourse. As a result, he's already engaging critically with two of them. But in order to engage fully with the discourse, he needs to use journal articles (sometimes referred to as 'research articles' by tutors).

Journal articles in whatever discipline you're studying sit at the cutting edge of research. They contribute to the discourse by adding to or extending knowledge within the discipline. They *are* research: they usually present fresh interpretations relevant to the topic, often based on original research, depending on the discipline involved. Plus, many are *peer-reviewed, meaning that the content has been through rigorous editorial checks by other academics working in the discipline. It's for these reasons that tutors are so keen for you to make use of them. Without them, it's very difficult to address the marking criteria we highlighted at the beginning of this chapter. A lack of journal articles in the references list points to a lack of engagement with discourse.

Journal articles can look different depending on which discipline you're studying. In humanities subjects, for example, articles tend to look like long essays. There might be an abstract (see below) at the start, for example, but other structural elements are not distinctly set out. Students sometimes ask us where the literature review section is in a humanities essay. The answer, of course, is that the literature is reviewed throughout such an essay and often forms the focus of the investigation. In other disciplines, however, the literature review forms one of several core sections to a journal article. These sections, in the order in which you'll meet them as you read through an article, are set out in Table 8.1.

As you can see, each section fulfils a specific purpose within the article as a piece of writing. The introduction, for example, is key in setting the

Table 8.1 Structural elements of a journal article

Abstract	Provides a concise summary or overview of the article, written by the author
Introduction/ Literature review	Establishes the 'problem' or research questions that underpin the article; sets out the academic context by discussing relevant parts of discourse
Methodology	Sets out method or approach used to collect the data
Results	Presents the results of the investigation
Discussion	Discusses the significance of the results, including their relevance in the context of the discourse
Conclusion/ implications	Sets out what may be concluded from the investigation and – depending on the discipline – any implications it might have on practice

scene. The methodology is important in giving the reader an insight into how the investigation was conducted and why certain decisions about the data collected, for example, were taken. The discussion is vital in establishing the value of the research within the relevant discourse. It's different from the conclusion, which simply provides a neat summary of what the investigation has achieved.

Reading through a journal article can be exhausting and time-consuming. When you're up against a deadline (probably more than one), you need to think strategically about how you engage with this genre of source. Understanding how an article is structured and what each section contributes to the whole is therefore very important to how you engage with it.

Let's consider how John makes use of an article in the research for his assessment on creativity in primary education. The article he has found looks very useful from its title: 'Classroom and music teachers' perceptions about the development of imagination and creativity in primary music education' by Sehnaz Sungurtekin (*Journal of Pedagogical Research*, 5(3), pp. 164–186).

John begins by (i) reading the abstract. This section not only gives him a good idea of how useful the article might be in relation to his assessment; the keywords that follow it provide him with search terms for his research (e.g., 'musical creativity'). He then (ii) looks at the introduction which, in this article, also functions as a literature review. He spends some time reading it, adding to what he has already found out about the relevant themes within the discourse. There are useful in-text references here, the full versions of which he finds in the references list at the end of the article (e.g., those by Webster). In relation to the (iii) methodology, John reads the first subsection on research design, to get a clearer idea of what the investigation looks like, but he skips over the rest at this stage to look in more detail at the (iv) results (called 'Findings' here). These are helpfully summarised in a series of tables, which he looks at carefully. He notes that there are also accompanying explanations. He then moves on to the (v) Discussion, which gives him a clear sense of the significance of the results. One of the headlines he notes, which he can link to the evaluative judgement he has already made about the importance of establishing how teachers think of creativity before considering their view of imagination, is that 'music teachers perceive imagination as vital in primary music education' (Sungurtekin, 2021, p. 178). This is supported by the examples of practice given in a subsection of the Discussion. He notes other points about the significance of the results before scanning the (vi) Conclusion and implications section. One point that catches his eye is that the author is calling for a more 'thorough understanding of developing a creative pedagogy in primary music education' and that teachers need more examples of creative activities to help promote creativity in the classroom (Sungurtekin, 2021, p. 183). The article's conclusions are therefore very important in looking at the issue of creativity with teaching practice in mind.

John's example represents what we might call a savvy approach to engaging with a journal article: taking what you need without spending too long on the less necessary sections. If John has concerns about the methodology, for example, then he should go back to that section in order to read it properly. Conversely, if he reads the introduction/literature review and finds that it simply repeats much of what he already knows, he needs to skim over it rather than read through it all again carefully. Like John, you need to be pragmatic and flexible when it comes to engaging with the journal articles.

Writing critically

Much of the critical thinking you do will take place as you research and plan your response to an assessment task. The challenge when writing is about articulating that understanding and critical thought. In this section, we consider this challenge in more detail by looking at the approach to writing we recommend and some of techniques you can use to flag up what we call the 'critical edge' of your work. Making your understanding and critical engagement with the discourse as visible as possible is essential if your writing is to be effective.

Active and passive approaches to engaging with discourse

The first point to make about your approach to writing critically is that you need to have a clear idea about what you're going to argue, how you're going to make that argument, and how your argument sits within the existing discourse. Answers to all of these questions should be found *before* you start writing. Why is this so important? Because if you're going to create a clear and convincing argument, that is well supported and grounded in discussion of the discourse, then it needs to be thought out and structured in the planning and research stages. Students who start writing without having properly planned what they're going to argue end up creating answers that lack focus, where understanding is less clear, and in which there is less evidence of critical thought, simply because they're not sure what exactly they're trying to say. Writing like this tends to veer from point to point, is lacking in coherence, and often appears muddled. Plan first; write second.

To illustrate the difference between what we call the active and passive approaches to engaging with discourse, let's consider two writing exemplars. Both exemplars concern the issue of 'classroom management' and its impact on learning. Read the first exemplar, by Susie.

> Classroom management is essential to learning. Lots of research has been done on it over the decades. As a concept, it has developed from 'practitioners' wisdom' on addressing disruptive student behaviour to the different ways teachers set up a suitable learning environment (Brophy, 2006). Classroom management is generally seen as referring to the steps teachers can take to create positive conditions for learning (Korpershoek et al., 2016). Teachers must check on what is happening in the classroom and address disruptive behaviour (Anderson & Taner, 2023). In this view, the responsibility for classroom management sits with the teacher. Different ways of looking at it have been suggested. Eccles and Roeser (2011) have looked at the role of other factors. The context of each class is important, as well as the behaviour of the students in that class (Wang et al., 2020). The teacher's control over the classroom is about more than the actions of management. As Keskin et al. (2024) have noted, it is also about knowledge and experience. Teachers need to know when to act to maintain order and to make sure students are concentrating on their work and how to do so. Since students' behaviour is difficult to predict, teachers need to be ready to make quick decisions as situations arise (Grub et al., 2020). Teachers also need to think about the impact of negative behaviour on the lesson. As Doyle (2006) has shown, attempts to address negative behaviour can sometimes just make things worse. Teachers therefore need to think carefully about the decisions they make to manage classrooms well.
>
> [Adapted from Marder, J., Thiel, F. and Göllner, R. (2023). Classroom management and students' mathematics achievement: the role of students' disruptive behavior and teacher classroom management. *Learning and Instruction, 86*, 1–13, at p. 2]

Think back to our discussion of the marking criteria at the start of this chapter. At a glance, Susie's writing meets some of these criteria: there are a number of references which point to a fairly broad engagement with the relevant discourse; there is some evidence of disciplinary knowledge; and the writing itself is fairly clear. Yet, at the same time, other aspects of the marking criteria are less clear. For example, while there is some disciplinary knowledge, is there much evidence of an understanding of it? Is there an argument? What point is Susie trying to make? The answer, of course, is that there is little clear-cut evidence of understanding and there is little sense of an argument beyond the fairly general point made in the final sentence about teachers needing to think carefully about their decision-making in relation to classroom management.

This exemplar illustrates what we call the *passive* approach to engaging with discourse. Susie has done what many new or less experienced students do when writing: she's prioritised reporting to the reader all the different interpretations she's found ahead of presenting her own view. Each sentence, beginning with 'As a concept', reports a different aspect of the discourse. It's followed by the Korpershoek et al. interpretation, then Anderson and Taner's. There's a brief bit of explanation in the next sentence, which is the closest Susie gets to engaging critically with these interpretations. This is followed by Eccles and Roeser's view, then Wang et al. – and so on. Susie is simply listing the different interpretations. In doing this, any point she wants to make is lost. What is she arguing? It isn't clear. It lacks what we can call an authorial voice.

From a tutor's perspective, this type of writing is frustrating to assess. Susie might have a good understanding of the discourse and the issues she raises; but she hasn't made that understanding clear. She's not *using* the interpretations to support or enhance her own viewpoint. Her treatment of them is too passive. 'Here's what I've read; there are some links between them, but I haven't been able to synthesise these interpretations into my own argument.'

Let's consider the next example, taken from John's work. How is his treatment of the discourse different from Susie's?

As researchers have consistently demonstrated, effective classroom management is key if learning is to be successful. Although, as a concept, classroom management has moved away from 'practitioners' wisdom' on addressing disruptive student behaviour to more research-led techniques used to create a suitable conditions for learning, it is still generally seen as the responsibility of the teacher, maintained through decisions taken in the classroom. Korpershoek et al. (2016), for example, highlighted actions a teacher might take to encourage constructive student behaviour, while Anderson and Taner (2023) noted the importance for a teacher of checking on activities in the classroom and addressing negative behaviour when necessary. However, alternative perspectives have emerged in recent years, as researchers have recognised the complexities of classroom management (e.g., Eccles & Roeser, 2011). For example, understanding the context of each class forms a key element of classroom management since it shapes what might be expected of the teacher, as does the behaviour of the students (Wang et al., 2020). Furthermore, effective classroom management requires not only a set of management actions, but also deeper understanding of when to intervene in order to maintain a positive learning environment and how to ensure that students remain focused on the learning at hand (Keskin et al. 2024). In addition, since student behaviour is unpredictable, teachers need to be proactive when it comes to responding to disruptive behaviour, while also considering the potential impact any intervention might have on the lesson itself (Grub et al., 2020). Sometimes, as Doyle (2006) points out, attempts to address negative behaviour might actually make it worse. Recent research has therefore reiterated the centrality of the teacher's role in ensuring that the classroom is managed effectively. While the complexities of classroom management have been stressed as a challenge facing teachers, it is the need for the teacher to be proactive and flexible when addressing negative student behaviour that is the most important factor in effective classroom management. Research has shown that unless teachers adopt an assertive attitude towards managing the classroom, such negative behaviour can be very difficult to overcome.

[Adapted from Marder, J., Thiel, F. and Göllner, R. (2023). 'Classroom management and students' mathematics achievement: the role of students' disruptive behavior and teacher classroom management'. *Learning and Instruction*, 86, 1–13, at p. 2]

In line with the marking criteria we used to review Susie's writing, John's work clearly demonstrates broad engagement with the relevant discourse, as evidenced by the in-text references. There's also evidence of disciplinary knowledge here, as there was in Susie's writing. In addition, though, there is more evidence of understanding. This is revealed in the way that the different interpretations have been presented. For example, when John notes that different perspectives have emerged in recent years, he is quick to explain this broadening of the discourse by referring to the recognition by researchers of what he calls the 'complexities' of classroom management. This statement is supported by the reference in the brackets – Eccles and Roeser. Another example can be seen in the second sentence, where John notes the evolution of classroom management as a concept before stating that it is usually seen as the responsibility of the teacher to achieve via effective decision-making. There's a lot of understanding in this sentence and it's conveyed quite simply by contrasting two related but slightly different points. The writing is clear, as Susie's is, but unlike Susie's writing, John's makes a point. This can be seen in the judgement in the final two sentences, where John highlights the importance of the teacher's role in maintaining classroom management and the need for teachers to be proactive when addressing student behaviour.

John's writing highlights what we call the *active* approach. In contrast to the first example, John puts his view, the point he's trying to make, first, and then uses the interpretations carefully to develop the discussion and support that point. The opening sentence is similar to Susie's: effective classroom management is essential to learning. In the sentences that follow, however, John guides the reader through the relevant interpretations, building towards the point he makes in the final two sentences. He's effectively synthesising the interpretations into his own argument, as reflected in those last two sentences.

John's work has a greater impact on the reader because he makes a point. Since he is using the interpretations to support and develop that point, the work has a sharper critical edge. It also highlights an important point about critical writing which lots of students struggle to grasp. Developing that critical edge doesn't necessarily involve any drastic steps. It's subtle and nuanced. At the heart of it lies the issue of how you present the interpretations you've found, and your thoughts on them, to the reader.

Forming judgements

As we've just noted, John's writing exemplar ends with a judgement, a clear statement of his interpretation of this part of the discourse:

> *Recent research has therefore reiterated the centrality of the teacher's role in ensuring that the classroom is managed effectively. While the complexities of classroom management have been stressed as a challenge facing teachers, it is the need for the teacher to be proactive and flexible when addressing negative student behaviour that is the most important factor in effective classroom management. Research has shown that unless teachers adopt an assertive attitude towards managing the classroom, such negative behaviour can be very difficult to overcome.*

It's indicated by the use of 'therefore', which provides just one example of what we call the 'language of criticality' (see below). Whenever you see 'therefore' in a text, you know that what you're about to read will offer some kind of judgement on the issue under discussion. In this example, John provides a judgement in two parts. To begin with, he notes the centrality of the teacher's role in effective classroom management, an observation that reflects much of the recent research. He then expands on this observation by noting two aspects of this issue relevant to the teacher's ability to manage the classroom: the complexities of classroom management facing teachers and the need for teachers to be proactive and flexible when confronting negative behaviour in the classroom. John presents these points using the language of criticality: 'While' one has been stressed, the other is 'the most important factor' because research has emphasised the value of teachers having an assertive attitude.

A judgement is evaluative because it assesses the *relative* importance of two factors; it also provides an explanation as to why one factor is more important than the other. Thus, it follows this formula:

X is more important (or significant or valuable – etc.) than Y because ....

Judgements act as powerful statements of your understanding. They also reflect critical engagement with the discourse, since in order to reach a judgement, you need to apply critical thought to the sources you're using.

Beyond their value in communicating understanding and critical thought, judgements also play a role in articulating an argument. By acting as clear statements of understanding, judgements effectively signpost elements of your argument to the reader as you write. In the example above, John makes clear that he believes the teacher's attitude towards negative or disruptive behaviour is the most important factor in ensuring that classroom management is effective.

How often do you use judgements in your writing? Reviewing a recent piece of writing, can you identify anywhere in the work where your argument might have been clearer if you had used judgements?

Applying synthesis in your writing

Key to the active approach taken by John to engaging with the discourse is the ability to synthesise those interpretations included to support the point he is making.

Synthesis refers to the ability to draw together different interpretations or evidence in the formation and expression of your own argument. It is a characteristic of very good, high scoring pieces of writing because students who are capable of writing at this level usually write with confidence. They have a good understanding of the relevant discourse and a very clear idea of what they are going to argue and how it fits into this discourse. Students who find it difficult to develop synthesis in writing are often less confident about these important aspects of their work.

Synthesis is about controlling the interpretations and evidence you use to support and develop your argument. You can see this control in John's writing. He clearly understands the significance of each of the interpretations he refers to and it's clear that he has carefully selected each one to develop the point being made. Consider the following extract:

> *For example, understanding the context of each class forms a key element of classroom management since it shapes what might be expected of the teacher, as does the behaviour of the students (Wang et al., 2020). Furthermore, effective classroom management requires not only a set of management actions, but also deeper understanding of when to intervene*

in order to maintain a positive learning environment and how to ensure that students remain focused on the learning at hand (Keskin et al. 2024). In addition, since student behaviour is unpredictable, teachers need to be proactive when it comes to responding to disruptive behaviour, while also considering the potential impact any intervention might have on the lesson itself (Grub et al., 2020).

The synthesis is expressed in the writing through the use of 'For example', 'Furthermore', and 'In addition'. Compare John's synthesis of interpretations in this extract with the lack of synthesis in Susie's:

The teacher's control over the classroom is about more than the actions of management. As Keskin et al. (2024) have noted, it is also about knowledge and experience. Teachers need to know when to act to maintain order and to make sure students are concentrating on their work and how to do so. Since students' behaviour is difficult to predict, teachers need to be ready to make quick decisions as situations arise (Grub et al., 2020).

It might be argued that there is some synthesis where Susie links the Grub et al. interpretation with that of Keskin et al. through the use of 'Since', but her writing is in general defined by a lack of synthesis. Interpretations are collected with little attempt to draw them together in support of a point she is trying to make. In this sense, the absence of synthesis, and any difficulty she might have experienced in developing it, may be attributed to the lack of purpose in her work.

The language of criticality

With that in mind, let's turn to another feature of John's writing: the use of what we call 'the language of criticality'. John, as we have seen, doesn't just report the interpretations he includes in his writing; he makes use of them to support and develop the point he is trying to make. It's clear John has a really good understanding of these interpretations. The impact of his writing, however, lies in the way that he communicates this 'critical edge' to the reader. How does he do it? Read through the exemplar again; consider how John presents the interpretations he discusses. What do you notice?

We said above that this critical edge is subtle and nuanced. As you can see in John's writing, it is expressed through the words and phrases you find at the beginning of certain sentences. These words and phrases point to the relationship between the interpretations under discussion. In doing so, they communicate John's understanding of the discourse and his attempts at engaging with it critically.

Consider this extract:

> However, alternative perspectives have emerged in recent years, as researchers have recognised the complexities of classroom management (e.g., Eccles & Roeser, 2011). For example, understanding the context of each class forms a key element of classroom management since it shapes what might be expected of the teacher, as does the behaviour of the students (Wang et al., 2020). Furthermore, effective classroom management requires not only a set of management actions, but also deeper understanding of when to intervene in order to maintain a positive learning environment and how to ensure that students remain focused on the learning at hand.
>
> (Keskin et al., 2024)

It begins with the word 'However', which carries great significance in the context of 'being critical'. Whenever you use 'However' at the start of the sentence, it flags up for the reader that what you are about to say qualifies or even contradicts what has come before. 'For example' is used to illustrate some of the alternative perspectives mentioned in the previous sentence, thereby demonstrating deeper levels of understanding. 'Furthermore' implies that what follows adds to or extends the previous point. All in all, such terms, although simple, help to highlight for the reader the critical edge of your writing.

There are others in the exemplar: 'although', 'in addition', and 'therefore'. And there are more that aren't used by John, some of which are set out in Table 8.2.

All such words and phrases, which constitute 'the language of criticality', help to communicate to the reader your understanding and critical engagement with the discourse.

At the same time, these words and phrases help to develop the *flow of your writing. If you compare John's writing with Susie's, you'll notice that Susie's sentences appear quite disconnected. There is a lack of logic or progression – flow – in their arrangement, so that the reader is almost stumbling through the paragraph. This works against any attempt Susie is making to convey understanding or to demonstrate critical engagement with the discourse. John's use of the language of criticality helps to link each sentence together. The flow here is much stronger; the writing, as a result, is much easier to read and John's understanding of the discourse and his critical engagement with it is enhanced by the arrangement of sentences. Compare the two exemplars and you'll see the difference. Using the language of criticality will significantly improve the quality and impact of your writing.

Table 8.2 Examples of the language of criticality

However	Used to imply a contrast or qualification between two ideas.
Because	Indicates to the reader that an explanation and some sort of analysis follows.
Although	Similar to 'however' in that it implies a contrast between two ideas.
Moreover	Implies that what follows holds greater significance or importance than what came before.
furthermore	Suggests that what follows provides additional, supporting evidence.
Therefore	Particularly useful in introducing judgements, 'therefore' helps to highlight synthesis, where you are drawing together knowledge, understanding and interpretations as you express your own viewpoint.
Indeed	Adds emphasis to a specific point; reiterates significance or importance.
But	Functions grammatically as a conjunction, linking two ideas together, but works in the language of criticality to imply a qualification to an idea.
While	Links two ideas together; can be used to imply a contrast.
in addition	Similar to 'furthermore', above.
in contrast to	Implies not only a comparison but also that there are differences between two factors.

Discipline-specific vocabulary

Linked to the 'language of criticality' and the way that these words and phrases can be used to create flow and to flag up critical engagement with sources is the use of disciplinary-specific vocabulary. What constitutes discipline-specific vocabulary? Included here are individual words or terms that carry meaning within the disciplinary discourse. They don't have to be scientific or abstract in nature; they might actually be fairly simple, everyday words, which pick up greater value when used in the discourse related to your discipline.

In the exemplar of John's writing, there are several examples. 'Classroom management' is one, which, to someone unfamiliar with the education discipline, might look less significant than it actually is. There is a whole body of research sitting behind this term. 'Practitioners' wisdom' is another, which isn't unique to education. Others include: 'research-led techniques', 'negative student behaviour', 'management actions', 'learning environment', and even 'intervention', in the context in which it is used here. By using these terms in his writing, John is making his engagement with the discourse very clear. He's also making it clear to the reader that he has a good understanding of these terms.

Using discipline-specific vocabulary, therefore, adds to the development of the critical edge of your writing. Just as you do when you're using the 'language of criticality', you're effectively flagging up your understanding and critical engagement with the discourse, making it easy for the reader to assess its extent and the quality of that engagement. As we said above, the critical edge of your writing rests in the way you present the points you're making and the interpretations that support, illustrate or qualify them.

Task: Identifying the critical edge of writing

Here is another extract from John's work on classroom management. Using the discussion above, can you identify how John develops the critical edge of his writing?

Teachers' management actions are often highlighted as being key to ensuring that the classroom functions as a positive learning environment. For example, Harlacher (2015) has stressed the need for the teacher to establish clear rules and expectations within the classroom, while Ruzek et al. (2016) have highlighted the importance of teachers offering students emotional support. In light of the challenging nature of the classroom context highlighted by Doyle (2006), student behaviour is seen as being reflective of the impact of the teacher's management actions. Disruptive behaviour is seen as evidence of the ineffectiveness of these actions. An absence of such behaviour, on the other hand, can be seen as evidence of the effectiveness of management actions. However, recent research has looked more closely at the different elements of classroom management that can be linked to teachers' management actions on the one hand and those associated with student behaviour on the other (Göllner et al., 2021). It is therefore possible to conclude that teachers are not solely responsible for ensuring effective classroom management; rather, it should be seen as the joint responsibility of both teachers and students.

[Adapted from Marder, J., Thiel, F. and Göllner, R. (2023). 'Classroom management and students' mathematics achievement: the role of students' disruptive behavior and teacher classroom management', *Learning and Instruction*, 86, 1–13, at p. 2]

Here are our observations:

1 John clearly takes an active approach to engaging with the discourse. As the opening sentence makes clear, the extract concerns

the role of teachers' actions in managing the classroom. The point he is making though, as reflected in the judgement at the end, is that ensuring effective classroom management is a joint responsibility shared by teachers and students.

2 John also presents the interpretations he includes carefully by using the language of criticality. He uses the phrase 'For example'; further on, he qualifies the point he makes about the focus within the discourse on student behaviour as a means of assessing the effectiveness of classroom management by pointing to more recent research.

3 There is discipline-specific vocabulary which helps to convey John's understanding of the discourse. For example, terms like 'management actions', 'classroom context', and 'disruptive behaviour'.

Summary

The main point of this chapter is to get across to you that if you're going to excel you must see 'being critical' as a mindset, a key part of self-regulated learning, that will shape your approach to studying. It's not simply a set of skills; nor are these skills flicked on and off as and when you do an assessment. You need to develop a critical mindset so that you are engaging critically with the discourse at all times.

Critical thought should inform the decisions you make when conducting research and the planning of your response to an assessment task. Mapping the discourse, which is fundamental to engaging critically with it, involves applying that critical thought as you build up a clear picture of what the discourse looks like – its key works and authors, themes, contentious areas, and so on. Having mapped the discourse, it becomes much easier to develop your own view on the topic of the assessment and then establish where it sits in relation to other interpretations. Writing is then about articulating that view and its position within the discourse in such a way as to make your understanding of it and your critical engagement with it clear to the reader.

The critical edge in your writing is developed through the way you present interpretations in your work. An active approach is needed, in which your argument comes first; interpretations are then used to support and develop the point you're making. The language of criticality is key in highlighting your understanding of the discourse; it also flags up your critical engagement with it. Similarly, use of discipline-specific vocabulary and academic phrasing does the same.

References

Anderson, J., & Taner, G. (2023). Building the expert teacher prototype: A meta-summary of teacher expertise studies in primary and secondary education. *Educational Research Review*, *38*, Article 100485.

Brophy, J. (2006). History of research on classroom management. In C. Evertson & C. Weinstein (Eds.), *Handbook of classroom management: Research, practice, and contemporary issues* (pp. 17–43). Lawrence Erlbaum Associates.

Doyle, W. (2006). Ecological approaches to classroom management. In C. Evertson & C. Weinstein (Eds.), *Handbook of classroom management: Research, practice, and contemporary issues* (pp. 97–125). Lawrence Erlbaum Associates.

Eccles, J., & Roeser, R. (2009). Schools, academic motivation, and stage-environment fit. In R. Lerner & L. Steinberg (Eds.), *Handbook of adolescent psychology: Individual bases of adolescent development* (pp. 404–434). John Wiley & Sons.

Grub, A.-S., Biermann, A., & Brünken, R. (2020). Process-based measurement of professional vision of (prospective) teachers in the field of classroom management. A systematic review. *Journal for Educational Research Online*, *12*(3), 75–102.

Harlacher, J. (2015). *Designing effective classroom management*. Marzano Research.

Higgins, C. (2008). Modest beginnings of a radical revision of the concept of imagination. In R. Fitzgerald & T. Nielsen (Eds.), *Imaginative practice, imaginative inquiry: Proceedings of the sixth international conference on imagination and education* (pp. 36–47). University of Canberra.

Keskin, O., Seidel, T., Stürmer, K., & Gegenfurtner, A. (2024). Eye-tracking research on teaching professional vision: A meta-analytic review. *Educational Research Review*, *42*, Article 100586.

Korpershoek, H., Harms, T., de Boer, H., van Kuijk, M., & Doolaard, S. (2016). A meta-analysis of the effects of classroom management strategies and classroom management programs on students' academic, behavioral, emotional, and motivational outcomes. *Review of Educational Research*, *86*(3), 643–680.

Sungurtekin, S. (2021). Classroom and music teachers' perceptions about the development of imagination and creativity in primary music education. *Journal of Pedagogical Research*, *5*(3), 164–186.

Trivedi, S. (2017). *Imagination, music, and the emotions: A philosophical study*. State University of New York Press.

Wang, M.-T., Degol, J., Amemiya, J., Parr, A., & Guo, J. (2020). Classroom climate and children's academic and psychological wellbeing: A systematic review and meta-analysis. *Developmental Review*, *57*, Article 100912.

Wilson, A. (Ed.). (2015). *Creativity in primary education*. Sage.

Chapter 9

Writing for assessment

Since most assessment tasks require written responses and it's through assessed work that you get your marks and then your degree classification, the ability to write effectively for assessment is key to excelling. For lots of students, however, it represents a particularly challenging aspect of studying at university.

In this chapter, we unpick the difficulties associated with writing for assessment. First, we set out the theory underpinning support in this area. You need to understand that tutors' expectations regarding writing are shaped by conventions associated with writing within your discipline. Writing in one discipline looks different from writing in another. You need to recognise these conventions. Second, we look at writing in practice to help you to improve your own writing. The guidance we offer here is informed by the questions students have asked us over the years.

By the end of the chapter, you'll have a much clearer understanding of the principles of writing for assessment and the practice of improving your writing. Our intention is not only to give you insights into tutor expectations; it's also to build up your confidence when it comes to writing. There's no quick fix for improving your writing. It takes practice, determination, and, above all, a willingness to read widely in your discipline area to better understand those conventions mentioned above.

Learning Objectives

By the end of this chapter, you will have gained:

- a clear understanding of the idea of 'writing within disciplines' and the importance of identifying 'writing conventions' within each discipline to excelling;
- an awareness of the different genres of writing that exist under the term 'academic writing';

- an understanding of the writing process that informs the creation of assessed written work;
- an understanding of the techniques that are available for bringing about an improvement in the quality and impact of writing.

Keywords

writing within disciplines; writing conventions; genres of writing; structure; expression; writing process; language of criticality

Writing in theory

In our experience, students tend to make assumptions about writing for assessment which can act as significant obstacles to their attempts at improving the quality of their writing. There are three main assumptions:

1. 'Academic writing' is a genre in itself, with its own defining features.
2. These features make 'academic writing' different from other types of writing students may be familiar with.
3. 'Academic writing' is inherently complex and more difficult to do because it sits on a higher intellectual plane than other types of writing.

Needless to say, all three assumptions are false! 'Academic writing', as a concept, is not a monolithic thing that sits astride all disciplines; it's more nuanced than that, with different genres of writing existing next to each other, linked to the different types of assessment you'll meet as you move through your course. Second, 'academic writing' is not different from other types of writing. Whatever you're writing, it needs to be clear, the expressions should be precise, and the text itself needs to be accessible to the reader. Third, it isn't complex, even if it is difficult for some students to get grips with at the start of their courses. In broad terms, some of the best academic writing is characterised by simple sentence structure and everyday vocabulary with careful use of discipline-specific terms. As a result, it is highly accessible, even though it might have been written by experienced academics at the top of their respective fields.

Before we look in any detail at the practice of writing effectively, we need to consider two important ideas that underpin our approach to writing in both parts of this chapter: (i) writing within your discipline and (ii) recognising the different genres that sit underneath this umbrella term of 'academic writing'. Exploring these ideas will help you to gain a better understanding of writing at this level, tutors' expectations when it comes to student writing, and the different ways you might be able to improve your writing as you go about creating assessed pieces of work.

We should add that what we're talking about in this chapter is writing *for assessment*. Writing is not just something you need to do in assessment contexts; you need to write effectively as you prepare for tutorials, for example, when you communicate with tutors, and as you do your research in the library. But it's in assessment contexts that the effectiveness of writing is most important because it's through the work created that you get your marks, find success, and then go on to excel. Writing in these other situations provides opportunities for you to practise some of things we set out in the second part of this chapter.

Writing within your discipline

It's now generally acknowledged by academics researching writing practices in higher education that support for students aimed at enhancing the ability to communicate in writing needs to be situated within the discipline in which you are studying (Halliday & Hasan, 1985; Somerville & Creme, 2005).

Disciplines might share certain conventions, such as the need to engage with quantitative rather than qualitative data or the practice of using the third person rather than first (i.e., 'it has been suggested ...' instead of 'I think that ...'). But it is important to acknowledge that writing in any discipline is defined by its own set of conventions related to such things as writing style, vocabulary, and structure. At a deeper level, these conventions are also related to the types of sources used, the way knowledge is presented and handled in the work, and the objectives of the writing, with work in some disciplines, for example, culminating in practical recommendations. Each discipline is therefore unique and so it's important for students to be able to recognise and understand the conventions that shape writing within it.

To illustrate this point, let's look briefly at our discipline, history. To many people, all history is the same – it's the study of the past. Yet within the broader discipline area of history are a number of different 'sub-disciplines' associated with distinct time periods; for example, medieval history, from *c.*500 up to *c.*1500, early modern history, from *c.*1500 up to *c.*1700, and modern, from *c.*1700 up to 1945. Writing within each of these sub-disciplines is quite distinct due to the extant source material and expectations over how that material is used. An academic working on early twentieth-century British history might include in their writing a direct quote, as recorded in a radio address, from Neville Chamberlain, British Prime Minister (1937–1940). A scholar working on Roman history, on the other hand, might want to include a quote from Julius Caesar, as recorded in the work of Suetonius, but the way he would be expected to handle that quote would be very different from the academic working on Chamberlain. Suetonius lived many years after Caesar and so much of what he recorded about the famous Roman dictator is hearsay, passed down the generations. Any quotes he attributed to Caesar were likely embellished or invented. You can therefore see the differences in expectations when it comes to using this evidence. The historian of the ancient world is almost using a different skillset.

Let's take a look at examples of writing from three very different disciplines: chemistry; education (primary); and history. We suggest seeing them as representative of broader collections of disciplines: sciences; social sciences; and humanities.

Example 1 – chemistry/sciences:

[Sokovic, M., et al. (2010). Antibacterial effects of the essential oils of commonly consumed medicinal herbs using an *in vitro* model. *Molecules, 15,* 7532–7546; at pp. 7541 and 7545.]

This extract is taken from the article cited above; it is from the 'Results and Discussion' section, which makes up the bulk of the article. Read through the two paragraphs below and consider the characteristics of the writing. How would you define its style? What do you make of the language used? What sources does it refer to? We've included items 15 and 16 from the references list at the end of the article.

It seems evident that there is a relationship between the high activity of the Thymus *and* Oregano *type oils and the presence of phenol components, such as thymol and carvacrol. The high antimicrobial activity of these essential oils could be explained by their high percentage of phenol components. It seems likely, that carvacrol interferes with the activity of cell wall enzymes like chitin synthase/chitinase as well as α- and β-glucanases of fungi [15,16]. Consequently, the high content of phenolic components may account for the high antifungal activity of oregano-type oils.*

It can be seen that the growth of tested bacteria responded differently to the essential oils and their components, which indicates that different components may have different modes of action or that the metabolism of some bacteria is able to better overcome the effect of the oil or adapt to it. Gram negative bacteria are in general more resistant than Gram positive. Some of the oils (Citrus *species, M. chamomilla, S. officinalis) and components (linalyl acetate, limonene, α-, β-pinene) tested in here and even more so streptomycin did not affect P. aeruginosa and P. mirabilis.*

15. Adams, S., Kunz, B., & Weidenbörner, M. (1996). Mycelial deformations of *Cladosporium herbarum* due to the application of eugenol and carvacrol. *Journal of Essential Oil Research, 8,* pp. 535–540.

16. Adam, K., Sivropoulu, A., Kokkini, S., Lanaras, T., & Arsenakis, M. (1998). Antifungal activities of *Origanum vulgare* subsp. *Hirtum, Mentha spicata, Lavandula angustifolia* and *Salvia fruticose* essential oils against human pathogenic fungi. *Journal of Agricultural and Food Chemistry*, 46, pp. 1739–1745.

The style of this writing can be described as 'matter-of-fact'. Science writing is often characterised by what we might call a 'clipped' style: authors get to the point quickly and although the writing is discursive to some extent – in that it engages in a discussion of the results – this aspect of the work is less developed than in our other examples. There is a tendency to state things as they are, without much further comment: 'Consequently, the high content of phenolic components may account for the high antifungal activity of oregano-type oils'. This shouldn't be taken as criticism; it's simply a reflection of the conventions associated with writing in this particular discipline. Another point is related to the vocabulary. Beyond the phrases that are typical in writing across many disciplines (tenative phrases like 'It seems evident that …' and 'It can be seen that …') there is careful use of discipline-specific vocabulary (e.g., 'Gram negative bacteria', 'phenol components', and '*P. mirabilis*') and certain verbs and phrases that would resonate with an informed reader (e.g., 'may account for' and 'responded differently'; you wouldn't expect to see 'responded' in history writing). Such words and phrases, as well as the techniques that underpin their use, help to illuminate the range of vocabulary associated with that discipline which you will be expected to use as a participant within that discourse community.

In respect of the sources used, you'll notice the numbers '15' and '16' within the squared brackets which refer to the two sources listed from the references list. As such, these references point to the authors' attempts to set their findings in the context of existing research, something that is to be expected, in principle, across most, if not all, disciplines. It's also to be expected here since this extract comes from the 'results and discussion' section of the article. These research papers represent one type of source used. The evidence which underpins the authors' comments, however, is made up of data gathered through chemical analyses of the essential oils under discussion. The extract above is preceded by a commentary on this data, which is set out for the reader in a series of tables. For example:

The results of the chemical analyses of the essential oils of the different herbs are presented in Table 1. The yield of M. piperita *oil is 3.2% (v/w), and its main components are menthone (12.7%), menthol (37.4%) and methyl acetate (17.4%). The yield of* Mentha spicata *oil is 1.5% (v/w), and the main components are menthone (21.9%) and carvone (49.5%).*

(Extract at p. 7533)

The substance of this research therefore – its currency, if you like – is data produced by the analyses. In addition to its particular style and the vocabulary it uses, writing in chemistry is also characterised by the importance of data of this sort as a source type. Together, such features define writing in this discipline.

Example 2 – education/social sciences:

[Prince, H. & Diggory, O. (2023). Recognition and reporting of outdoor learning in primary schools in England. *Journal of Adventure Education and Outdoor Learning*, 24(4), 553–565, at p. 559.]

> *The data in this research give evidence about how attention to outdoor learning is reported to a greater extent on the EYFS during Ofsted inspections than in other phases of primary education. This is unsurprising as the Early Years Framework (DfE, 2021) not only actively promotes the use of the outdoors during this phase of a child's development but it also makes it a statutory requirement. Early years setting attached to schools, like the ones considered as part of the primary school inspection reports in this study, are also obligated to adhere to the Early Years Framework. Interestingly, although 72% of the schools identify outdoor learning in their EYFS provision, this means that 28% do not, or that this employment of this research methodology has not identified such practice.*
>
> *In the Framework, three characteristics that promote teaching and learning are identified: opportunities to play and explore; learning actively with concentration; and learning to think and create critically. If outdoor learning provides children with freedom and opportunities to learn and problem solve (Joyce, 2012), it becomes apparent that outdoor learning has the potential to promote the teaching and learning characteristics listed in the Framework. The Ofsted reports sampled in this research show recognition that outdoor learning contributes to enjoyment and learning development for EYFS children supporting the notion that the outdoors is an effective learning environment for children in this phase of development (Bilton, 2010; Knight, 2011, 2013; Ouvry & Furtado, 2020; Watts, 2013). Due to their focus on the quality of education, inspectors also identify areas for development such as the need for learning activities outside to be integral to the whole learning experience for children and that the activities and opportunities inside and outside should be equally demanding and stimulating.*

This extract is about the role of 'outdoor learning' in primary schools in England. With the writing in Example 1 in mind, how does the writing here compare? What does it tell us about the conventions and expectations associated with writing in the discipline of education?

The extract is taken from a section providing a discussion of the results. It shares the same objective as Example 1: to draw meaning out of the results of the research by setting them in a broader context provided by the relevant discourse. However, the way that it does this, the style of the writing, and the extent to which it establishes these links differs. You can also see clear differences in the type of sources used. Overall, even though Example 1 is discursive, the writing in Example 2 is more so, in accordance with the conventions of this discipline.

The sentences are longer, less matter-of-fact, and, as a result, lend themselves more to a fuller discussion of the significance of the research. It is clear that the views of the authors expressed here are more interpretations of the evidence and less statements of fact. Notice, for example, in the second paragraph, the sentence beginning 'If outdoor learning provides children …'. This is not a clear and unassailable position; it reflects a connection made by the authors between Joyce's (2012) view about learning providing children with freedom and opportunities to learn and the possibility that outdoor learning might be used as a means of delivering the learning and teaching identified in the Early Years Framework under discussion. It is their *contention*, as reflected in the use of the tentative 'If' at the start of the sentence, but it might be challenged by another author, in a future study, who might have found evidence that contradicts it. In the next sentence, they point to positive evidence taken from the Ofsted reports used in the research of early years children's enjoyment of outdoor learning which supports, in their view, the idea put forward by several scholars that the outdoors is an effective learning environment for children of these ages. But this again is a contention. The verb used is 'supports', which allows for the possibility that contradictory evidence might exist. The authors avoid using a verb like 'proves', for example, because it is just their interpretation of the evidence that is on offer.

These examples highlight an important point about writing in education when compared to writing in the sciences, as in Example 1. In the former, conclusions are rarely black and white. There isn't a clear result from the research; the result doesn't definitely prove or disprove something. When writing in the social sciences, you're dealing with the interpretations you find in the discourse. One interpretation might be more favourable than another, but that doesn't mean that one is right while another is wrong. These authors are adding to the discourse related to outdoor learning. The way this is done is by examining and critiquing existing interpretations in the course of forming new, fresh ones. Hence it is important to be tentative and to allow for the possibility of alternative perspectives.

There are other differences, such as the way that the 'data' in the research is presented. Here, in Example 2, the data is presented in broader terms, in the form of general observations, and is integrated more seamlessly into the discussion. In Example 1, it is presented without any elaboration in a number of short, sequential sentences. Links to relevant literature also feature more prominently in Example 2 than in Example 1. In the sentences cited above, such references are integral to the shaping of the discussion. In the first, Joyce's view that outdoor learning provides children with freedom and opportunities to learn is used to posit that it has the potential to promote the learning and teaching in the Framework. In the second, the authors use the collective view of a number of researchers of the effectiveness of the outdoors as a learning environment to highlight the significance of the conclusion they draw from the Ofsted reports linked to this idea.

The writing in Example 2 also includes discipline-specific terminology, as in Example 1 – 'outdoor learning' being the main one. It uses particular verbs and phrases in the course of the discussion to emphasise the tentativeness of the remarks, as we have seen. One final point concerns the nature of the source evidence. Rather than statistics, the authors in this example use reports from Ofsted, a government body, and a framework created by the Department for Education. Using such sources clearly requires a different set of skills to those needed to interpret data. This in itself is one of the reasons why the writing has to be tentative rather than definitive.

Example 3 – history/humanities:

[Milne-Smith, A. (2016). Shattered minds: Madmen on the railways, 1860-80. *Journal of Victorian Culture*, 21(1), 21–39, at pp. 24–25.]

The following extract comes from a journal article exploring the moral panic surrounding the impact of railway travel in the mid to late nineteenth century on the sanity of men. In history (and humanities) research articles, it's unusual to have discrete sections addressing a different aspect of the research (e.g., 'Methodology' and 'Results and discussion'). This, in itself, is of significance because of its impact on the way that writers are expected to engage with the relevant discourse in such disciplines. The extract below is taken from the article's fourth and fifth pages.

> *Victorians had a complex relationship with their railways; they were simultaneously the ultimate symbols of progress and technological triumph and a focus for the anxiety and horrors of modern life.*[23] *The expansion of railway traffic around the mid-century is staggering: in 1850 the railways carried over 64 million passengers a year, rising to 320 million by 1871.*[24] *Wolfgang Schivelbusch's masterful* The Railway Journey *demonstrated how the railway shaped almost all aspects of life across Europe in the nineteenth century.*[25] *It was a disruptive innovation that transformed how people lived, establishing modern patterns of urban and suburban life.*[26] *From the establishment of standardized time to disrupted social interactions or the legislation of limited liability joint stock*

companies, few areas of life were untouched by the railway.[27] *And yet the mid-Victorian railway had a bad reputation, riddled with safety concerns and accusations of corruption and collusion at the highest levels.*[28] *This status persisted into the 1870s despite the fact that the actual safety records were strong, and continued to improve throughout the century.*[29] *Scholars have highlighted this dark side of the railway, tracing how tales of massive railway fares, derailments, and collisions with their large-scale destruction and high mortality rates were a staple of newspaper coverage from the earliest days of the railways.*[30] *The railways thus added new concerns to everyday life, and they could also add extra* frisson *when combined with other incipient fears.*[31] *The railway journey was neither benign nor routine in the popular imagination. The railway was an unstable setting, often full of danger and a focus of anxieties.*

References (*amended from original text):

23. Harrington, 'Railway Accident', p. 31.
24. Evans, *Forging of the Modern State*, p. 420.
25. Schivelbusch, *Railway Journey*.
26. Carter, *Railways and Culture in Britain*, p. 10.
27. Carter, *Railways and Culture in Britain*, p. 10.
28. Kent, 'Containing disorder in the 'Age of Equipoise', p. 310.
29. Harrington, 'Railway safety and railway slaughter', pp. 187–188.
30. For example, Daly, 'Blood on the tracks', pp. 47–76.
31. Barrow, 'Rape on the railway', pp. 341–356.

On reading through Example 3, you should be able to see immediately its differences when compared to the previous two examples. The style of writing, for example, is very different. Sentences tend to be longer. Some also have a more complex structure, with semi-colons used to connect two independent clauses. For example, 'Victorians had a complex relationship with their railways' is followed by a semi-colon which links it to 'they were simultaneously the ultimate symbols of progress and technological triumph and focus for the anxieties and horrors of modern life'. The first effectively provides the context for the second. Sentence constructions like this one leave the writing with a more sophisticated appearance.

In terms of 'evidence', you might be surprised to see the author referencing statistical data as evidence for the dramatic expansion of the railway network. Otherwise, one thing that distinguishes writing in history is that the interpretations of other scholars lie at the heart of the discussion. Whereas the currency of the research in Example 1 is the data collected, and the substance of the discussion in Example 2 is the evidence drawn from Ofsted reports and policy documents, here, in Example 3, the discussion is focused upon what others have said about the topic. In this sense, the views of scholars are not only included to situate the research in the wider discourse; they also play a vital role in shaping the argument offered by the author. You can see this process at work clearly in the sentences ending in footnotes 24–27, and 28–31. In the first group (24–27), each sentence builds on the point made in the preceding one, working towards the overall point that railways lay at the centre of Victorian life. This point is then contrasted with a collection of interpretations (28–31) highlighting the negative reputation of the railways at the time, which builds towards the final sentence that emphasises the instability surrounding the idea of the railways in the Victorian mind.

Discipline-specific vocabulary is not as easy to identify in this example. Here, certain words take on greater significance in the context of this writing. Words like 'complex', for example, which aren't exclusive to history, carry much greater meaning in this example, as do others like 'horrors' and 'anxieties'. These words are key to the topic and therefore recur within the discussion. They also represent fairly specific ideas in relation to the topic. In the opening paragraph of the article (not provided), for example, the author refers to the level of panic in Victorian society caused by the speeds at which trains travelled. 'Anxieties', therefore, in the context of this research, refer to such concerns.

Familiarising yourself with writing in your discipline

It's very important for you to get to know how knowledge is articulated within your discipline. This means understanding the conventions attached to writing within it. Grasping this idea, and then identifying these conventions, represent a significant challenge facing you as a student. Excelling in writing is not only about getting across your ideas clearly; it's about doing so in a way that is consistent with the conventions associated with writing in your discipline.

How do you do this effectively? The simplest answer is to read, read, and read. Don't just read anything; read good quality research in the discipline. As you do so, consider the following aspects of the writing, all of which we've identified in the discussion above:

1 Writing style
   Writing in the sciences (Example 1) tends to be characterised by short, matter-of-fact sentences, whereas the style associated with the humanities (Example 3) is more sophisticated, with longer sentences and more complex sentence structure.
2 Evidence
   Sciences (Example 1) make more use of quantitative data. In social sciences, quantitative and qualitative data are used, but in the education example (Example 2) the specific source type used by the authors is essentially government reports. In the humanities (Example 3),

we can see – surprisingly – some quantitative data used, but here there is a much greater emphasis on the use of interpretations drawn from the discourse.
3 Discipline-specific vocabulary
In each discipline, there will be words and phrases (linked to the way that evidence is presented) considered as typical within that discipline. This might be technical vocabulary, such as that found in Example 1, or words that carry a specific meaning in the context of the writing itself, as seen in Example 3.
4 Discourse
Finally, as we've seen, in all disciplines, you'll be expected to engage with the relevant discourse. Generally, this is about the need to locate your own views or research in the broader academic context. We saw this in particular in relation to Example 1, but it could also be seen in Example 2. In Example 3, there is an element of this; but, as we noted above, in history, the discourse itself takes on greater significance as the author tries to build an argument by engaging with it.

Genres of writing

There is a lot of variety now in the types of assessment tasks used in higher education. This means that there are more genres of writing that students have to become familiar with if they're looking to excel in their academic work. Developing the ability to write effectively is not enough in itself to reach that level of success. It's now just as important that students demonstrate what might be called 'writing agility', an ability to write successfully across genres by completing different types of assessment.

In the following discussion, we look at a sample of genres, the ones we think a discussion of will be most useful to you:

- the essay;
- a research proposal;
- a literature review;
- a report;
- reflective writing.

The essay

The essay can be defined as a continuous piece of writing which sets out a response, usually in the form of an argument, to a question or assessment task. Although it's often used, its usefulness as a means of assessment in higher education has come into question in recent years due to the ease with which it has become possible for some students to 'beat' it. For example, some students have used essay-writing companies to produce work for them to submit in their own name, while, more recently, AI has allowed others to generate portions of text to include within essays. Despite this, the essay has endured, particularly in humanities disciplines, where it remains core to student learning. The form of the essay lends itself to the development and assessment of the literacies we've been discussing in this book. For the tutor, the essay makes it easy to assess the progress of your development as a learner and to measure your overall performance against that of other students more generally. As a genre of writing, the essay is clearly and easily assessable.

In some handbooks on writing you'll find different types of essay identified. In what follows, we're looking at the argumentative (sometimes called 'analytical') essay. This is an essay built around an argument, a response to a question set that is shaped by an understanding of the relevant discourse and supported by relevant evidence.

All essays follow a simple and logical structure which you'll have come across before: it needs a beginning (an introduction), a middle (the body of the essay), and an end (the conclusion). What should you include in each of these sections?

The introduction should do just as it says: it should *introduce* the reader to the topic of the essay, the approach taken, and the direction of your argument. The following questions might help you to create an introduction:

- What is the subject of your essay?
- What has been said about it in the discourse?
- What are you going to argue?
- Why are you arguing this?
- How does it fit into the existing discourse surrounding the issue?

Let's look at an example. The passage below is an introduction to an essay addressing the following question: 'Assess the potential impact of the use of generative artificial intelligence on learning in higher education.' Read the example and consider how effective it is as an introduction.

> *The impact of generative AI in today's society is often discussed in the media. Much of this coverage is about the potential dangers of AI, as if it is something to be feared. One reason for this is that it is not well understood amongst the general population. There is also a growing awareness of it invading our lives in a number of different ways. This is highlighted very clearly in the field of higher education where the use of AI, principally amongst students, has created a great deal of concern. This concern can be attributed to the assumption that students will use generative AI, like ChatGPT, as a means of cheating in assessed work, generating large amounts of text for their essays, for example, with little thought or input from the students themselves. Whilst there is evidence to suggest that this is*

a valid concern, much less attention has been given to the potentially positive impact generative AI might have in higher education as a learning tool. It will therefore be argued that whilst the use of generative AI might, on the surface, appear to have a negative impact on learning, once tutors and higher education professionals develop a better understanding of how this technology might enhance the learning experience, it will act as a force for good in the sector.

When you review the example above in light of the questions we listed, it's clear to see how this piece of text works as an introduction. Here are some points to consider:

1 It starts broadly by introducing the reader to the topic of generative AI and the largely negative way it is depicted in the media. This is neatly reflected in the view that AI is presented as something to be afraid of. An explanation is then provided, which leads logically into the topic of AI and higher education.
2 Higher education is presented as a case study which highlights the author's general observations about AI: professionals in this field are generally afraid of its influence. An explanation is offered: there is an assumption that students will use it to cheat.
3 The author then alludes to the discourse by referring to evidence which supports this contention.
4 This point, however, is qualified by noting that literature on the potentially positive impact of AI on learning is less developed.
5 This supports and leads into a clear statement of what the author intends to argue: that, superficially, it looks like AI has only a negative impact on learning, but that once you take a closer look, you'll see that it has the potential to act as a powerful learning tool if tutors are willing to embrace it as such.

The author has indicated the line of argument at the end of the introduction. In the body of the essay, you need to set out the argument, which is built, paragraph by paragraph. Planning, therefore, is critical. If your argument is going to be easy to follow and to have impact on the reader, you need to plan it.

Here's an extract from the body of the AI essay. Can you find the argument? If you can, what techniques does the author use to convey it?

AI has the greatest potential to impact positively on learning by disrupting traditional modes of teaching. Its potential to act in this way has been noted in a number of studies, since it effectively makes it easier to access key knowledge and understanding (e.g. Gilbert, 2024). Lectures, for example, can often provide students with a dry, unimaginative and passive learning experience, particularly if the lecture has been pre-recorded and made available via a VLE. Such experiences might be transformed through the use of AI, with student-led sessions in which knowledge found via generative AI might be tested or critiqued. Similar learning activities might be used in tutorials or seminars. AI therefore has the potential to act as a tool for tutors to use to develop a more active learning experience for students. This will only benefit student learning because it will help to improve engagement and student participation in learning.

AI stands to have considerable influence over assessment practices. There are growing concerns about the number of students who are willing to take advantage of technology, including AI, when creating written work (Sweeney, 2023). The reaction of many universities to these trends has been to update unfair practice regulations so that students can be penalised if they use technology like AI. Yet, in this area, AI also has the potential to stimulate fresh ways of engaging students. There has been less attention given to how assessment practices might be changed to incorporate the use of generative AI in some way. One example of how this might be done effectively is in teaching new undergraduate students about research. By comparing the results returned on a specific literature search using an AI search engine next to a library discovery service, students might be encouraged to discuss the benefits and drawbacks of using AI in this context. Such a task might help to shape student behaviour when it comes to conducting research.

At a more basic level, generative AI also offers students the opportunity of receiving a more personalised learning experience. Chatbots, powered by generative AI, have the potential to act as facilitators of learning, just as tutors do. Indeed, this is how a large proportion of university-level students in Hong Kong, recently surveyed, viewed the role played by chatbots in their own learning (Chan & Hu, 2023). Chatbots might even take on the role of 'critical friend' when asked more specific questions about aspects of learning. International students, for example, use generative AI to help refine their English-language skills, while researchers have also established its usefulness in marking student work (Chan & Lee, 2023; Crompton & Burke, 2023; Steiss et al., 2024). Advances like these will have a significant effect on learning and teaching, particularly at universities.

The argument emerges first and foremost out of the structure of the writing. Here, we have three separate points about the positive influence AI might have, each made in its own paragraph. Within each paragraph, you can see a microcosm of the essay structure: an introductory sentence setting out the topic of that paragraph (often called a 'topic sentence'); a body, in which the point of the paragraph is developed; and a conclusion, where the point is summarised. The argument is also developed through the arrangement of these paragraphs. The author clearly thinks that the impact of AI is at its greatest when it is disrupting traditional modes of teaching. Its influence over assessment practices is next in importance, followed by the potential role of chatbots in supporting the learning of individual students. There is a hierarchy here. The argument is also reinforced by the vocabulary used. In the first paragraph, for example, the author contrasts active and passive learning in order to emphasise its positive impact. AI is also described as a learning tool and its use is linked to the broader issue of student engagement. Such terms carry significance and meaning in the discipline of education, and their use helps to clarify and strengthen the points being made.

The point of the conclusion is to summarise the argument. It represents a golden opportunity for you to make your argument or key points as clear as possible for the reader. What you shouldn't do is simply repeat the points you've made in the essay. Some students, to save time, copy and paste the first sentence of each paragraph into the conclusion. But this is a wasted opportunity when it comes to ensuring that your reader has fully grasped your argument. You need to synthesise the points you've made without repeating yourself. Consider the example below. What makes this an effective conclusion?

> *Generative AI will undoubtedly impact upon learning in higher education. It is a widely held view in the sector at the moment that this impact will be negative because generative AI has the potential to undermine assessment practices and even to discourage student engagement in learning. However, as set out here, AI has the potential to enhance the learning experience at university by stimulating new ways of thinking about student engagement in learning and alternative approaches to assessment. It is by disrupting traditional modes of teaching in higher education that AI has the greatest potential to impact learning. However, if this potential is to be realised, tutors and professionals working in higher education need to recognise its value as a learning tool rather than seeing it simply as danger to existing practices.*

The effectiveness of this conclusion lies in the way that it acknowledges the prevailing view in the discourse before emphasising the alternative presented in the essay of the potential value of generative AI in learning. The author goes on to explain that it is as a disrupter of learning practices that AI is likely to have its greatest impact. It ends by looking to the future: the positive impact of AI will only be realised once tutors and other professionals working in higher education embrace it as a means of enhancing learning. It does all the things we highlighted in the preceding paragraph: it summarises the argument; it expresses the argument clearly; it has synthesised the key points; and it reflects a broader understanding of the relevant discourse. It's much more effective than copying and pasting the first sentences of each paragraph!

Research proposal

A research proposal forms part of a larger research project, like a dissertation. In a sense, the proposal acts as a plan for your research; but, through its design, it actually does a lot more than that. The proposal is often made up of a series of questions which have been carefully created to encourage you to engage with the topic and its associated discourse at a deeper level – but in a guided and structured way. By answering each of these questions as fully as you can, you're creating a framework for the entire project. Each question will help to define or articulate key elements of the research: its focus; its aims and objectives; the approach you intend to take; and its contribution to existing knowledge. Given its potential for supporting the development of your work, it's important to use it! Treat a research proposal as a live document, something you can edit and update as the project progresses.

In terms of how it's written, some of the same principles we've already met apply here. Clarity, in the sense of making your points as precisely as possible, is very important in a research proposal because you'll be referring to specific viewpoints or pieces of knowledge. Such precision helps to convey the depth of your understanding. Generalised comments, on the other hand, tend to give the opposite impression. Avoid unnecessary detail or digressions; say just enough without saying any more. This isn't easy, but once you've drafted the proposal, consider whether all that you've included is needed. If you cut anything out, it won't be wasted; keep it in a separate document for use when writing up the research later on.

Another important point relates to the vocabulary you use. We've already noted the significance of discipline-specific vocabulary in writing for assessment more broadly. Here, it takes on added importance since its use in the proposal will help to demonstrate to your tutor the depth of your understanding of the topic. Using such vocabulary is also a function of being clear and precise: to be as specific as possible, you need to make use of terms that carry meaning in the context of the topic area and wider discipline.

Let's consider some of the questions often included in research proposals. We've also got an example to show you. How effective is this example in answering these questions?

The questions discussed here have been distilled from a range of proposals we've discussed with students. These proposals come from a variety of disciplines and relate to work at both undergraduate and postgraduate levels. The questions are:

- What is the title or research question of the project?
- What is the rationale for the research?
- What are the aims and objectives of the research?
- What is your approach or methodology?
- How will you organise your research? (i.e., a chapter outline)
- Indicative bibliography

What is the title or research question of the project?

Establishing the title or research question for your project can be very difficult – and frustrating! To phrase it properly, it helps to identify the topic first before pinning down the specific title or research question.

How do you identify a topic? Put simply, by engaging with the discourse, just as your tutors would do when they're preparing their own research. This means that you need to read, read, and read in your discipline area. The more you read, and the more you think about what you're reading, the easier it will be not only to find that topic but to establish the angle or approach you're going to take. You'll find that as you become more familiar with the discourse, questions about what you're reading will come to mind. How does this view relate to the one I read about in the article yesterday? What is the significance of these findings on my understanding of this aspect of the topic? Keep a record of these questions as they occur.

In marking criteria, you might see, as a characteristic of pieces of work in the highest band of marks, reference to its 'originality'. There is a misconception among undergraduates in particular that dissertations, for example, *must* include original research. This isn't true. Much research across the disciplines cannot be described as 'original', in the sense that it is entirely new. Imagine you are researching a topic in the discipline of history. It's possible that you might, for example, include a source text that has never been published before, or you might be writing about an event that has barely been studied. Most of the time, however, you are providing a different perspective on something that has been written about before. Rather than talking about originality, therefore, we prefer talking about the *freshness* of a perspective. How innovative is the approach? Does it build on or extend approaches taken elsewhere? Is it distinct, in that does it represent an approach unique to the author and their work?

A title or research question should reflect the topic you're investigating and the approach or angle you intend to take. Whereas the topic area might be expressed in a general statement, the title or research question needs to have a specific focus. What aspect of the topic are you looking at? The process of defining a title or research question is about moving from the general to the specific, as illustrated in Table 9.1.

Notice how in each example we move from the general topic area to the specific title or RQ. The latter clearly emerges out of the former.

What is the rationale for the research?

A tutor or prospective supervisor might ask you *why*? Why are you looking at this topic? What interests you about it? Why are you adopting this approach? What contribution will it make to knowledge in the discipline?

Table 9.1 Topic areas and research questions

General (Topic area)	Specific (Title or RQ)
Coastal erosion in Europe	A case study of the impact of storms and storm waves on coastal erosion in south-western France, 2010–2020
The use of social media in marketing for small businesses	An assessment of the relative value of Facebook as a marketing tool for UK-based SMEs
France and the causes of the First World War	To what extent did ultranationalism in France during the Third Republic contribute to the outbreak of the First World War?

Why, in other words, should your research exist? All of these questions are related to the *rationale behind your project. Your focus here should be on justifying the decisions you've taken to carry out the research you've identified.

In the example below – on France and the causes of the First World War – you'll notice that in this section the student has provided some observations on the way nationalism has been approached within the discourse. These comments are combined with questions about the role of ultranationalism in shaping French political culture. In other words, we've got a broad awareness of the main threads of the discourse, together with questions that point to how this research will contribute to our overall understanding of the topic.

What are the aims and objectives of the project?
The background reading you've done relating to the topic will give you a deeper understanding of the relevant discourse, which you'll need when identifying the aims and objectives of the research project. Your title or research question will highlight an overarching objective for your work. Within that objective, however, there will be a small number of 'mini' objectives which you will need to address as you work towards the overarching one. Each one will be related to a subtopic of the main topic area.

You can see this in the example provided. The student has highlighted several aspects of the topic for further consideration, such as the need to define 'ultranationalism'. Note that the student has turned each one into a clear and achievable objective: 'To define ultranationalism and to trace its development in France during the Third Republic'. The clarity here is important because it will help to provide the final piece of work with greater coherence.

There isn't a recommended number of aims or objectives to have in a research project. The student in our example might need to add one or two more. Our advice is to keep it manageable. Much depends on the discipline in which you're working, the topic area, the nature of your investigation, and even the length of the piece of written work you're producing. It's normal to have three, four, or five.

What is your approach or methodology?
Expectations regarding this question will vary according to the discipline in which you're working. Across all disciplines, explaining your approach or methodology means setting out how you intend to address the project's aims and objectives. What data will you be using? How will you analyse this data? What theoretical lenses are you applying to this analysis? What theory underpins your approach?

The nature of the data you will be using will depend on the discipline in which you're working. For a social media and marketing project, you might be looking at several different types of data, including social media posts, interviews with stakeholders, and government policy documents. Some of this data will be quantitative (i.e., numerical data), while other types of data will be qualitative (e.g., interviews). The nature of the data involved in your research will impact upon the methodologies you use. For this project, a mixed-methods approach – one that is used when you have both quantitative and qualitative data sets – will be needed. In the social sciences, for example, greater weight is placed upon your explanation of the methodology you will be using.

In our example below, the student has set out the approach they intend to take to the project as a whole, explaining how each element is linked together. In addition, they've also highlighted what sources they intend to use and how to access them. You can see here how different such a project is from, say, the social media one.

How will you organise your research?
In this section, you'll provide an indication of what chapters you're likely to include. These chapters will reflect the aims and objectives you've identified above. When setting out the chapters, try to think of the flow of the work. How are the subtopics related to one another? In what order should they be included? How is your research presented most effectively? In the example below, the organisation of the chapters closely resembles the approach set out in the preceding section. Remember, this is not the final version of the work. The organisation of the research will

evolve as the project develops. You might add a chapter, change the focus of another, or even remove one.

Indicative bibliography
In the final part of the proposal document, you'll be expected to set out an indicative bibliography – items you have read, plus those that you intend to read. It's good practice to keep a 'to read' list which you can update as and when you come across something relevant. In our own research, we've sometimes divided up this list into sections relating to each subtopic. It's up to you. The important point to have in mind here is that you're trying to demonstrate to the reader that you have a sound grasp of the landscape of discourse relevant to the topic, as well as its contours. It doesn't have to be complete (and won't be), but try to include all that you think is relevant, from key works to the most recent pieces of relevant research you can find.

Below is the example of a research proposal relating to history:

Topic/title

<u>Topic</u>: France and the causes of the First World War

<u>Title</u>: To what extent did ultranationalism in France during the Third Republic contribute to the outbreak of the First World War?

What is the rationale for the research?

Nationalism is often identified as a primary cause of the First World War. Usually, it is Serbian nationalism that provides the focus of this view. However, the growth of German nationalism, following the creation of the German Empire in 1871, has also been highlighted as a prominent cause of the conflict. This study aims to examine the part played by the rise of ultranationalism in France in the build-up of tension in Europe which led to the outbreak of war. Following the country's defeat in the Franco-Prussian war in 1871, right-wing sentiments grew among the populace, driven by a desire for revenge against the new German Empire. While the impact of *revanchism* on the French political mindset at the end of the nineteenth century has been contested in modern historical discourse, its importance in the rise of ultranationalism cannot be played down, as the popularity of Georges Ernest Boulanger, Général Revanche, suggests. How far did the popularity of ultranationalism influence political culture in France in the late nineteenth century? What part did it play in shaping France's actions in the crucial years leading up to the outbreak of war?

What are the aims and objectives of the project?

1 To define ultranationalism and to trace its development in France during the Third Republic.
2 To assess the popularity of ultranationalism and its significance in French political culture during this period.
3 To assess the impact of ultranationalism on France's foreign policy in the years leading up to 1914, notably its relationships with Germany and Russia.

What is your approach or methodology?

It is important to first define ultranationalism, identify its origins, particularly as they are related to the Franco-Prussian war, and to trace its development. The latter might be achieved by considering some well-known episodes of French history, such as the Dreyfus affair, as well as the careers of individual figures associated with ultranationalism, such as Boulanger. These events will provide windows onto the rise of ultranationalism. Its popularity will be considered by reference to such events and by using evidence from contemporary newspapers. All of this information will then be used to assess how far ultranationalism influenced popular politics and how these sentiments might have influenced French politicians in the lead up to the war.

This study will make use of a range of primary sources, many of which are only available in French, such as newspapers and political pamphlets (available via gallica.bnf.fr). Scholarly websites, such as that devoted to the Dreyfus affair (www.dreyfus.culture.fr/en), also provide access to some of these sources, some of which are available in English translation. Use of primary sources will obviously be complemented by information, ideas, and interpretations gleaned from modern discourse. The university's library collection includes many of the items listed below. Those that I cannot find there will be requested via Inter-Library loan or accessed directly at the British Library.

How will you organise your research?

- Definition of ultranationalism, its origins, and the context provided by France's defeat in the Franco-Prussian war.
- The development of ultranationalism: mini case study of Boulanger's career.
- Ultranationalism, revanchism, and the popular political culture.
- Ultranationalist sentiment and French foreign policy in the early twentieth century.

Indicative bibliography

- Burns, M. (1984) *Rural Society and French Politics L Boulangism and the Dreyfus Affair, 1886-1900*. Princeton: Princeton University Press.
- Bury, J. (2003) *France, 1814-1940*. 5th edn. London: Routledge.
- Fortescue, W. (2000) *The Third Republic in France, 1870-1940: Conflicts and Continuities*. London: Routledge.
- Goodliffe, G. (2012) *The Resurgence of the Radical Right in France: From Boulangism to the Front National*. Cambridge: Cambridge University Press.
- Hanson, S. (2010) *Post-Imperial Democracies: Ideology and Party Formation in Third Republic France, Weimar Germany and Post-Soviet Russia*. Cambridge: Cambridge University Press.
- Hutton, P. (1976) 'Popular Boulangism and the advent of mass politics in France, 1886-1890', *Journal of Contemporary History*, 11, pp. 85-106.
- Irvine, W. (1979) *French Conservatism in Crisis: The Republican Federation of France*. Baton Rouge: Louisiana State University Press.
- Irvine, W. (1989) *The Boulanger Affair Reconsidered: Royalism, Boulangism, and the Origins of the Radical Right in France*. Oxford: Oxford University Press.
- Passmore, K. (2013) *The Right in France from the Third Republic to Vichy*. Oxford: Oxford University Press.
- Passmore, K. (2014) 'The historiography of 'fascism' in France', *French Historical Studies*, 37, pp. 469–499.
- Rémond, R. (1966) *The Right Wing in France: From 1815 to de Gaulle*. Philadelphia: University of Pennsylvania Press.
- Tombs, R. (ed) *Nationhood and Nationalism in France: From Boulangism to the Great War, 1889-1918*. London: Harper Collins Academic.

Literature review

Most of you reading this will encounter the literature review as part of a dissertation (or any longer piece of research-based writing), whether that's at undergraduate or postgraduate level. In some disciplines, such as in history, the literature review doesn't form a discrete section within a dissertation. In other disciplines, it forms a distinct and key element of a written up piece of research.

What is it, therefore, and why is it so important? The literature review provides a review of the literature relevant to your research. It does this by establishing key works and authors, important themes, key debates, and controversial elements of the discourse, what topics are currently being looked at, and gaps in the literature. It's not just a description of who said what, when. It establishes the landscape of the discourse relevant to your research, its 'intellectual context'. In this sense, it's necessary in order to position your own research within that discourse.

It's created through extensive reading of the discourse, considered thought about it, and careful planning. You need to read widely in order to fully engage with the discourse. This needs to be done in a structured way, so that – in keeping with some of the ideas we've already discussed – you build your knowledge and understanding logically. Avoid just jumping into a journal article that looks relevant if you don't have sufficient background knowledge to fully understand it. This will impact upon the type of source you look at first. Textbooks provide background knowledge; journal articles open up research. Plan your research, in other words, with the principle of building knowledge in mind. At the same time, think carefully about what you're reading. How do ideas relate to each other? What themes link the research together? What is missing or underdeveloped in the discourse? Keep asking questions of what you're looking at; don't just passively accept what's in front of you with a view to 'reporting' it in the literature review.

When writing a literature review, your objective should be to critique the discourse – to analyse, evaluate and synthesise it in such a way as to make the value of your research absolutely clear. A number of techniques are available to help you do this, some of which are highlighted below in the exemplar. This is an extract from a literature review concerning the links between rising levels of plagiarism and the stress experienced by many university students. Read through it; how does the author engages with the literature?

> *Recent research has highlighted the large numbers of students whose studies in higher education are affected by stress and wellbeing issues. For example, one study on students in the US found that the number of students reporting mental health problems only increased as a result of the*

negative impact of the COVID-19 pandemic (Son et al., 2020), while another, on students at Australian institutions, highlighted the low levels of wellbeing recorded amongst undergraduate students in particular (Dodd et al., 2021). In an investigation into the impact of COVID-19 on medical students in the Philippines, Baticulon et al. (2021) noted how the changed mode of learning, with a greater focus on online learning, caused anxiety amongst a significant proportion of the students surveyed. Stress and wellbeing issues clearly form important issues which universities across the world need to address.

Setting aside the impact of the pandemic, research has highlighted several key causes of stress amongst university students. The most significant are stress related to academic expectations (e.g. Berdida, 2023), financial worries and concerns over funding (Usman & Banu, 2019), and the pressure associated with balancing the demands of an academic course with familial and other non-academic commitments (Narwal et al., 2021). These concerns reflect the changing make-up of the student population, with many more students returning to education after a break and therefore carrying with them a host of other commitments that traditional school leavers are less likely to have.

It is recognised that these concerns have made many students vulnerable to choosing easy options linked to plagiarism when it comes to completing assessed academic work. Data suggests that commercial contract cheating, for example, has been on the increase since 2014 (Newton, 2018; Hill et al., 2021). This rise has been attributed to the increased pressure university students are under; one study has even highlighted the significance of peer influence in explaining the increased incidence of academic dishonesty (Zhao et al., 2022). The impact of technology on learning has also been cited as an important factor, since online learning resources have made it much easier for students to cut corners by engaging in unethical practices (Kampa et al., 2025). There is great concern about the impact of, for example, AI on learning (e.g. Guo et al., 2024), with practice suggesting that universities on the whole are struggling to keep pace with developments in this field.

However, the reality is that the reasons for the rise in the incidence of plagiarism are complex and multi-faceted. Furthermore, what motivates an individual student to engage in unethical behaviour varies from person to person according to circumstance. The decision to commit plagiarism cannot be attributed to one or two factors, such as AI or the academic demands of a course. Moreover, there is a tendency to view AI almost entirely negatively in the literature, largely because of the fears of academic staff about its potential impact on assessment (Michel-Villarreal et al., 2023). Comparatively little research has been done on the positive effects

it might have on enhancing learning. It this aspect of AI that will form the focus of this study.
[Adapted from: Crawford, J., Cowling M., & Allen, K. A. (2023). Leadership is needed for ethical ChatGPT: Character, assessment, and learning using artificial intelligence (AI). *Journal of University Teaching & Learning Practice, 20*(3), 1–19, at pp. 1–2]

The first thing to notice is the clarity of the writing – its organisation and structure. Each paragraph deals with a slightly different point. By doing this, the author successfully builds a discussion which effectively contextualises the point in the final paragraph, on the need to examine the positive impact of AI on learning. This point is key, since it sets out the objective of the research.

Each paragraph is also effectively linked together. This gives the writing a sense of logic, coherence, and flow. This is achieved by repeating ideas or keywords from the preceding paragraph in the opening sentence of the next one. Note, for example, how the second paragraph begins with a reference to the pandemic mentioned in the first one.

A critical edge is added through the language of criticality. This is clearest in the final paragraph, which opens with 'However', a powerful word that implies to the reader that some critical thought is about to appear. It's followed by two more words that are loaded with similar meanings: 'Furthermore', which implies that an additional or supporting example is about to be introduced, and 'Moreover', which carries with it the implication that the point being introduced is more convincing and impactful than the previous one.

Linked to the point about the language of criticality is the use of verbs. Well-chosen verbs can help to add clarity to your argument. Consider the use of 'highlighted' and 'attributed' in the exemplar. 'Highlighted' is used here to indicate that recent research has brought these issues to the surface. It provides a more precise way of saying that certain researchers have 'shown' you something or have simply 'stated' it. 'Attributed' is used to indicate that in the work cited the researchers have linked the rise to specific factors. As such, it helps to demonstrate to the reader that you have a clear understanding of the factors that underpin the increase in the number of students who admit to engaging in plagiarism. Using such verbs helps you, as the author, to put your view first and then to demonstrate how it is related to what has already been published about this topic.

A final point concerns the way the literature has been integrated into the discussion. We've just mentioned how the author is careful to put their view first. This is recommended, since it suggests an active rather than passive approach to the use of the sources; it encourages the author to critique the literature instead of simply describing it. Many of the sources included here are therefore used to support or to illustrate observations relating to the literature made by the author. Such a characteristic is typical of a literature review that is discursive and analytical, and which includes evidence of an ability to synthesise the interpretations found in the creation of the author's own argument or perspective.

Reports

In science-related disciplines, for example, you'll be assessed at some point on your ability to write up a report on practical work (e.g., in the laboratory). In the sciences, the report resembles a research article, in that it is structured along similar lines, as set out in Table 9.2.

In other disciplines, such as business-related disciplines, the report might look slightly different. You'll still include core elements – introduction, methodology, results, and discussion – but it will include several other elements, depending on context. For example, you might have an executive summary rather than an abstract, and the conclusion might include recommendations, again, depending on context. The introduction might be more focused on explaining the context for the report rather than its purpose as such.

Table 9.2 Report structure

Title	What was the purpose of the practical work? What were you doing? Try to summarise the work itself in a sentence – this sentence will then form the title of the work.
Abstract	The abstract provides a summary of the report: what did you set out to do? How did you do it? What did you find? How significant were these findings? What were your overall conclusions?
Introduction	Here, you should set out the purpose of the work – what are you trying to do? – and explain its significance.
Methodology	How did you go about working towards the objectives identified above? Consider what you did step-by-step.
Results	What data or results did the practical work yield? In this section, you need to present this data, usually in tables or as graphs. Include some explanation of what each table or graph shows.
Discussion	Here, you'll set the results in their broader context. How do the results relate to your intentions when starting the work? You might also include some links to relevant literature, if it's appropriate.
Conclusion	In the conclusion, you'll be summarising the preceding two sections in particular. The conclusion should be short and concise.
References List	A list of all those items you've referenced in the report.

For a fuller discussion of the structural elements that underpin the creation of a report, see our discussion of the way John engages with a journal article in Chapter 8.

Reflective writing

Reflective writing stands out from the other genres of writing discussed here because it is (i) less formal in style and expression and (ii) focused almost exclusively on experience. This often means that you don't need to include references to academic sources. The writing style is less formal because it is characterised by the use of the first person ('I' rather than the third person, 'he, she, it') and the expressions you use will more likely reflect everyday spoken English. The absence of references is because in reflective writing you're not expected to engage with relevant discourse. Instead, you're expected to reflect on (critique) an experience in order to gain a greater understanding of you (the self). The reflection is meant to bring about an improved performance when you undertake a similar task in the future.

Reflective writing is still meant to be critical. One mistake students often make is that they concentrate on describing the experience without offering any critique of their own performance, actions, or decisions. The value of reflective writing – its worth to you, as an analysis of what you did – lies in the insights it can provide into your performance. For the tutor, it provides a means of assessing your ability to engage effectively in personal development, to take responsibility for it, and to regulate your own academic performance.

Being critical is just one of the characteristics that reflective writing shares with the genres of writing we've already looked at. Your expression still needs to be clear and precise even if the style itself is less formal. Structure is also important; it comes from the use of a reflective cycle to organise the writing. In the example that follows, we'll be using the three-step, ERA cycle (Jasper, 2013):

- Experience
- Reflect
- Take action

What might a piece of reflective writing look like which uses the ERA cycle as its structure? Read through the exemplar below, which does just that. It's the reflection of a student, Will, who has just completed the 'marshmallow challenge'. This is a much used team-building exercise. The challenge is to build a structure using uncooked spaghetti, Sellotape, and string; the structure has to be solid enough to carry a marshmallow on top once it's standing. Google it, if you need to!

Experience

On Tuesday, I took part in the first session of a two-day course on 'Reflective Practice'. There were ten students on the course. The course itself was made up of four sessions across two days. There was an optional assessment task we could do after the course, which was credit bearing, and a further day later in the summer when we could discuss the assessment with the tutor. In the first session, the tutor split us into two groups and set us a group exercise to do. This was called the 'marshmallow challenge'. He gave us a packet of spaghetti, a roll of sellotape, some string, and a marshmallow. He asked us to work together to create a tall, freestanding structure. We could only use the materials provided and the marshmallow needed to sit on top of the structure. The structure had to stand. The purpose of the challenge was to get to know the other students, but it also provided an experience for us to reflect on during the course. For the next half an hour, we worked together, discussing ideas and experimenting with the materials – some contributed more than others. It wasn't easy, but we managed to create a standing structure that was about thirty centimetres high. However, when the marshmallow was put on top, it collapsed. The other team's structure was higher and so we lost the challenge.

Reflect

I think the lack of input from certain team members might have just been the 'luck of the draw'. The other team seemed to be chattier. I might have just had quieter people. I also think the situation might have been unusual for some people. The task itself is a bit odd if you haven't done anything like it before and I'm not sure that everyone understood why they were doing it. I think that reflection itself was something very different for the students on my team. I don't think they'd ever done anything like it before and so they were already feeling a bit lost. We were on campus in a large university building, with lots of proper students around. This might have intimidated some of the students on the course. Because I was speaking a lot, trying to get the task done, I think some team members thought, 'why not leave it to him?' This obviously didn't help when it came to creating ideas because there was only me coming up with anything. Maybe the fact that we could see the other team getting on with the task didn't help either. By comparison, we were a bit stuck! The fact we created a structure was great, but the fact it collapsed highlights, I think, how limited our approach was. We didn't have great ideas because not everyone was contributing and so it was inevitable that our structure wouldn't work properly.

Take action

If I could do the task again I would consciously take a back seat pretty quickly. This would allow others to step forward – even force them to – and I could then perhaps influence the discussion by adding my own thoughts at the right moments. Alternatively, I might have done what the tutor ended up doing in the discussion after the completion of the task – asking individual students for their thoughts. If I had done this in the group, it would have involved everybody and it would have meant no one could hide! Another way of sharing out the responsibility for completing the task would have been to have agreed, as a group, on specific areas of responsibility. For example, team member B, who was quite arty, might have focused on building, while others could have looked at design. This approach would have given us a more organised way of working. I think I'm confident enough to be a good leader. I get on with people and I can motivate others. I think it's important to be aware of the circumstances in which you're working and the way that might make others feel. If, for example, someone isn't contributing to a team task, there's no point getting frustrated. I should think about why they might feel shy and what I can do to help them engage more with the work.

I would

- *be more aware of the circumstances in which the group task is taking place;*
- *think carefully about how these circumstances might affect others;*
- *take a more organised approach to a group task, working with others to assign areas of responsibility;*
- *try to avoid dominating the conversation, even when I don't mean to – putting a lid on it!*
- *read up on project management theories and working with others resources.*

You can see in this exemplar some of the core characteristics shared by reflective writing with other genres: the structure, as we noted above, which emerges out of the application of the ERA cycle, and the clarity of the writing. You can also see a critical edge. Will doesn't simply describe what happened; he does attempt a critical assessment of his own actions within this scenario. The characteristics that are unique to reflective writing can also be seen: the use of the first person and the less formal writing style. Its most striking feature, however, is linked to its purpose. This comes into sharper focus in the final section, 'Take action', which provides a conclusion together with a short action plan. Reflective writing, as we noted, is meant to support you as you engage in personal development. It's vital therefore that you link the observations you make about your performance during the reflective process to the positive steps you intend to take. In this way, the action plan neatly captures the benefits to you, as a learner, of reflective writing.

The four pillars of effective writing

If you look at the relevant marking criteria for each of the genres we've discussed, you'll notice that certain features recur. Think carefully about the following four features, regardless of the genre in which you're working:

1. Clarity and precision of expression
   It's here where we can remind you of a maxim we press on the students we teach: 'say what you mean; no more and no less'. If what you're trying to say isn't fully clear to you, change the expression.
2. Structure
   Writing needs to be organised if it is to be effective. Plan your work carefully. Use paragraphs in your work and think carefully about their arrangement.
3. Effective engagement with relevant discourse
   Almost all assessed written work requires some engagement with discourse. Where you're expected to make critical use of it, make sure you're not simply reporting what you've found. How is it related to what you want to say? What is its significance in light of the question?
4. Presentation (including references)
   This refers to the font size and spacing, for example, as well as how you've set out the references list. It will also likely include reference format. All of these things contribute to the overall impression made by your work.

The following discussion of the practice of writing will help to bring the importance of each one into sharper focus.

Writing in practice

How do you go about creating a piece of written work? What techniques can you use to enhance your writing? Let's begin with the reality that faces lots of students when trying to complete a piece of assessed written work. Consider the case of Emma, a second-year marketing student, in the following scenario:

> *Emma gets to university early on Monday morning and goes straight to the IT suite (via the coffee shop) to claim her favourite PC in the corner. Her intention on arriving at the desk is to spend all day and evening writing the essay due in at the end of the week. She turns on the PC, gets out her folder with the notes she's made in lectures and tutorials, as well as a pen and notebook, and lines up everything in front of her next to her coffee and water bottle. She logs-in, opens Word, types out the question, her name and the date – and then freezes. She stares at the flashing cursor*

on the white background and panics. *How do you start an essay? What are you going to say?* After several gulps of coffee and a long stare out of the window she types out four or five words. She stops. She reads them back. And then deletes them. She looks at her watch; she's already been at university for forty-five minutes. *This is not going to plan.*

The dreaded blank, white background of a Word document without any text. We've all been there at some point. For Emma, it was even worse, because after writing a few words, she immediately deleted them. A general principle which is always worth having in mind is that *it's better to have a draft of something to work with than nothing at all*. Try to avoid immediately deleting what you've written. Emma's objective should not be to write up the essay due in at the end of the week in a day; it should be to get a draft of her work down, on the screen, as quickly but as completely as she can. But how do you get started? What is Emma doing wrong?

Writing is a process consisting of distinct stages. The most important of these stages is planning. Underneath any effective piece of writing of whatever genre is a structure created in the planning phase. What Emma needs to do first all, before she starts drafting her response, is to develop a plan. Spending a few hours on this will make the task of writing much easier. Let's begin, therefore, by looking at what we call the 'writing cycle', which is set out in Figure 9.1.

The writing cycle represents the process in which you need to engage in order to have the best possible chance of creating a really effective piece of writing. Let's take a look at each of its stages.

Understanding the task:

It's vital that you fully understand the question you're being asked or, more broadly, the assessment instructions, if your writing is going to be effective. Consider carefully (i) the steer of a question and (ii) its keywords. The steer of the question refers to the opening phrase which points to the approach you need to take when answering it, as well as any specific 'skills' being tested. For example:

To what extent has coastal erosion in south-western Europe between 2010 and 2020 been caused by storm waves?

The phrase 'To what extent' requires a judgement. You need to produce a substantiated (i.e., supported with evidence and grounded in your knowledge and understanding of the relevant discourse) judgement in response to the question or assessment task. To reach that judgement, you'll need to evaluate a range of factors, including the one named in the question. Why is X more important than Y? This steer is asking you to weigh up the significance or importance of a factor next to that of others. A question

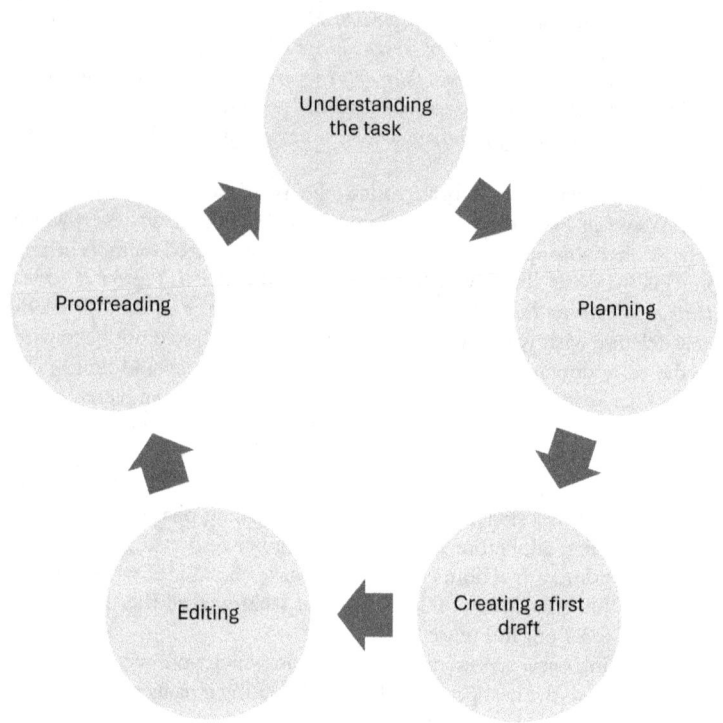

Figure 9.1 The writing cycle.

beginning in this way is not asking you to describe all that you know about the topic. Its focus is much sharper; in order to respond to it successfully, you need to take an evaluative approach.

In Emma's case, she needs to get to grips with a slightly different question:

Assess the potential value of social media to the marketing strategy of a typical SME.

The steer is 'Assess'. As a directive, it's similar to 'To what extent', in that Emma will be expected to weigh up the benefits and drawbacks to an SME of integrating social media into their marketing strategy. A successful answer will therefore look at both sides of the 'potential value' before reaching a substantiated judgement, just as with the coastal erosion question. It's perhaps a bit harder than that question because it doesn't identify a named factor for you to focus on (the coastal erosion question mentions 'storm waves'). In terms of keywords, there are two levels of complexity here. Taken at face value, the keywords are 'value', 'social media', 'marketing strategy', and 'SME' (small, medium-sized enterprises). At another level, though, we've also got 'potential value' and 'typical' SME. 'Potential' gives you a clue about looking at both the benefits and drawbacks. 'Typical' will require some sort of definition. What does Emma understand by a 'typical' SME? Keep an eye out for such keywords that may not be immediately obvious when you look at a question or assessment task. It's with the steer and keywords in mind that Emma needs to start her plan.

One final point when it comes to understanding the assessment task is to look carefully at the marking criteria your tutors will use to assess your work. This will be provided in the assessment brief, module handbook, or perhaps online via Moodle or Blackboard. Typically, the criteria will include the clarity of the writing, the extent to which you've made critical use of evidence and sources – and so on. In some marking criteria, however, there is a weighting. For example, making critical use of evidence might account for 30% or 40% of your mark, while referencing might be 10%. Have such things in mind as you plan and write up your work.

In summary:

1 Identify the steer and keywords in the assessment question or task.
2 Consider carefully what sort of approach the steer requires.
3 Read the marking criteria carefully and consider any weighting within it. What – exactly – are your tutors looking for?

Planning:

Planning acts as the bridge between the research you do – identifying and engaging with suitable academic sources found via your library's discovery service – and the actual writing. The plan you create as you do your research – an outline of your work – provides a framework on which your written response will sit. It's for this reason that planning represents such an important stage in the writing cycle. A good plan, one that's well-thought through, with detailed supporting knowledge, can make the next stage, writing a first draft, much easier.

How do you create a plan? It's important to remember that a good plan is a live document. In other words, it's something that can change. You can move points around, add more to it, delete anything that you think has become unnecessary, and use the plan almost as a sand pit for you to practise your expression, sentence structure and paragraph organisation. A plan begins by setting out the work's core elements: its introduction, its main part, and its conclusion. Under the introduction, try to set out, succinctly, your response to the question. This may change as you develop the plan, but it's important to define what might be called a 'line of reasoning', the argument in its basic form. Doing this will help to shape the rest of the plan, in terms of selecting the key points you want to make as you explore your response. The main part of the plan should consist of these key points. We find it's useful to express each point as a sentence, as if you're writing the opening sentence of each paragraph. In this way, you can practise writing clearly. Underneath each of the key points you can add in any supporting evidence you find or links to the discourse surrounding the topic – anything, in short, that helps to develop your argument. The organisation of these key points will be up to you. What works best? You might change the order of the points as you do more research. Try to find the most coherent structure you can. Under the conclusion, try to summarise the argument in the work. Phrase it differently to any statements you've made in the introduction. Again, this is an opportunity to practise your expression. Try to be as clear and to the point as possible.

The core elements of Emma' plan might look like this:

Assess the potential value of social media to the marketing strategy of a typical SME.

Introduction

- Use of social media in marketing strategy by SMEs is open to debate – is it worth it or not given the resources needed to use it effectively (human resources, training, technology, etc.).
- Define SMEs and links to traditional approaches to marketing – unique context.
- Traditional modes of marketing often work better for SMEs, but in some industries, such as tourism, it may help to extend reach of business.

Main part

1 Social media and marketing.

- How widespread is its use?
- How is it used/for what purpose?
- What are its benefits, in the literature?
- What are its drawbacks?

2 The uniqueness of the SME context.

- What are its benefits?
- What are its drawbacks?

3 SMEs and the use of social media.

- How has it been used well?
- How has it been used badly?

Conclusion

Integrating social media into marketing strategy for many SMEs isn't effective due to the resource cost outweighing any potential benefit. However, much depends on what industry the SME is operating in – careful use of social media can be beneficial, as long as it is used in conjunction with more traditional modes of marketing.

It's recommended to use bullet points in a plan, to give you greater flexibility over the way you organise it. Emma will need to find examples and supporting evidence to go underneath each of the main points, but you can see here the principles discussed above at work. The key points in the main part reflect the bullet points made in the introduction, while the conclusion emerges out of the discussion in the main part. You can use the above example as a template for your own plan.

In summary:

1 A plan is the bridge between research and written work.
2 Use the core elements of a piece of written work – introduction, main part, conclusion – as the foundation for a plan.
3 Create a live document, one that you can update and amend as you get deeper into the research.
4 Set out the line of reasoning in your plan, under the introduction, as soon as you can; it might evolve as you do more research, but that's a good thing!
5 Add in as much detail as you can, so that the writing becomes easier.
6 Use the plan as an opportunity to practise writing clearly and effectively.

Creating a first draft:

You'll get to a point in the planning stage where you'll feel more confident about the writing. Now it's time to type! Remember Emma: you're not writing the finished version of the essay; the objective here is get a draft of it down, on the screen, as soon as you can. It won't be perfect (no piece of writing ever is), but that's not a problem. You need a decent draft to work with in the following stages of the cycle. As you write, you may notice bits that need more work or points you need to check. That's fine – just keep writing. You can always flag up these bits using the highlighter option or the comments box under 'Review' on Word. Above all, use the plan to structure your writing. If something doesn't work, you can always amend the plan; but try to stick to the broad outline you've already established at the planning stage. Don't get too bogged down in writing either the introduction or conclusion. If you're finding it difficult to write the introduction, for example, move on to the first paragraph of the main part. You can always go back to the introduction.

In summary:

1 Focus on completing a good draft of the work. You need something to work with; you're not creating the finished version from the off. There's an editing stage to come.
2 Use the plan to structure and organise your writing.
3 Avoid writing traps: if you're trying to write the introduction, for example, but it just isn't happening, move on to a paragraph in the main part of the work. There's no point writing and re-writing the same piece of text or just staring at a blank screen.

Editing:

At the editing stage, you're going to be making substantive changes to the first draft. There's a distinction to draw here between proofreading and editing. Proofreading is more about polishing the text, eliminating typos and superficial errors that are easy to correct. Editing is about deleting text, adding it, changing the expression you use, creating new paragraphs, and so on. It's at this stage where you can make significant improvements to the first draft. The first thing to do on completing the draft is to read it through. Identify where you can make improvements. Are any of your points less clearly expressed? Does a point need more supporting evidence? Only you can make these decisions. It's your argument and your work; does it have the impact that you intended? If not, how can you heighten its impact?

How might Emma heighten the impact of her writing through editing in the example below?

> *Social media marketing (SMM) has been around for a long time, certainly since at least 2003 when LinkedIn started, which is a social media platform for building a network of contacts with shared professional interests. SMM has been used in marketing strategies to target specific groups of people who might be interested in a product or service and then to promote that product or service. It's used to build brand awareness and it's for this reason that SMM has become popular as a way of marketing these things (Charlesworth, 2015). But it's very difficult for SMEs to use SMM because they need resources. Bigger businesses use SMM for this reason (Meier & Peters, 2023). They have more resources available than SMEs. One platform that has been useful is Facebook. Lots of research has proved that it is popular with SMEs (Fink et al., 2020; Nobre & Silva, 2014). This is because it is easier for SMEs to use. Therefore SMEs can use social media and SMM if it's looked at properly.*
>
> [Adapted from: Kraus, S., Gast, J., Schleich, M., Jones, P., & Ritter, M. (2019). Content is king: How SMEs create content for social media marketing under limited resources. *Journal of Macromarketing, 39*(4), 415–430, at pp. 416–417]

The point of this paragraph is that despite the difficulties caused by a lack of resources, SMEs can make effective use of certain social media platforms in their marketing. Is it clear to you as the reader? It's hinted at in the final sentence, but Emma could make it clearer. The question is, how?

1 The first sentence, which makes a general point about how long SMM has been around, might be focused more sharply on this key point. Contextual information about how long it's existed as a feature of marketing strategy might follow a clearer statement about the purpose of the paragraph.
2 Certain sentences need shortening, including this first one which is just too complex in its structure. Meaning in shorter sentences tends to be clearer. This first sentence in particular requires the reader to work much harder in trying to follow the point being made.
3 There are also some of what we call 'congested sentences' in the middle of the paragraph which might be arranged in a more effective way. The sentence beginning 'SMM has been used ...' is followed by the one starting 'It's used to build ...'. There are unnecessary words here, as well as some repetition. The point is surely that marketing strategies have been used to target specific groups of people in order to build brand awareness. It looks like Emma could make this point clearer by combining these sentences.
4 The point that follows about larger businesses and their resources is also a little congested.
5 The brief discussion of Facebook is too imprecise in its expression. It works to a certain extent, but it could be more effective if it is re-phrased.

Let's take a look at the edited version of this paragraph. Emma's made changes in line with our comments above. Can you see how she's improved it?

The use of social media marketing (SMM) by SMEs is not widespread, but research has shown that it can play a part in the marketing strategies of these businesses. As a marketing tool, SMM has existed since at least 2003, with the launch of the professional networking platform LinkedIn. SMM has been used to promote products or services amongst specific groups of people. In this way, it has been effective in building brand awareness (Charlesworth, 2015). However, as Meier and Peters (2023) have shown, SMM is usually associated with larger businesses because of the amount of resource it takes to implement. Its use by SMEs, which tend to have less resource, has been limited in comparison. Yet research has shown that some SMEs have effectively made use of Facebook in their marketing strategies, since the platform is easier for the owners to engage with (Fink et al., 2020; Nobre & Silva, 2014). Therefore it is possible for SMEs to make use of SMM but it is important that they choose the right platform for their business.

There are further ways to improve the text – such as that final sentence where a judgement is attempted – but the writing is certainly clearer in this version.

In summary:

1   Read through your draft carefully once it's complete.
2   Identify where you can make improvements by editing.
3   Make those changes, but don't be a perfectionist!

Proofreading:

The final stage, once you've edited the draft and you're feeling more confident about your work, is proofreading. Proofreading is about making superficial changes, such as correcting typos. It includes reference format. It's important to leave sufficient time for careful proofreading. Superficial errors can detract from the overall quality of your work; it's important to eliminate them as far as possible. Pay particular attention to the format of your work. We've seen assessments where presentation can count for as much as 10% of your final mark. It's easy to make mistakes with font type or size. Check these things carefully during the proofreading stage. Once again, though, don't be a perfectionist by spending too long tinkering with the text. No piece of writing is perfect!

Common errors in student writing

Over the years, we've built up a detailed picture of student writing and the sort of mistakes that are made. What follows is a list of the most commonly occurring errors in ascending order. We haven't got the space here to explore each one in detail. We suggest looking each one up in a good grammar book. If you use Google to find out more about any of these errors, try to look at the guidance offered by universities (URLs ending in ac.uk.edu, etc.).

5   Misuse of the apostrophe

   Lots of students struggle with the use of the apostrophe. Often, it's missing; at other times, the singular version ('s) is used where the plural (') should be, and vice versa. Double-check your work: are your apostrophes where they should be, and can you distinguish between the singulars and plurals?

4 Confusion over semi-colon/colon
It's not uncommon to see students using the semi-colon (;) where they should be using the colon. The reverse is less common, but it does happen. A semi-colon is used to connect two independent clauses together. It's similar to a full stop. A colon, on the other hand, is most often used to introduce a list. You shouldn't be using a semi-colon in this context; it's in this way that confusion between the semi-colon and colon occurs most often.

3 Use of articles
This is more common in the writing of students who don't have English as their first language, but we see lots of examples where the article – either the definite (the) or the indefinite (a, an) – is missing or sometimes confused. There's a difference in meaning when talking about *the* book you need to read as opposed to *a* book you need to look at. In the former, you're referring to a specific book, whereas in the latter you're talking about one book of many.

2 Sentence structure
Put simply, some students write sentences that are far too long or complex. As a result, the meaning of their writing is less clear and their work, overall, is more difficult to follow. As we discuss below, shorter sentences tend to be more effective, since their meaning is clearer to the reader.

1 Comma splice
By far the most common error we see in student work is the comma splice, where two sentences are connected by a comma rather than a full stop (or perhaps a semi-colon). The sentences produced as a result are longer and are often not as clear in their meaning as separate sentences would be. Comma splices make writing more difficult to read because there is a lack of natural pauses; the work reads as a stream of consciousness, or even as notes, with little structure. Look over your work for comma splices. Can you find anyway? The comma splice is a symptom of a lack of understanding about the proper function of commas in writing. Look up both things if necessary.

Can you spot any of these commonly occurring errors in the extract below taken from Emma's work? Read through the extract carefully first before looking at our discussion below.

> *The biggest advantage to SMEs of using Facebook is in its functions and the way it works. The posting feature allows users to post content easily even if they have little technological knowledge, this in turn gives SME owners the opportunity to start conversations with potential customers (Lim et al., 2022). Other aspects of it's functionality can also help SMEs; by clicking on the 'like' button, SMEs can develop awareness of its brand, also the fact that content is likely to be shared widely in a Facebook*

community helps to raise the profile of an SME. Facebook can therefore be a valuable tool for SME owners looking to develop their business and it does not require a great deal of training or technological knowhow.

[Adapted from: Kraus, S., Gast, J., Schleich, M., Jones, P., & Ritter, M. (2019). Content is king: How SMEs create content for social media marketing under limited resources. *Journal of Macromarketing, 39*(4), 415–430, at pp. 416–417]

1 The first minor change we would suggest making with this extract is to replace the word 'biggest' in the first sentence with the more acceptable 'greatest'.
2 The second sentence includes a *comma splice*. We would replace the comma with a full-stop after 'knowledge'. 'This' would then come at the start of a new sentence.
3 There is an incorrect apostrophe in 'it's' in the next sentence. It needs to be removed. (The apostrophe in 'it's' is used as a contraction, to abbreviate 'it is'. Here, however, we're talking about aspects of Facebook's functionality, and so no apostrophe is needed.)
4 Shortly after 'it's', there's a semi-colon (;) at the start of a list, where there should be a colon (:).
5 The use of 'also' to introduce the second factor needs replacing. We suggest using 'while', to link the two factors together more effectively.

In summary:

1 Read through the edited draft carefully.
2 Identify any superficial errors. Pay particular attention to typos, basic points of grammar (e.g., capital letters and the apostrophe), the consistency of font type and size used, and spacing.
3 Check the format of your references in the references list or bibliography. Ensure that the format is correct and that you have applied it consistently throughout.

Techniques for enhancing your writing

We often get asked by more experienced students how they can improve the overall quality and impact of their written work. There are lots of techniques available to help you achieve this. In this section, we cover some of the most useful ones based on our own experience of advising students, our understanding of the common features of marking criteria (which you should have some knowledge by now), and the most common bits of feedback students get from tutors on their writing.

Expression: improving clarity and precision:

Let's begin with the need for clarity and precision in your expression. Or, in short, saying what you mean. Clarity of expression is something that can always be improved or sharpened; it's never perfect. However, there's a difference between tweaking the text to make its expression more aesthetically pleasing and re-writing or re-phrasing it because the meaning of the point you're trying to make is less clear. We're more concerned with this latter scenario. Consider the following example:

Less clear sentence:

SMEs have never really got to grips with technology in marketing for lots of reasons, the main one being that the owners of SMEs lack the knowledge to use technology properly.

Improved version:

Many SMEs have found it difficult to make use of technology in marketing. One reason for this is the lack of technological knowledge among the owners of such businesses.

How is this sharpened clarity achieved? The most obvious way lies in the vocabulary used. The improved version is more effective because there is more careful use of vocabulary. For example, rather than 'never really got to grips', we've got 'found it difficult', and instead of 'the knowledge to use technology properly', there's 'lack of technological knowledge'. There's a greater precision here which, in turn, provides the work with a heightened impact.

Another way is to use shorter sentences. This is particularly useful for less experienced writers because it helps you to keep a tighter grip on what you're trying to say. Lots of new students get lost in the writing process by trying to create longer and – what they think are – more convincing sentences. But you don't need to do that. Short, sharp, and to the point. This is a good maxim to have in mind when writing.

One of the simplest yet most effective ways of structuring your sentences is to use the SVO model. Consider the following example:

Watkins (2019) proposed a different solution.

Subject (Watkins) – verb (proposed) – object (solution).
You can build more complex sentences around the SVO model. Consider this revised version of the sentence above:

Watkins (2019), who studied a range of factors, proposed a different solution.

We've got the same SVO arrangement here, but we have additional 'who' clause between the subject and verb. At its heart though is still the SVO model.

Another is to move from the passive to the active voice. The active and passive voices are simply different forms of a verb that reflect whether the

subject of the sentence is performing the action of the verb (active) or is being acted upon (passive). For example,
Active: Ollie completed the project.
Passive: The project was completed by Ollie.
Which of the following examples is clearer and has more impact on you, as the reader?

a   An attempt was made to integrate Facebook into the business's marketing strategy. It was developed by the owner.
b   The owner made an attempt to integrate Facebook into the business's marketing strategy.

By combining the two sentences and using 'the owner' as the subject (in other words, using the active rather than passive voice), sentence (b) has greater impact. Its meaning is clearer and the reader isn't left hanging at the end of the first sentence to find out a bit more about the inquiry.

Some tutors discourage students from using the passive voice. We're not suggesting that you shouldn't use it, but we do think that it's worth considering what impact its use has on the clarity of your writing. Look at a piece of work you've recently completed. Are there any instances where you've used the passive voice, perhaps by making a point using several sentences when you could have made the same point using only one? If so, can you re-write these sentences in the active voice. Is the meaning any clearer?

The most obvious technique available for sharpening the clarity of your expression is by removing any text that isn't crucial to the point you're trying to make. Some students try to cram as much as they can into a sentence; others write in a 'stream of consciousness' way, without punctuation, which leads to long, unwieldy sentences where the meaning is less clear. Adding too much to a sentence will often water-down the meaning – the exact opposite of what you're trying to do. That's why you need to remove any unnecessary text in the editing stage of the cycle.

Take a look at the example below. It is unedited; there is text here which is unnecessary to the point being made. Try to identify this text. Have a go for yourself before looking at our revised version.

> *Use of Facebook by SMEs differs. Some use it a lot whereas other business owners make little use of it. This is because of a number of reasons, including the different levels of technological knowledge of the owners, the type of business it is, and the industry involved. As Lim et al. (2022) have pointed out in their detailed study of the use of social media marketing by SMEs, there is a larger problem with the use of social media by SMEs linked to the problem of actually getting a better understanding of the extent to which it is used and the different ways it is used. The social media companies themselves can provide businesses with lots of data about the*

> content posted, such as the number of visits and the types of people making those visits, but SMEs need more data if they are going to made effective use of social media.
>
> [Adapted from: Kraus, S., Gast, J., Schleich, M., Jones, P., & Ritter, M. (2019). Content is king: How SMEs create content for social media marketing under limited resources. *Journal of Macromarketing, 39*(4), 415–430, at p. 417]

The expression in this paragraph could be clearer. Take the second sentence, for example, beginning 'Some use it a lot …'. How important is that sentence to the point being made? Emma has already said that the use of Facebook by SMEs differs. Does this sentence not simply repeat that statement? A clue to where improvements can be made is often found in the length of the sentences. Here, the final sentence, which is quite long, is muddy. It can be trimmed down. Here's a revised version of the text:

> *Use of Facebook by SMEs differs for a number of reasons, including the different levels of technological knowledge of the owners and the nature of the business involved. As Lim et al. (2022) have noted, it is also difficult to measure its use by SMEs. Social media companies can provide businesses with data related to the content posted, such as the number of visits. However, SMEs need more detailed information if they are going to make more effective use of social media in their marketing strategy.*

Certain sentences and phrases, which add little to the point being made and are therefore considered as unnecessary, have been deleted. The resulting text is leaner, clearer, and more precise.

Developing structure and organisation:

We've already stressed the importance of planning in our discussion of the writing cycle. Long pieces of writing like essays need to be thought out carefully first; it's essential to plan your work properly if it is going to be successful. If you ask most students about how important structure is in writing they would all agree that it is. Yet we still see pieces of work which include repetition, inconsistent arguments, where it isn't clear that the student knows what they want to say, or overly descriptive writing that lacks a meaningful argument. All of these problems can be ironed out in the planning stage, just as more careful planning can help to strengthen an argument.

Structure operates at two levels: the macro level refers to the arrangement of the points in the main part of the work or the overall organisation of your response; the micro level, on the other hand, refers to the structure of individual paragraphs, including the introduction and conclusion. Improvements can be made to both. You might find that by rearranging the points in the main part of the work, you can bring greater clarity to your argument. Adding another point might do the same, just as removing one might. You might also heighten the impact of an individual paragraph by improving the expression in the first sentence or in the judgement at the end, or by adding stronger supporting evidence.

There isn't a single, universally applied model for how to organise the sentences in a paragraph. Certain structural elements are very important: the first sentence, for example, is key in conveying to the reader a clear sense of (i) what the paragraph is about and (ii) how it is related to the paragraphs either side of it, and to the overall argument in the piece of work. Equally, the final sentence, in which you will usually express some kind of judgement related to the argument, is key in giving clarity to that argument. An uninspired final sentence, which makes no effort to provide a judgement, represents a missed opportunity to get your view across to the reader. This isn't to say that the sentences in between are less important. Their content and arrangement will be determined by the marking criteria for that piece of work. In assessments where you are expected to engage critically with the relevant discourse, it's vital that in these sentences you refer to the academic sources you've looked at. These sentences should therefore inform the judgement you make at the end. In this way, all the sentences in the paragraph should be linked together through sense and logic.

Let's look at an example. Here's a paragraph we've already seen in the discussion of 'editing' above. It's reasonably effective; why?

> *The use of social media marketing (SMM) by SMEs is not widespread, but research has shown that it can play a part in the marketing strategies of these businesses. As a marketing tool, SMM has existed since at least 2003, with the launch of the professional networking platform LinkedIn. SMM has been used to promote products or services amongst specific groups of people. In this way, it has been effective in building brand awareness (Charlesworth, 2015). However, as Meier and Peters (2023) have shown, SMM is usually associated with larger businesses because of the amount of resource it takes to implement. Its use by SMEs, which tend to have less resource, has been limited in comparison. Yet research has shown that some SMEs have effectively made use of Facebook in their marketing strategies, since the platform is easier for the owners to engage with (Fink et al., 2020; Nobre & Silva, 2014). Therefore it is possible for SMEs to make use of SMM but it is important that they choose the right platform for their business.*
>
> [Adapted from: Kraus, S., Gast, J., Schleich, M., Jones, P., & Ritter, M. (2019). Content is king: How SMEs create content for social media marketing under limited resources. *Journal of Macromarketing, 39*(4), 415–430, at pp. 416–417]

To begin with, we've got a clear first sentence which identifies the potential role of SMM by SMEs in marketing strategy. If we look at the final sentence, the judgement, beginning 'Therefore', is directly related to this topic. This immediately gives us a sense of the coherence of the paragraph and the likely clarity of the point being made. In between these two sentences, there is a discussion of the relevant academic discourse. It begins with a brief reference to the origins of SMM, followed by its use. This is qualified (note the use of 'However') by the view of Meier and Peters which, in turn, is contrasted with the research of Fink et al. and Nobre and Silva who have highlighted the use of Facebook by SMEs. This provides a neat context for the judgement in the final sentence. The discussion flows naturally. The sentences lead into one another, thereby building a discussion. All the sentences are related to that key issue identified in the first sentence. As a result, the writing has clarity and coherence, both of which make it easier for the reader to engage with.

A final point here concerns the introduction and conclusion to any piece of writing. What should be included in an introduction and what shouldn't? What makes a good conclusion? Here are some general points for you to think about. An introduction should do just that: introduce the topic of the assessment task and your take on it. Usually, this means providing an explanation of the scope of your response together with some indication of the line of argument you're going to take. 'X depends on a range of factors, including …. However, it can be argued that Y is the most significant because …. '. The conclusion provides an opportunity for you to reiterate your argument to the reader. To spell it out, in other words. Make sure that the reader puts your work down (or closes it) with a clear sense of your response to the assessment task.

Integrating academic sources:

Paragraph structure, like the one suggested above, provides one way of integrating academic sources into your work. Another is to use a popular technique called 'voices'. We've mentioned how important it is to take an active approach to the way you engage with academic sources in your work. This means *using* the sources to support or enhance your argument. It requires you to put your view first, ahead of those you find in the academic sources, rather than doing what some students do, which is to report the contents of the sources they find. For example: Smith says this …. Rogers says this …. etc. This kind of approach is too passive; it's as if the author is being led by the sources rather than the other way around. The advantage with using 'voices' is that it effectively forces you to adopt an active approach. Your voice needs to come at the start of a paragraph before it reappears again, logically, towards the end. Consider the following paragraph on the relationship between SMEs and technology when it comes to marketing:

> The relationship between SMEs and technology, including social media, in the context of marketing is a difficult one. *Zamani (2022) has highlighted the problems many SMEs experience when adopting new technologies. Often, the owner of an SME lacks the technological knowhow to make use of such technologies (Indrawati et al., 2020).* As Gilmore (2011) has observed, this problem is made worse in some cases where owners have an underlying lack of knowledge about marketing. *However, in more recent years, SMEs have started to make more use of social media (Bruce et al., 2023). But there are still challenges facing SMEs looking to engage with social media effectively, not least the need to create interesting and attractive content (Kraus et al., 2019).* There is therefore much research to be done on how to make it easier for SMEs to integrate social media and technology into their marketing strategies.
>
> [Adapted from: Kraus, S., Gast, J., Schleich, M., Jones, P., & Ritter, M. (2019). Content is king: How SMEs create content for social media marketing under limited resources. *Journal of Macromarketing, 39*(4), 415–430, at pp. 415–416.]

Here, we can see the active approach to using academic sources and you can also see the importance of the author's voice within it (in normal font rather than italics). The first sentence, beginning 'The relationship', provides the author's voice, a clear statement of the subject of the paragraph. Then, we get the voice of Zamani, followed by that of Indrawati et al., which effectively supports it. Next, we get Gilmore's voice, and then we have the contrasting voice of Bruce et al. This, in turn, is contrasted with the voice of Kraus et al., before we return to the author's voice, with a concise summary judgement, informed by the discussion of the other voices.

In terms of its effectiveness, you can see how useful the voices technique is if you remove the author's voice from the text. It then becomes simply a list of different viewpoints. This would therefore reflect the passive approach, where the author is simply reporting views taken from the academic sources they've tried to engage with. If such an approach is taken in assessed work in which you're expected to demonstrate an ability to critique these sources (as revealed in the marking criteria), you won't get a mark in the higher levels.

In summary:

1 Review a piece of work you've recently submitted; how have you engaged with the sources? Are you reporting the views you've found, or are you making use of them?
2 Identify a paragraph that you think is less effective in getting across the point you intended. Can you re-write it using the 'voices' technique?
3 Reflect, more broadly, on how critical you are when engaging with academic sources.

Developing a critical edge:

Being critical when it comes to engaging with academic sources begins the moment you pick up (or open) one to read. In other words, don't just sit back and passively read through something without trying to set it in the broader context provided by everything else you have read about on the topic. This means linking the different viewpoints together, comparing and contrasting them, analysing the data used in one source, evaluating the recommendations in another – and so on. The difficulty lies in articulating this critical engagement with the sources in writing.

First, take an active approach to engaging with the sources in your work. Don't just report or describe what you've read; use it to build your own argument. Your argument, the points you make, need to be front and centre in your work; it can be supported and given greater meaning by elements of the discourse.

Second, flag up where you are being critical by making use of the language of criticality. The words or phrases, through their meaning, indicate to the reader that some use is being made of the knowledge or viewpoint under discussion. In other words, you are being critical. They act as beacons that grab the attention of the reader. Their use throughout a piece of written work helps to provide your writing with a sharper critical edge. Look at a piece of work you've recently completed. How might you incorporate this language into your work to give it that critical edge?

Summary

In this chapter, we've looked at the theory and practice of writing for assessment. In terms of theory, it's important to identify the conventions of writing associated with your discipline. Writing for assessment is nuanced and tutors' expectations concerning your work are shaped in part by these conventions. It's also important for you to be aware of the different genres of writing and the expectations associated with each one. If in doubt as to what tutors expect to see, review the marking criteria for that assessment. When it comes to writing in practice, engage fully in the writing cycle. Prioritise getting down a first draft – something you can work with – and then consider improving it through editing. Identify where you can improve your writing by reviewing it critically. Consider the pillars of effective writing: does the structure work? Is the expression clear enough? How might you engage with the discourse more critically?

There is no quick fix when it comes to writing. It requires patience and determination; improvement comes with practice, as well as an ability to reflect critically but constructively on your work. We want to leave you with a reminder of one of our key messages: read as much as you can within your discipline. It's only by doing this that you can build up a clear picture in your mind of what tutors expect to see in assessed written work in your discipline.

References

Baticulon, R., Sy, J., Alberto, N., Baron, M., Mabulay, R., Rizada, L., Tiu, C., Clarion, C., & Reyes, J. (2021). Barriers to online learning in the time of COVID-19: A national survey of medical students in the Philippines. *Medical Science Educator, 31,* 615–626.

Berdida, D. (2023). Resilience and academic motivation's mediation effects in nursing students' academic stress and self-directed learning: A multicenter cross-sectional study. *Nurse Education in Practice, 69,* Article 103639.

Bruce, E., Keelson, S., Amoah, J., & Bankuoru, S. (2023). Social media integration: An opportunity for SMEs sustainability. *Cogent Business & Management, 10*(1), Article 2173859.

Chan, C., & Hu, W. (2023). Students' voices on generative AI: perceptions, benefits, and challenges in higher education. *International Journal of Educational Technology in Higher Education, 20,* Article 43.

Chan, C., & Lee, K. (2023). The AI generation gap: Are Gen Z students more interested in adopting generative AI such as ChatGPT in teaching and learning than their Gen X and millennial generation teachers? *Smart Learning Environments, 10,* Article 60.

Charlesworth, A. (2015). *An introduction to social media marketing.* Routledge.

Crawford, J., Cowling M., & Allen, K. A. (2023). Leadership is needed for ethical ChatGPT: Character, assessment, and learning using artificial intelligence (AI). *Journal of University Teaching & Learning Practice, 20*(3), 1–19.

Crompton, H., & Burke, D. (2023). Artificial intelligence in higher education: the state of the field. *International Journal of Educational Technology in Higher Education, 20,* Article 22.

Dodd, R., Dadaczynski, K., Okan, O., McCaffery, K., & Pickles, K. (2021). Psychological wellbeing and academic experience of university students in Australia during COVID-19. *International Journal of Environmental Research and Public Health, 18,* Article 866.

Fink, M., Koller, M., Gartner, J., Floh, A., & Harms, R. (2020). Effective entrepreneurial marketing on Facebook – A longitudinal study. *Journal of Business Research, 113,* 149–157.

Gilbert, T. (2024). Generative AI and generative education. *Annals of the New York Academy of Sciences, 1534*(1), 11–14.

Gilmore, A. (2011). Entrepreneurial and SME marketing. *Journal of Research in Marketing and Entrepreneurship, 13*(2), 137–145.

Guo, K., Pan, M., Li, Y., & Lai, C. (2024). Effects of an AI-supported approach to peer feedback on university EFL students' feedback quality and writing ability. *The Internet and Higher Education, 63,* Article 100962.

Halliday, M., & Hasan, R. (1985). *Language, context and text: Aspects of language in a social semiotic perspective.* Deakin University Press.

Hill, G., Mason, J., & Dunn, A. (2021). Contract cheating: An increasing challenge for global academic community arising from COVID-19. *Research and Practice in Technology Enhanced Learning, 16,* Article 24.

Indrawati, H., Caska, & Suarman (2020). Barriers to technological innovations of SMEs: how to solve them? *International Journal of Innovation Science, 12*(5), 545–564.

Jasper, M. (2013). *Beginning reflective practice.* Cengage.

Kampa, R., Padhan, D., Karna, N., & Gouda, J. (2025). Identifying the factors influencing plagiarism in higher education: An evidence-based review of the literature. *Accounting Research, 32*(2), 83–98.

Kraus, S., Gast, J., Schleich, M., Jones, P., & Ritter, M. (2019). Content is king: How SMEs create content for social media marketing under limited resources. *Journal of Macromarketing, 39*(4), 415–430.

Lim, H., Bright, L., & Wilcox, G. (2022). Is repetition really the key to success? The impact of ad repetition and the power of 'likes' on Facebook. *Journal of Interactive Advertising, 22*(3), 238–248.

Meier, A., & Peters, M. (2023). Limited engagement of SMEs with social media: A structuration and sensemaking perspective. *Information & Management, 60*, Article 103853.

Michel-Villarreal, R., Vilalta-Perdomo, E., Salinas-Navarro, D., Thierry-Aguilera, R., & Gerardou, F. (2023). Challenges and opportunities of generative AI for higher education as explained by ChatGPT. *Education Sciences, 13*, Article 856.

Narwal, S., Narwal, P., Leung, Y., & Ahmed, B. (2021). Stress and work-life balance in undergraduate dental students in Birmingham, United Kingdom and Hong Kong, China. *Journal of Dental Education, 85*(7), 1267–1272.

Newton, P. (2018). How common is commercial contract cheating in higher education and is it increasing? A systematic review. *Frontiers in Education, 3.* https://www.frontiersin.org/journals/education/articles/10.3389/feduc.2018.00067.

Nobre, H., & Silva, D. (2014). Social network marketing strategy and SME strategy benefits. *Journal of Transnational Management, 19*, 138–151.

Somerville, E., & Creme, P. (2005). 'Asking Pompeii questions': A co-operative approach to writing in the disciplines. *Teaching in Higher Education, 10*(1), 17–28.

Son, C., Hegde, S., Smith, A., Wang, X., & Sasangohar, F. (2020). Effects of COVID-19 on college students' mental health in the United States: interview survey study. *Journal of Medical Internet Research, 22*(9), Article e21279.

Steiss, J., Tate, T., Graham, S., Cruz, J., Hebert, M., Wang, J., Moon, Y., Tseng, W., Warschauer, M., & Olson, C. (2024). Comparing the quality of human and ChatGPT feedback of students' writing. *Learning and Instruction, 91*, Article 101894.

Sweeney, S. (2023). Who wrote this? Essay mills and assessment – considerations regarding contract cheating and AI in higher education. *The International Journal of Management Education, 21*(2), Article 100818.

Usman, M., & Banu, A. (2019). A study on impact of financial stress on students' academics. *Journal of Business & Economic Policy, 6*(1), 58–64.

Zhao, L., Mao, H., Compton, B., Peng, J., Fu, G., Fang, F., Heyman, G., & Lee, K. (2022). Academic dishonesty and its relations to peer cheating and culture: A meta-analysis of the perceived peer cheating effect. *Educational Research Review, 36*, Article 100455.

Chapter 10

Academic integrity and referencing

It is becoming more important in higher education to discuss academic integrity as a literacy in itself rather than as an aspect of academic practice specifically related to the ethics associated with sound research. With the advent of generative artificial intelligence like ChatGPT, it is vital for all students, undergraduates, and postgraduates, to have a sound understanding of academic integrity and what it means in practice for you, as a student. This is not to say that it wasn't important before we all started talking about AI; it was, particularly in recent years as the number of students using 'essay mills' to produce assessed work increased. But there are now more ways through which academic integrity might be compromised without you necessarily realising that what you've done is unethical. Resolving this problem therefore begins with building up your understanding of academic integrity as a literacy.

In this chapter, we define the literacy of academic integrity by examining the values which underpin it. We consider how each value is related to the work you do on your course; we also think about the significance of these values to your graduate identity by considering how they might inform your conduct in professional contexts. We then move on to a more detailed discussion of referencing, the practice most associated with academic integrity. We cover the main points, including reference format, before urging you look at more detailed resources to develop your knowledge in this area.

Learning Objectives

By the end of this chapter, you will have gained:

- a clear understanding of what the literacy of academic integrity is and what values underpin it;
- an understanding of how each value might impact upon the practice of studying;

- an understanding of the role of academic integrity in ethical research;
- an appreciation of the value of effective referencing, not simply in acknowledging the sources you use, but as a tool in helping you to address marking criteria;
- an appreciation of when to include an in-text reference;
- an understanding of how to format references – within the text and in the references list.

Keywords

academic integrity; values; referencing; plagiarism; in-text references; citations; references list; quoting; paraphrasing

Defining academic integrity

If we think back to Chapter 3, which looked at learning at university, we conceived of learning as the journey you undertake as a student as you move from the edge of a discourse community to the centre. At the edge, you are a novice, a new or less experienced learner; by embarking on a learning journey, you gradually take on the identity of an expert who sits at the heart of that community. Academic integrity refers to the *values* that underpin not only the scholarly work of such a community, but also the work you complete on your learning journey as you move from the edge to its centre, from being a novice to an expert.

Different universities will have different interpretations of these values, but the International Center for Academic Integrity (ICAI, 2021) has helpfully identified six of what it calls the 'fundamental' values of academic integrity. These are:

1 Honesty
2 Trust
3 Fairness
4 Respect
5 Responsibility
6 Courage

The meaning of each of these values should be fairly clear. The difficulty lies in identifying the significance of each one in the context of your learning experience.

Task: Understanding the fundamental values of academic integrity

> Consider the significance of each of these values in relation to the work you're doing on your degree programme at the moment. What does each one mean in the context of the way you approach your studies – your application of academic literacies? Try to define each value first.
>
> We recommend doing this task with a friend or in a small group. Try to come up with an answer for each value before reading on!

Honesty is about being honest! Being truthful rather than trying to deceive your peers or your tutors. An example of *honesty* in practice is the need to reference your sources accurately (more on this below).

Trust is linked to honesty, in that you're more likely to trust someone who is honest. An example of trust in the context of your own academic work might be in relation to a group project in which you need to trust other members of the team to complete their work on time. Trust here is a two-way process: all team members need to trust each other if the project is to be successful.

Fairness is linked to impartiality or the need to keep an open mind about the importance of alternative interpretations. In an essay, for example, you will need to consider different perspectives on an issue by evaluating each one in a balanced and objective way. This represents fairness in action.

Respect is about your own self-esteem as well as the esteem in which you hold others. Scholarly communities are diverse, with members from different cultural backgrounds who might hold very different views to your own. Respect is about recognising the diversity of these opinions and listening to them carefully. A practical example of when respect is important in a learning context is when you're receiving feedback. You might be tempted to dismiss feedback that is critical; but it's important that you engage with it by respecting the view of the tutor rather than simply ignoring it.

Responsibility is about ensuring that you are actively observing – and encouraging others to observe – the values of academic integrity. It begins with taking responsibility for your own decisions and actions; but it also lies in holding others to account in a professional and constructive way. An example of responsibility at the level of the self is reflecting on your experiences, learning from them, so that you can hold yourself to account before others.

Courage is, as the ICAI note, an aspect of character. It's almost related to leadership, in that courage, in the sense of strength of character, is needed if you are to act on your values by holding others to account.

It's about being willing to make difficult decisions, upholding the values we've discussed here, and protecting academic integrity.
What other examples did you come up with?
Academic integrity, as a set of values, therefore conditions the way you engage with the work of the discourse community to which you belong. It's a pre-requisite of working effectively as a self-regulating learner. It's important to recognise its significance beyond simply 'plagiarism' and the need to avoid it – but that's not to say that this isn't important! As the broad applicability of the values set out above indicate, academic integrity is just as important to how you conduct yourself as a graduate, in a professional context, as it is to your conduct as a student. All of the six values highlighted above should together inform your graduate identity, since all are expected of graduates and the way you work, regardless of what field you eventually enter.

Research and the handling of data

We often get asked by students about the use of data collected in the course of research, as well as the broader issue of research ethics. Most queries we get on research ethics are related to the task of completing a research ethics form. All institutions will follow a similar process when it comes to the governance of data collected as part of a research project. Usually, students undertaking research that requires data collection will be expected to complete some sort of research ethics module in preparation for completing a research ethics form. On this form, students will essentially set out the nature of their research, as might be expected in a research proposal, as well as any ethical issues linked to it. We're not going to guide you here on how to complete such a form; instead, we're going to set out the key principles of ethical research, in keeping with the values of academic integrity set out above.

Put simply, when it comes to collecting, using and sharing data as a part of a research project, you have a legal obligation to ensure that any data not in the public domain remains confidential. If you need to share any collected data, it is your responsibility to secure the consent of the participants. This is usually done by getting each participant to sign a consent form; your university may provide this form or you will need to create one for yourself. It may be appropriate when sharing data for which you have consent to do so to anonymise participants' responses. Rather than mentioning a participant by name, you would refer to them as 'Participant A' or 'Participant B' – and so on. If children are involved, further consideration is needed; your tutor, or the university's research ethics committee, can provide you with more advice on this issue.

The principles that underpin sound practice in ethical research have been helpfully set out by the Economic and Social Research Council

(ESRC), one of the largest funding bodies in the United Kingdom, for research into the social sciences. It identifies six (UKRI, 2021), all of which contribute to the maintenance of research integrity:

1 research should aim to maximise benefit for individuals and society and minimise risk and harm;
2 the rights and dignity of individuals and groups should be respected;
3 wherever possible, participation should be voluntary and appropriately informed;
4 research should be conducted with integrity and transparency;
5 lines of responsibility and accountability should be clearly defined;
6 independence of research should be maintained and where conflicts of interest cannot be avoided they should be made explicit.

These principles are aimed at shaping your research conduct. In any research ethics form designed to secure approval for your research, you will need to acknowledge the issues raised by these principles. Ensuring that your research conforms to these good practice guidelines therefore forms an important part of academic integrity.

Referencing

The clearest example of where academic integrity meets learning at university is in referencing. Put simply, referencing refers to the practice of acknowledging where the knowledge you are using in your work comes from. Students usually see referencing in the context of plagiarism (using the work of another author without crediting it appropriately): in order to avoid accusations of plagiarism, you need to include references in your work. When seen only in this light, referencing is reduced to a technical aspect of writing that you need to use if you're going to pass an assessment task. There is clearly an ethical imperative behind the principle of acknowledging the work of an author when you use it; it's essential for you to do it if your work is to have any academic integrity. Yet referencing is about much more than avoiding plagiarism. When looked at in the context of marking criteria, referencing becomes a highly valuable tool which can help you to evidence your competencies against it. In what follows, we set referencing in the broader context provided by marking criteria.

Referencing styles

Before we begin, however, it's important to note that a number of different referencing styles are used in higher education. Much depends on the discipline in which you're studying; but, that said, on some programmes, particularly at postgraduate level, you might be expected to use more than one style.

In our experience, the most commonly used referencing styles are (in no particular order):

- Author-date (usually referred to as 'Harvard' in UK institutions) – used widely across a number of disciplines;
- MHRA (Modern Humanities Research Association) – mainly used in humanities disciplines;
- Chicago (Chicago University Press) – again, often used in humanities disciplines;
- APA (American Psychological Association) – principally, psychology, but also social sciences and some business-related disciplines;
- Vancouver – for medical/clinical-related disciplines;
- IEEE (Institute of Electrical and Electronic Engineers) – for engineering, computer science, and related disciplines;
- OSCOLA (Oxford University Standard for Citation of Legal Authorities) – for law.

*It's important to check in your module handbook(s) or directly with your tutor which style is needed.

The style we're going to focus in the rest of this section is author-date/Harvard. The principles we're going to discuss about the 'why' and the 'when' of referencing apply to all of the above styles. However, when we discuss format, the details will reflect the requirements of the author-date style rather than the others. Author-date/Harvard is a tricky style to use here because there are so many ever-so-slightly different interpretations of it in use. Tutors often talk about 'Harvard' as if it is a clearly defined style in itself, but it isn't. Pick up a selection of books in the library published by different publishers and you'll see slight variations in the format of author-date references. For example, in one book, you might find a comma between the author and date in an in-text reference; in another, there won't be one. When it comes to formatting references, it's important to be consistent. If you put a comma between the author and date of your in-text references, use a comma in *all* of these references. Needless to say, you also need to be accurate. As long as you are both consistent and accurate, there shouldn't be a problem.

In the examples you'll find in this section, we've tried to use a generic form of author-date/Harvard which reflects the format preferences of lots of tutors we've worked with. We flag up any variations as we go.

What do references look like?

Many of you reading this will already know what references look like, but, for the benefit of those who are less certain, let's take a look at a writing exemplar we've seen in a previous chapter. It's from Susie's work on 'classroom management'. The content is irrelevant; what matters is the references and their position.

> Classroom management is essential to learning. Lots of research has been done on it over the decades. As a concept, it has developed from 'practitioners' wisdom' on addressing disruptive student behaviour to the different ways teachers set up a suitable learning environment (Brophy, 2006). Classroom management is generally seen as referring to the steps teachers can take to create positive conditions for learning (Korpershoek et al., 2016). Teachers must check on what is happening in the classroom and address disruptive behaviour (Anderson & Taner, 2023). In this view, the responsibility for classroom management sits with the teacher. Different ways of looking at it have been suggested. Eccles and Roeser (2011) have looked at the role of other factors. The context of each class is important, as well as the behaviour of the students in that class (Wang et al., 2020). The teacher's control over the classroom is about more than the actions of management. As Keskin et al. (2024) have noted, it is also about knowledge and experience. Teachers need to know when to act to maintain order and to make sure students are concentrating on their work and how to do so. Since students' behaviour is difficult to predict, teachers need to be ready to make quick decisions as situations arise (Grub et al., 2020). Teachers also need to think about the impact of negative behaviour on the lesson. As Doyle (2006) has shown, attempts to address negative behaviour can sometimes just make things worse. Teachers therefore need to think carefully about the decisions they make to manage classrooms well.

In this exemplar, we can see examples of the author-date/Harvard style. The references are easy to spot: they're within the brackets, as indicated above. These are called in-text references or citations. Make a mental note of these terms. One of the challenges when it comes to referencing for less experienced students is getting to grips with the vocabulary associated with it. We've highlighted four, slightly different, in-text references used by Susie. The first is quite simple: (Brophy, 2006). Brophy is the author; 2006 is the year of publication. Note that both appear between the brackets and that the reference itself comes at the very end of the sentence. In the second, the reference comes at the end of the sentence, as we would expect, but there are two authors, linked together by the ampersand (&); in some versions of 'Harvard' referencing, you're expected to use 'and' instead. Whether you use the ampersand or not, just be consistent throughout your work. The third differs because Susie has used the authors' names at the start of the sentence: Eccles and Roeser. In this case, only the year, 2011, is needed inside the brackets, and this comes immediately after Roeser. In the fourth example, the author is noted as Wang *et al.*; *et al.* is an abbreviation for the Latin phrase *et alia*, meaning 'and others', which is used in in-text references where there is more than three, four, or five authors (depending on which version of 'Harvard' referencing you're using – again, just be consistent).

Susie's use of in-text references therefore highlights several key points:

1. in-text references are usually added at the end of a sentence but *before* the full-stop;
2. an author's name can be used within the sentence, as in the Eccles and Roeser example; if you do this, only the year is needed within the brackets and this is placed immediately after the author's name;
3. *et al.* is used to indicate that there are more than three (or more) authors, depending on which version of author-date referencing you're using.

Each of the in-text references in Susie's exemplar corresponds to the full version of that reference found at the end of her work in the 'References list'. The 'References list' provides a complete list of all those sources used in the work, set out in alphabetical order by author surname. The Brophy reference, for example, looks like this in the references list:

Brophy, J. (2006) 'History of research on classroom management', in C. M. Evertson and C. S. Weinstein (eds), *Handbook of Classroom Management: Research, Practice, and Contemporary Issues*. New York: Routledge, pp. 17–43.

This is a chapter in an edited book. Note that the author's surname comes first, followed by their initial. The title of the chapter is in normal font but the title of the edited book is in *italics*. Note that we've used capital letters at the start of all keywords. This is not required in all versions of 'Harvard'.

It is in the 'References list' where most mistakes can be found. Take care to set out each reference correctly. Avoid – at all costs! – copying and pasting references in from your library's discovery service or any pdf document. If you create the list in this way, it's highly likely that you will introduce inaccuracies or inconsistencies.

Why are references so important?

We've already mentioned what we described as the ethical imperative behind conscientious referencing. Acknowledging that an idea, a theory or an interpretation belongs to another author is ethically appropriate and forms a core part of 'academic integrity'; if you don't credit the original author then you are presenting that idea, theory or interpretation as your own, when, of course, it isn't.

It's this function of referencing that causes many less experienced students to look on the practice of referencing with some anxiety. This is because it's wrapped up with the 'p' word, *plagiarism*, which some students get very worried about. Plagiarism refers to the practice of presenting the work of another author as your own without properly acknowledging its source.

Broadly speaking, when you're writing up an assessment, you know when you're using an idea or interpretation that isn't your own. When you do, just add in the appropriate in-text reference. The problem is that plagiarism isn't always deliberate; it can happen unintentionally. But unintentional plagiarism comes about because you're not doing things as efficiently as you should be. You're probably cutting corners. For example, you might copy and paste text from a pdf into your own work and then decide to come back later to add in the in-text reference; but then, as the deadline approaches, you forget, and you end up submitting a piece of work which, in part at least, has been plagiarised from other sources. Working efficiently by taking the time to do things in the most effective way will minimise the possibility of committing unintentional plagiarism.

We've often been asked by students, 'how do you know that something you're arguing in your work hasn't already been argued by someone else?' The answer to that is that you don't know. However, each piece of assessed work sits in its own context. If you're a first-year undergraduate student then you clearly don't possess the deeper levels of knowledge and understanding of your discipline that a master's-level student would be expected to have. Consequently, when a tutor marks your work, they don't expect you to know all about the different interpretations of a particular topic that exist. On the other hand, if they're marking the work of a master's student, they will have higher expectations as to what that student will know about the discipline and its discourse. In other words, don't panic! Remember, you're working in a context, and your tutors are aware of that as much as you should be.

Beyond the issue of plagiarism, referencing acts as a highly valuable tool for you to use as a means of evidencing the extent and depth of your engagement with the relevant discourse. First, in-text references and, more importantly, the references list at the end of your work, indicate to your tutor (the reader) the scope of your research. Think back to our discussions of marking criteria: one criterion is about the extent to which you've engaged with relevant discourse. When assessing student work, many tutors turn to the references list first, to get an impression of the scope of the student's research. Depending on the discipline and the nature of the assessment task, a list of four or five books might, at first glance, suggest that only a limited amount of research has been done. A list of four or five books, complemented by several journal articles, on the other hand, would suggest a more thorough attempt at engaging with the discourse. Tutors will obviously look more closely at the titles of these sources, but, as an initial impression, the references list is very important.

Within the work itself, in-text references indicate to the tutor the way you have used these sources. For example, they highlight which pieces of work have shaped your argument, what evidence you've used to support the points you're making, and how your argument fits within the broader discourse. Thus, when you're writing, you need to think about how your use of in-text references communicates your argument and the knowledge and understanding that underpins it to the tutor. At a more basic level, if you've taken the time to read and think carefully about a particular journal article, for example, make sure you refer to it in your work so that you can include an in-text reference to it. Only by doing this will your tutor recognise the effort you've put in to engage with it.

Your use of in-text references also helps to highlight for the tutor that critical edge we spoke of in an earlier chapter. Sometimes, you'll be flagging up an interpretation to illustrate a particular point. On other occasions, you'll be referencing an interpretation as you express your own point. It's by doing this that references serve to signpost for the tutor your critical engagement with the discourse. Again, it's important to have this function of referencing in mind as you write, so that you can write with the reader in mind.

Finally, in-text references also help to convey disciplinary knowledge and understanding. As we noted above in the point made about how references help to demonstrate the scope of your engagement with the relevant discourse, in-text references also provide clear and unequivocal evidence of a basic level of engagement with disciplinary knowledge. This, too, as we've seen in our discussions of marking criteria, forms a key element in what tutors are looking for in your work.

Quotation and paraphrase

As we've established, in-text references are needed whenever you are referring to the work of another author. That might be when you are directly referencing the interpretation of a particular author or when another author's work has influenced your own. You also need to include in-text references when you quote directly from a source and when you paraphrase.

Quotation refers to the practice of including the exact words from another source, within single speech marks (according to UK convention). The in-text reference is usually placed after the second single speech mark at the end of the quotation but before the full stop:

For many teachers, 'classroom management ranks as a top concern' (Pinto, 2013, p. 4).

In cases where the author's name forms part of the sentence itself, the in-text reference is placed immediately after the author's name:

As Pinto (2013, p. 4) has noted, 'classroom management ranks as a top concern' for many teachers.

[*Taken from Pinto, L.E. (2013) *From discipline to culturally responsive engagement: 45 classroom management strategies*. Thousand Oaks: Corwin.]

One question we often get asked by students is 'what's the difference?' In truth, there isn't really much of a difference. It's more of a stylistic choice. In the second example, there is, perhaps, more emphasis placed on the author's name; but it's open to debate. Use whichever approach comes more naturally as you're writing.

Another question we're often asked is 'how many quotations should I include?' Quotations can be useful if you've got, for example, a short bit of text that neatly illustrates a point, particularly if it comes from a well-known author; such a quotation can have significant impact on the reader. However, quotations should be kept to a minimum. Why? Because depending on quotations in your work undermines your ability to demonstrate understanding of whatever the quotation is about and, thus, your critical engagement with the discourse. If you think about it, quoting from a source doesn't really involve much in the way of skill. Anybody can type out some text between a couple of speech marks and then add a reference on the end. Doing so doesn't necessarily mean that you have understood what the author is saying. Furthermore, when your work is submitted through plagiarism and originality checking software like Turnitin, a high percentage score will be returned. This score isn't taken as clear proof of plagiarism; but it will certainly lead to a potentially awkward conversation with your tutor about the need to 'be more critical' when it comes to using academic sources. Your objective should be to paraphrase text.

Paraphrasing refers to the practice of expressing the work of another author in your own words, without changing the meaning, often by simplifying the original text. When compared to quoting, as described above, paraphrasing is clearly far more skilful. In order to transform the words of another author into your own, you need to process the original text. In other words, you need to think about it, understand it, and then explain your understanding of it in your own words. Here's an example:

Classroom management requires careful planning if it is to be effective (Roth, 2015). The reason for this is that a teacher needs to have ready-made measures in place if an intervention is needed. For example, what do you do if a student's behaviour becomes disruptive? A teacher who has

not created a plan to address such a situation is more likely to flounder when it comes to managing the classroom environment. Those who are prepared are more capable of containing such behaviour so that the rest of the class remain focused on the learning task at hand.
[Adapted from: Pinto, L. (2013). *From discipline to culturally responsive engagement: 45 classroom management strategies.* Thousand Oaks, at p. 5]

A paraphrased version of the paragraph above might look like this:

At the core of effective classroom management lies a proactive approach in which responses to various scenarios are planned in advance.

This represents just one way the sample text might be paraphrased. It might not be perfect, but it's certainly paraphrased. How did we do it? All you're doing when paraphrasing text is (i) identifying the key point the author is making, (ii) disregarding anything that is surplus to this point, and then (iii) writing it out in your own words. Here, the key point is that a teacher needs to take a proactive approach to classroom management and that this approach involves planning ahead. The rest of the text can be put aside; this is the point to take from the exemplar.

Paraphrasing is a vital part of effective writing. It allows you to demonstrate your competencies against those key aspects of the marking criteria we've been talking about: knowledge and understanding, and critical engagement with discourse. But it's difficult – for all students, at all levels. That's why it takes practice. You must work hard at paraphrasing if you're going to do it routinely. Next time you begin to type out a quotation in your work, ask yourself, 'can I paraphrase this instead?' The answer is 'yes', but, to begin with, it'll take you just a little bit longer to do.

How do you format references?

So much for the principles behind effective referencing practice; how do you actually set out the references you need to include in your work? As we've seen, each reference you include is formatted in two different ways: (i) the in-text, shortened version, often called a citation; and (ii) the full version, included in the references list at the end of your work.

What is a 'References list'? A 'References list' is a list of all those sources you have used in your work. In other words, it presents each in-text reference in full, rather than in the abbreviated, 'author-date' form found in the work itself. It includes *only* those sources you've used; it does not include references to sources you might have looked at but haven't cited. The sources are listed in alphabetical order, by author surname, beginning with 'A'. Where you have multiple sources by the same author, all published in the same year, it is customary to add a letter after the year in each reference. Thus, Smith, B. (2022a), Smith B. (2022b) – and so on. These sources will also be listed in alphabetical order but, on this occasion, by the title of the work.

A distinction is sometimes made between a 'References list', which includes only those items you've cited, and a 'Bibliography', which is often broader in scope, listing sources you might have read but not cited as well. However, in some disciplines, 'Bibliography' can mean exactly the same as 'References list'! It's worth checking in your module handbook or with the tutor as to what is expected before you submit your work.

Let's look at how we set out references for three source types: books, journal articles, and web pages. Remember, there are variations in how author-date/Harvard references are set out. We're providing just one interpretation here; we recommend checking on the requirements for your work in any relevant module handbooks or by discussing referencing with your tutor.

Books:

On the theme of research ethics, how do we format a reference, in its full version, to Helen Kara's *Research ethics in the real world*? To do this, we need the following elements:

- author surname and initial;
- year of publication;
- title of work, and any subtitle;
- place of publication;
- publisher.

The reference, as it should be included in a 'References list', would look like this:

Kara, H. (2018) *Research Ethics in the Real World: Euro-Western and Indigenous Perspectives.* Bristol: Policy Press.

Note the use of punctuation and spacing; it's with these aspects of the reference that some students make mistakes. For example, there's a full stop after the initial (it's an abbreviation), as well as after the book title, and there's a colon after the place of publication. These bits of punctuation matter; if any are missing, the formatting of your references will be inconsistent.

The in-text version of this reference simply uses the author and date: (Kara, 2018).

Journal articles:

We've found an article on the effectiveness of research ethics committees at universities by Donald Sharpe and Julie Ziemer; what do we need to format the references list version of the reference?

- author surname and initial;
- year corresponding to volume of the journal;
- title of article;
- title of journal;
- volume number and issue number, if provided;
- page numbers.

The full version of the reference would therefore look like this:
Sharpe, D. and Ziemer, J. (2022) 'Psychology, ethics, and research ethics boards', *Ethics & Behavior*, *32*(8), pp. 658–673.

Punctuation is important here as well. Note that the article title is not in italics but the title of the journal is. It should also be noted that the US English spelling in the journal title has been preserved: *Behavior* not, for UK students, *Behaviour*. More commas are used here, there is no space between the volume and issue numbers, and 'pp.' is used for multiple pages (not p., which is for one page).

Most journal articles are reproduced digitally now. All of the information needed will almost certainly be available on the first page of this digital version. The author(s) and title will be obvious; the remaining elements will be found running across the top or down the side of this first page.

A DOI (Digital Object Identifier) number is sometimes provided with the information we've just mentioned in digital versions of journal articles. The article referenced above has one: after the page numbers, you can see, at the top of the page, the URL 'https://doi.org/10.1080/10508422.2021.2023019'. Where this is provided, it can be added after the page numbers, following the full stop, preceded by 'Available at:':

Sharpe, D. and Ziemer, J. (2022) 'Psychology, ethics, and research ethics boards', *Ethics & Behavior*, *32*(8), pp. 658–673. Available at: https://doi.org/10.1080/10508422.2021.2023019

In some online journals, no page numbers are provided; instead, you'll find an article number. Where this is the case, simply replace 'pp. XXX–XXX' with 'article number 12345'.

The in-text version of the reference would be: (Sharpe and Ziemer, 2022).

Web pages (with an organisation as the author):

How do you reference a web page? Let's look at an example where we've got an organisation as the author. For example, the UK Data Service's page on 'Ethical obligations'. The key elements here are the year of the page's publication, its URL, and the date you accessed that page:

- author;
- year that the page was published or last updated;

- title of page;
- URL;
- date of access.

Our reference looks like this:

UK Data Service (2024) *Ethical Obligations*. Available at: https://uk-dataservice.ac.uk/learning-hub/research-data-management/ethical-issues/ethical-obligations/ (Accessed: 3 December 2024).

The year of publication/last updated is sometimes difficult to find. In this case, it sits at the very bottom of the page. The in-text version of the reference, as you might have guessed, is: (UK Data Service, 2024).

There are obviously lots of other source types you might need to reference. Whatever the source type you're referencing, the required format will incorporate some of the elements outlined above. Use a referencing guide provided either internally, on your course or within your university, or externally, in the form of a published book or database. The only way to learn is to figure out for yourself how to format a reference for each different source type you meet. That way, once you've formatted different references once or twice, you'll gain in confidence and it'll soon become second nature. Above all, when referencing, take care to be accurate and consistent. As long as you do that, you shouldn't encounter any problems with your referencing.

Summary

In this chapter, we've introduced you to the broader literacy of academic integrity, in which referencing – a core aspect of academic practice which, for students, can cause great anxiety – sits. The values that underpin academic integrity – those set out neatly by the ICAI – are not only important in shaping research conduct; they hold a significance to your professional career after university, as key components of graduate identity. Use the information we've discussed in this chapter to inform your practice, not only when it comes to research, but in all other aspects of the way you participate in the discourse community you have joined. If you act like an academic, you'll become an academic; and you'll be able to take this understanding of the values that make up academic integrity into the workplace.

When it comes to referencing, we've looked at its importance in relation to avoiding plagiarism. But, at the same time, we've encouraged you to look beyond this rather obvious function of referencing to its broader value in relation to evidencing your competencies next to marking criteria. In-text references, for example, help your tutor to gauge the scope of your research. They also help to demonstrate the extent and quality of your critical engagement with different academic sources and the discourse they contribute to. There are different referencing styles and variations in the format of the most popular style, author-date (Harvard) referencing. This is nothing to worry about; what's important is that you are accurate when it comes to formatting references and consistent in the way you do it. As with all of the literacies discussed in this book, the more you do it, the easier it will become. Adopting a conscientious approach to referencing will ensure that you become adept at it as quickly as possible.

References

International Center for Academic Integrity (ICAI). (2021). *The fundamental values of academic integrity* (3rd ed.). Dayton.

Marder, J., Thiel, F., & Göllner, R. (2023). Classroom management and students' mathematics achievement: The role of students' disruptive behavior and teacher classroom management. *Learning and Instruction, 86*, 1–13.

Pinto, L. (2013). *From discipline to culturally responsive engagement: 45 classroom management strategies*. Thousand Oaks.

UK Research and Innovation (UKRI). (2021). *Framework for research ethics*. https://www.ukri.org/councils/esrc/guidance-for-applicants/research-ethics-guidance/framework-for-research-ethics/our-core-principles/

Chapter 11

Creating effective presentations and working in groups

Presentations and group work feature prominently in learning at university because of their value in helping you to develop aspects of graduate identity that are highly valued by employers. Presentations, for example, often form important elements of selection processes at interview; in many professions, you'll be expected to present information routinely to different audiences. Similarly, the ability to collaborate and to work effectively with others is needed across a wide range of professions; it, too, is often tested at interview, sometimes by a practical task. Communicating through public speaking and interacting with others are what we would call *'transferable skills' in higher education. These are skills or competencies that can be used across a wide variety of professional contexts. Creating effective presentations and working successfully in groups are therefore not only important as literacies in relation to finding success in your academic work; they also hold a broader value to your personal development, as you work towards becoming a graduate. In this chapter, we look in more detail at the process by which you can create an effective presentation. We then move on to working in groups, providing you with recommendations on how you can optimise your performance in group work.

Learning Objectives

By the end of this chapter, you will have gained:

- an understanding of the presentation as a form of assessment used by tutors in higher education;
- an awareness of the value of presentations and the transferable skills involved to the process of becoming a graduate;
- insights into how to create and deliver a presentation;
- an awareness of common presentation errors and how to avoid them;

DOI: 10.4324/9781003217527-11

- an awareness of the challenges involved in group work;
- an understanding of different personality types in the context of conflict resolution;
- insights into how you can optimise your performance in group work.

Keywords

transferable skills; academic voice; academic authority; graduate identity; personality types; leadership; collaboration; resilience

Defining the presentation

Presentations are activities which test many of the same literacies you would use when completing a piece of written work. For example, in a presentation, you're expected to articulate an argument, demonstrate an ability to critique relevant discourse, and to communicate clearly. The difference with presentations is that you are expected to communicate your ideas orally, in front of audience, and you might also be expected to create visual aids, like a PowerPoint slideshow, to complement spoken content. There are also usually certain constraints that you're expected to observe. There's often a time limit, for example, and sometimes even a limit on the number of slides you can use in your presentation. You might also be expected to respond to questions at the end of your presentation, some of which may be difficult to answer. In short, in terms of expectations, there are both similarities and differences between the presentation and other forms of assessment.

For the tutor, the presentation offers an alternative form of assessment, one that brings some variety to the way that students' progress might be measured. For you, as a student, the presentation holds value as learning tool. Creating a presentation involves many of the same literacies you would use when writing an essay. For example, you will need to do some research for it and then critically engage with the interpretations you find. Given the greater emphasis on the quality of your communication in a presentation, it holds particular value as a tool for helping you to develop your own 'voice'. In addition to having to deepen your knowledge and understanding as you prepare a presentation, you'll also need to assert and defend the argument you create by responding to the questions and challenges from an audience. This sort of engagement with other students and tutors is valuable in itself because it can provide you with further insights into your topic. It is therefore by creating a well-researched and confidently delivered presentation that you can exercise greater ownership of your understanding and disciplinary knowledge. As such, presentations serve as a key way of developing your academic voice.

Presentations and transferable skills

Presentations stand out from other forms of assessment because of their importance in developing transferable skills. Employers increasingly look to recruit graduates who can demonstrate excellent communication skills. The ability to articulate complex information clearly and confidently represents a highly valued competency. As you approach the end of your degree programme and prepare to enter your chosen profession, this competency becomes very important in determining whether you can successfully become a graduate. It's therefore vital that you take the opportunities presented by presentation tasks to develop this competency so that you can stand out from your fellow graduates.

Employers usually test your ability to communicate at the interview stage of a selection process. This process often includes a presentation task which is usually focused on a fairly general or straightforward topic. The reason for this, of course, is that employers are in general less interested in the content of the presentation than they are in the way that you communicate and present yourself. However, this is not to say that you can just make up the content! But the purpose of the task is to give you an opportunity to demonstrate your communication competencies.

What are employers looking for specifically? Like your tutors, employers want to see evidence of an ability to communicate complex information to different audiences and to tailor your communication according to the level of knowledge or expertise your audience might have. For example, the assessment task might ask you to present technical information to an audience who have little technical knowledge, or you might be expected to summarise data sets represented in tables or in graphs on accompanying slides to the same group. This is not as easy as it might sound; you'll need to use less technical vocabulary, for example, and find ways of making detailed information accessible. An effective presentation might also point to your ability to communicate in other ways, such as in formal correspondence with customers or clients, as well as interpersonal modes of communication like email. Such everyday activities are important in professional contexts. The content of your presentation might be used to assess your ability to do research. Similarly, it might point to your creativity and your aptitude for innovation and problem-solving. The use of visual aids highlight your proficiency in the use of software like PowerPoint, while the very fact that you've been able to create a presentation and then deliver it showcases your application and organisational skills. In short, presentations, when used in a selection process, function as a statement of your graduate identity. It's therefore important to practise and hone these skills through the presentation tasks you encounter on your course.

Presentations and assessment

It is as forms of assessment that presentations play such a significant part in the learning experience at university. Tutors, however, use different types of presentation, each with its own set of expectations when it is used for assessment. Broadly speaking, tutors are assessing the quality of your presentation's content, the clarity and appropriateness of your communication, your delivery, the effectiveness of your visual aids, and your ability to interact with your audience, as reflected in the way you handle any questions. Let's consider the different types of presentations used by tutors.

Individual presentations

This type of presentation is the most common. It involves you creating and then delivering a presentation on your own, usually in front of a tutorial or seminar group. Typically, you would be assessed on those features discussed earlier. Depending on the nature of the task – whether it's formative or summative – you might receive feedback on your performance which you can then use to bring about an improved performance the next time you tackle a presentation task. Sometimes, individual presentations are focused on research you might be doing, perhaps for a dissertation. In this situation, you'd be expected to communicate your methodology, some of your findings, and any conclusions you might be working towards. In other words, you're delivering an update on your progress.

Poster presentations

Posters are used much more often now, in part because they're often used at academic conferences. In a poster, you're expected to communicate some of the core elements of a research article, such as the problem you're investigating, highlights from the literature review, methodology, findings, and conclusion. The challenge with a poster is to display all of this in a visually effective way. It requires an ability to summarise and synthesise knowledge while maintaining the academic rigour expected in a research paper. There is also the challenge of how to create the poster using suitable software. This is not easy for everyone and it may take more time to transfer the knowledge collated into the software than it did to actually complete the research!

Group presentations

Often a cause of much anxiety among students, tutors use group presentations to help you to develop the interpersonal skills needed in the workplace. The challenge here is get each member to contribute then to reconcile these contributions in such a way as to create a coherent and convincing presentation. Preparation is key: all team members need to be committed to the project and to remain engaged throughout its duration. One way of achieving this is for a team leader to be nominated and for that person to delegate tasks according to each team member's preference, experience, and skillset.

Professional or practice-based presentations

In vocational disciplines or those more closely related to professional contexts, professional or practice-based presentations are used to mirror experiences students might face in the workplace. For example, students studying marketing might be expected to pitch an idea to prospective clients; social work students might be expected to present recommendations regarding a challenging case; sport science students might have to present a coaching plan to a group of swimmers. Here, the presentation meets authentic learning. Tutors may be assessing specific features of the presentation that are directly related to the professional context, such as an awareness of professional standards and ethical considerations. Such presentation tasks are intended to prepare you for professional practice.

Interview-based presentations/tasks

In interview-based assessment, tutors are trying to engage you in a dialogue about certain topics in order to test the depth of your disciplinary knowledge and understanding. It works in a similar way to a job interview with an emphasis on the need to evidence your knowledge and understanding. It resembles the *viva voce*, the oral exam PhD students have to take once they've submitted their theses.

Technology-based presentations

Digital platforms have transformed the way presentations can be delivered. For example, virtual presentations can be delivered via software like Zoom or Teams. For this type of presentation, assessment might focus on your ability to engage remote audiences using the different features of this software. Tutors might also ask you to create a video presentation using, for example, lecture capture software, or simply by recording it on your mobile phone or tablet. In this type of presentation, you might be assessed on your digital skills, such as your ability to engage an audience through the integration of different digital elements, including audio, video, animation, and interactivity.

Whatever form the presentation takes, it's very important to consider the instructions for its creation and the associated marking criteria carefully. This list is only meant to give you a flavour of the different types of presentations used in higher education. It's up to you to establish what exactly you need to do to excel by considering the marking criteria carefully.

Planning, structuring, and designing your presentation

Let's now consider the practice behind the creation of a presentation. The form of presentation we're going to look at is the individual presentation, which, as we said earlier, is the one used most often in assessment contexts at university.

The assessment task comes from Natalie and Jess' course on marketing. Students have been asked to design a social media marketing strategy for the university. Each student is expected to present their strategy to key stakeholders, consisting of the pro-vice chancellor for learning and teaching (a senior figure at the university), staff from the university's marketing department, the tutor responsible for the module to which the presentation task belongs, and two postgraduate students in the marketing department. Students are told that the presentation needs to be accompanied by a PowerPoint slideshow consisting of no more than eight slides. At least one slide needs to address: (i) the theoretical foundations of the strategy; (ii) the strategy itself, including its objectives; (iii) mocked up examples of content; (iv) student feedback, collected by each presenter; and (v) suggestions for how it might be implemented. The presentation itself is to be no longer than ten minutes, with up to ten minutes at the end for questions from the audience.

How do you go about tackling such a presentation task? Let's consider an account of Natalie's approach. What does it tell us about the steps you need to take in order to create an effective presentation?

Natalie hates public speaking. The thought of having to present a social media marketing strategy to an audience which includes some important people at the university fills her with dread. The sooner it's over, the better, as far as Natalie is concerned. She reads through the instructions. The first thing that comes into her mind is that she doesn't know how to use PowerPoint. She can probably just wing it by using the default format settings. She remembers looking at a model for social media marketing in a tutorial. Something about the Cs – but she can't remember how many there are. That's the theory slide sorted out. Then all she needs to do is talk about how to write posts on different social media platforms. The university is all about studying. She can talk about the library, the coffee shops and restaurants, and the bar! All of that will make good content;

she might even be able to make the audience laugh by joking about her priorities. Now that she's planned what she's going to do, she turns to PowerPoint. She sees so many different formatting options in the ribbon running across the top of the page that she just copies out some keywords relating to the 7 Cs model which she finds via Google in black font on a white background. She creates some images of social media posts by creating fake posts on her own accounts. The coffee shop is closed so she takes a picture of its entrance to use in one post. By the time she comes to creating the presentation, a lot of students have gone home. She asks her housemate what she thinks of her fake posts. All she gets back is 'brilliant', which she adds to the presentation. For implementing the strategy, she adds some notes to the PowerPoint about timing and the use of multiple platforms. She skims through her work and decides that she's done just about enough.

The first point to acknowledge about Natalie's experience is that many of you will find public speaking and delivering presentations nerve-wracking, particularly when the audience is made up of what Natalie calls 'important people'. You do get used to standing up in front of people, but there's always a bit of anxiety when you don't know the audience. The trick is to appear confident even when you're feeling nervous. For Natalie, her nerves get the better of her. She basically gives up before she's even started! She has little sense of the potential value to her personal development of the experience. Her attitude is reflected in her lack of preparation. The fact that she drops in some knowledge she's picked up of one particular model (which she doesn't get right to begin with) highlights one of the weaknesses her presentation will have: a lack of coherence. She doesn't do any research on the university's use of social media. She makes an assumption about the sort of content the university would post about. She then mocks up some social media content which isn't properly linked to the model she highlighted. She more or less manufactures feedback on what she's created. Underpinning it all is a lack of understanding of how to use PowerPoint. The slides she is creating will stand out for all the wrong reasons: plain and uninspired, they will immediately suggest to the audience that she hasn't put much effort into creating her presentation.

Natalie's poor performance highlights the different steps you need to take if you're going to create an effective presentation. Let's consider them one by one.

1   Read the assessment instructions carefully.
    As the details of Natalie's assessment reveal, instructions for assessment presentations are often more involved than for written forms of assessment. For example, she can only use a set number of slides. Each slide needs to address a specific aspect of the work. She needs to be

competent with PowerPoint in order to create these slides. All of these conditions inform the approach she needs to take.
2 Research the topic.
Natalie doesn't really do any research for her presentation. The content will lack depth as a result and it will be clear that she hasn't fully engaged with the underlying theory. Research is just as important for presentations as it is for written forms of assessment. There's much research to do for Natalie's presentation task. In addition to looking at theory, she also needs to consider how educational institutions like universities make use of social media marketing. Are there any case studies published? If not, why not look at the social media presence of different universities? She also needs to consider how social media marketing fits into a strategy which includes marketing through other media. Even though the presentation is only ten minutes long, its content needs to reflect an in-depth understanding of the relevant theory and discourse.
3 Plan the presentation.
Again, just as you would plan an essay, you need to set out the content of a presentation before you start creating it. Planning provides structure. It also helps to ensure that your argument is clear and that the presentation itself is coherent and easy to follow. Natalie doesn't really do any planning. You can tell that her presentation will lack coherence and her strategy won't be expressed clearly. A presentation will have an introduction, main body and conclusion, just as a piece of writing would. For Natalie's assessment, we suggest using the instructions about the content of the slides to form the basis of the plan. You might also draft a 'script' at this stage. This doesn't need to be written out in continuous prose. In fact, we urge you to make bullet points to act as prompts.
4 Design visual aids.
As you develop the plan, you'll have a clearer idea of what you intend to cover in each slide. You can then begin to add keywords, phrases, and images to the slides. In Natalie's case, there's a clear instruction about using PowerPoint to create the visual aids. For your presentation, you might have more freedom to choose which platform to create them on. There are many options, some of which require more technical knowledge than others. A Prezi presentation, for example, when done well, looks great; but not everyone has the skillset to make the most out of it. The key point to remember when designing visual aids is that they are meant to complement the spoken content of the presentation; if they distract, they're not fulfilling their purpose.
5 Putting it all together and practising.
Once you've got your visual aids, you need to link them to the spoken content. The easiest way to do this is by practising. You don't need an audience to practise your presentation; you can do it on your own, perhaps in front of a mirror. The more you practise, the better. It's

by practising that you find out whether each part of the presentation works. Use these practice sessions to iron out any problems with the presentation. If you speak for too long about one slide, edit the content down. You might fall short of the allotted time. If you think you need to add any content, do so, and then practise it again. Does the presentation run to time now?

Designing visual aids

In most forms of assessed presentations, you'll be expected to demonstrate your digital skills by creating visual aids to complement the spoken element. When used effectively, such aids can really help to enhance your argument and the points you're making. Conversely, when used less effectively, they can distract the audience, undermine their engagement, and disrupt the flow of the presentation. Broadly speaking, when the visual aids provide the focus of the presentation rather the spoken content, their effectiveness dwindles. Visual aids are an integral element of presentations; but they support rather than replace the spoken part.

You can create visual aids using a variety of different software. In our examples, our students are using PowerPoint, but there are others, one of which, Prezi, we mentioned earlier. Prezi offers dynamic slideshows which, when done creatively, can look spectacular. Without that technical know-how, however, they can have the opposite effect. If there's no specific direction as to which software to use to create the visual aids, we recommend using something you're more familiar with which does what you need. There's no need to impress the audience by trying to use something which you don't fully understand.

We've seen some terrible visual aids over the years – and we still do! What we set out here are general recommendations that can be applied across different pieces of software. The first and most important is 'less is more'. The ineffectiveness of some slides is down to how much content is displayed on it. It's difficult to make sense of cluttered slides. Keep it simple: a header, some brief keywords which can act as triggers for you when delivering, and perhaps an image, if it has impact. Other recommendations relate to the design decisions you make:

- Bold type: avoid overusing bold type, particularly when the font is quite large. It can feel like bold type is hitting you square in the face!
- Font size: avoid very small fonts. If you're having to reduce the font size so much that you can barely see it on the screen, there's too much content on the slide.

- Font type: try to use fonts that complement each other, one for headers, one for content. If in doubt, use the software's recommendations.
- Clashing colours: some colours simply don't work together. Have in mind recommendations about which colours to use for anyone who is visually impaired or has a learning difficulty like dyslexia.
- Minimise the number of words on each slide: avoid using unnecessary words; try to stick to keywords rather than adding complete sentences.
- Graphics: try to present information using graphics (SmartArt on PowerPoint); diagrams and images are easier for an audience to take in at a glance.
- Image resolution: not all images are produced in a resolution high enough to be used in a visual aid. Check to see how an image is displayed by a projector if you have any doubts.
- Remember the environment: be aware of the size of the room in which you'll be presenting. Check what technology is in there – is there a projector? If so, how big is the screen?

These are the main recommendations we would make when it comes to creating visual aids. Remember, less is more, and try not to use visual aids to show off your technical knowledge. Your presentation should not be about the visual aids; it's about the content, your argument, and the way you present it and yourself.

Tips on structure

The organisation of a presentation is key. It's at the planning stage that you determine the overall structure of the presentation; this can be refined later on, as you practise delivering it. But what are the defining features of the introduction, main body and conclusion?

Introduction

The introduction to a presentation, as in a written assessment, fulfils several important functions. The most important is to capture the attention of the audience. An effective way of doing this is by using a hook. For example, you might use a personal anecdote or a less well-known aspect of the topic to draw your audience in. Alternatively, you might challenge an accepted interpretation. Whatever it is, the hook is meant to engage the audience from the start. The difficulty lies in sustaining this interest! The introduction should also set out the presentation's aims and objectives; in doing this, it should effectively signpost content. You need to give the audience an idea of the direction of travel in your presentation if you're going to sustain that interest.

Main body

The main body is where you set out the core points of your presentation. As in a piece of written work, these points, taken together, will form your argument. As in the example of Natalie's presentation, it might be helpful to have one slide or visual aid per point; this will add to the overall coherence of the presentation as well as making it easier for you to deliver. The point is the main body should also be arranged logically, so that there is a flow to the content of your presentation. The flow will help to sustain the interest of your audience. It's therefore very important to think carefully about the links between the points. When it comes to discussing the evidence used to support your points, avoid adding in too much detail. Only reference the key pieces of evidence. It might be appropriate to include some interactive elements in the main body, but only if time allows. Encouraging interaction with an audience, perhaps by posing questions, is a very effective way of sustaining their interest. But it takes time to do it well; always have an eye on the clock in order to avoid running over your time limit.

Conclusion

The conclusion provides the final opportunity to articulate your argument and reinforce the key points of your presentation. Avoid simply repeating what you've said in the main body. Instead, refer back to the objectives you set out in the introduction. How have you addressed each one? Try to maximise the impact of your argument by, for example, demonstrating the broader significance of your research. Look beyond your presentation to the future. What contribution are you making? How might you extend the research? What future research projects are suggested by the work you've done?

Common presentation errors

Over the years, we've learnt a lot about the mistakes students often make in presentations. In this section, we just want to highlight a few of them, with a view building your awareness of where a presentation can go wrong and how you might avoid making similar mistakes. Let's consider the unfortunate example of Natalie's friend, Nasser, whose presentation didn't go to plan. What mistakes did Nasser make?

> *Nasser can't remember feeling this nervous before any form of assessment he's done before. He can literally feel himself shaking as he waits to be called into the room to deliver his presentation on social media marketing. Finally, his tutor opens the door and asks him to come in. He can see*

the audience on his right as he enters the room, but he doesn't look at them. He moves straight to the front to plug his USB drive into the PC. He's so nervous that he can't navigate to the USB drive, and so his tutor comes to the front to help him. Once the presentation is on both screens – it's a big lecture theatre; there are two screens at the front – he turns to the audience and gives them a quick glance. This makes him so nervous that he decides to look at the corners of the ceiling instead. The tutor begins the timer and Nasser, in a panic, turns to the index cards he's brought with him which have the presentation written out on them. He keeps his head down and reads off the cards. As he reads, he forgets to move to the second slide. This puts him into another panic as he clicks backwards and forwards to try to get to the right slide. He turns to the screen and begins to read off the slide with his back to the audience. The slide is so full of text that he can't really see it properly for himself. He is not even halfway through when the tutor gives him a two-minute warning before the end of the time allowed. He panics again, skips over much of the content of the fourth slide, before trying to make a new point – but then the tutor stops him. When the audience are invited to ask questions, Nasser doesn't understand the first one. He doesn't have an answer for the second question, but the third he does respond to. He leaves the room relieved that the experience is over.

There are a number of mistakes to highlight here. The first relates to his nervousness. This isn't a mistake, as such, but Nasser's inability to control his anxiety works against him even before he's walked into the room to begin the presentation. He can feel himself shaking, something that would be immediately obvious to his audience. Nervousness in a speaker might elicit sympathy. However, we've all seen presentations where the speaker is so nervous that you're almost willing it to be over as much as they are! Try to hide your nerves by projecting confidence. It's not easy, but it helps to put everyone at ease, including yourself. Nasser's nervousness leads to some confusion as to how to get his USB drive to work. It's also made worse by his unfamiliarity with the room he's in and the technology available. The fact that there are two screens throws him. If he'd prepared more thoroughly, he might have been more aware of the environment. His nervousness makes him less willing to look at the audience; he looks to his prompt cards instead, on which he is very reliant. He forgets to move through the slideshow which makes him turn his back on the audience (a big mistake – how are you going to engage an audience with your back to them?) and then read from the slides rather than his cards. His slides are poorly designed. He overruns; he's barely halfway through when he gets the two-minute warning. He then skips over some of the content which means that the presentation loses coherence. When it comes to answering questions, Nasser is so poorly prepared that he doesn't even understand one of the questions.

In summary, therefore, to avoid Nasser's mistakes, we recommend:

- trying to control your nervousness by projecting confidence even if you don't feel it;
- if you need the security offered by index or prompt cards, fine, but avoid reading directly off them; look at your audience to engage them;
- concentrate on utilising the visual aids at appropriate points;
- design visual aids carefully so that they complement rather than distract an audience;
- always look at a clock so that you stay on time; practise your presentation in advance so that you know, roughly, how long it will take for you to get through;
- think about the presentation's content as you move through it; try to ensure that you preserve its coherence by not missing out anything;
- prepare for questions;
- know your environment; check on what technology is available, the size of the room – and so on.

Working in groups

Group presentations provide just one example of an assessment task or activity where tutors expect you to work closely with other students. Group work, like presentations, is very closely linked to your graduate identity because it requires behaviours and competencies required in the workplace. Just as employers are keen to see strong communication skills in presentations, they also value highly interpersonal skills, an ability to collaborate with colleagues, innovative thought and leadership. This is why tutors in general incorporate group work into the learning you do on your course and why on some courses it figures prominently as a form of assessment. This assessment often takes the form of a group presentation, where the overall quality of the presentation serves as a reflection of how well you have all worked together as a team. This type of project can often be a very frustrating experience for students, for reasons highlighted below in the exemplar. But however frustrating you find it, working on a group project offers a rich learning experience, one that will directly influence your behaviours in the workplace as a graduate.

Why might you find the experience of working with others frustrating? First of all, in our experience, it's usually the conscientious students, those who are trying to excel, who get more frustrated by group work. This is because of their lack of control over the 'end product', such as a group presentation or project brief. In group work, your ability to excel depends on the contribution of others. If other team members are less motivated or lack the required knowledge and understanding to make a significant contribution to the project, then it will affect your mark as much as theirs. In other words, your mark is not simply determined by your own performance, and there may be little you can do to encourage others to engage fully in the project. Lots of students get frustrated by the challenge of working with others. Everyone is different. Your values and expectations when it comes to engaging with your course will be different from those of other team members. This can be a source of great tension, not least because you all need to work together if you're going to get a good mark. You might also be expected to mediate and resolve conflicts between team members. This can be tricky, and it adds to the pressure of an already stressful situation. Some students find the objectives of group work difficult to understand. This is often because they are too focused on that end product. For tutors, the value of group work lies in the processes behind the creation of that product rather than the product itself, but for students who are focused on marks and performance, this can be difficult to understand.

It is important for you to recognise the broader value of group work to your personal development if you are to get as much as possible out of the experience. Since tutors are interested in the process rather than the product, assessment linked to group work often includes a reflective element. In this exercise, you are expected to reflect on the experience of participating in group work as a whole. Tutors are looking to see what you have gained from the experience in terms of your professional development; for example, how well have you managed any conflicts within the group? Even if there is no formal reflective element associated with the group work, we would recommend that you reflect on it informally. Using one of the reflective cycles we've already discussed, you can produce a reflective account for your benefit. Doing so will ensure that you have made the most out of the experience. It will also give you valuable insights into your personality traits and behaviours which will inform your participation in similar activities in professional contexts.

What are tutors looking for from your participation in group work?

Tutors' expectations mirror those of employers. They are looking to see how you interact with others: your ability to communicate, to listen, to mediate, to empathise, to encourage, to motivate – and so on. The end product will inevitably reflect the ability of the group to work well together, but tutors remain more interested in process rather than product. In a reflective account of the experience, tutors will be looking at how you evaluate your performance in the context of the interaction you have with other group members. Below is a list of personality traits and behaviours you might like to think about as you reflect on your own experience of group work.

Communication and your ability to listen

Arguably the most important aspect of group work, tutors will be very interested to see how you communicate with other group members – whose personalities will be different to your own – and whether you listen to the contributions of other group members. Lots of students fail to recognise the importance of listening to others in group work, even if you don't share their point of view. However, an effective team member listens to alternative viewpoints and is willing to adopt suggestions that will benefit the team and enhance the quality of the end product. It should also be noted that there is a difference between *hearing* and *listening*. You can hear what another team member says without making use of it; listening, on the other hand, involves thinking about that contribution and doing something with it.

Collaborating with others

As noted earlier, tutors are looking for how you interact with other team members. It's often challenging to work effectively with team members who you find difficult to deal with. Tutors will be interested in how you manage such relationships and how you might have to mediate between other team members.

Flexibility and adaptability

Linked to the way you interact with others, tutors will also consider your flexibility and adaptability. You might, for example, be expected to take responsibility for another aspect of a group project if one team member falls behind or fails to do what is required. If some aspect of the project doesn't go to plan, you might have to revise the team's objectives. All of this points to your flexibility, adaptability, and your willingness to embrace change and uncertainty – all of which are highly valued by employers.

Resilience

Another characteristic valued by employers, tutors will look for evidence of your resilience. Conflict with another team member, for example, might be draining on you, personally, but a resilient student will remain focused on task. Similarly, you might face other types of obstacle – perhaps a team member is off sick, an absence that works against the completion of the project. Again, a resilient student would work twice as hard to ensure that the project was completed on schedule.

Leadership

Tutors might also look for evidence of leadership, particularly if they have instructed you, as a team, to allocate team roles to each member of the group. If you're given the role of 'project manager', for example, tutors will expect to see you making informed decisions about team affairs, such as who is responsible for each task and what to do in the event of an unexpected problem. As a leader, you might have to take control of disputes within the team, monitor progress, and organise team meetings; it might also be up to you to motivate other team members and to lead such assessment tasks as presentations.

Accountability

Linked to leadership is accountability, the ability to take responsibility for decisions made and the work produced by the team. Some team members will shy away from mistakes made by the team or poor performance overall, as reflected in a disappointing end product. Leaders will do the opposite; they will accept disappointments and make well-thought-out evaluative judgements on why such disappointments occurred.

Innovative thinking and problem-solving

Within any group work, there will be opportunities for you to demonstrate innovative thought and problem-solving skills. You might do this in a leadership capacity, or your contribution to the group's work might reflect your innovative thought.

Organisational and time-management skills

On a practical level, tutors will also use group work to assess your organisational and time-management skills. Inevitably, the quality of the end product will reflect how effectively the team has organised itself and managed its time. Your own proficiency in these areas may be judged through the reflection you provide or via updates provided to your tutor as the group work is completed.

With these personality traits and behaviours in mind, let's take a look at the example of Ross. He is a second-year hospitality management student. For this group activity, which is assessed, he is expected to work with three other students on a plan for expanding the hospitality offer of a local football club. The activity culminates in an assessed pitch which the team must deliver in the boardroom of the football club in front of its commercial management team and Ross' tutor. The account below refers to the preparation for the pitch. Ross has taken on the role of 'project manager'. Sandra is the team's researcher, David is responsible for the accompanying PowerPoint presentation, while Lucia has written the content with Ross.

> *Ross convenes the final meeting first thing on Monday morning, two days before the pitch takes place. He sets an agenda which is designed to give each team member an opportunity to set out how they think the pitch should be delivered. David, who is very good at presentation design, has come up with some unusual ideas about the colours and font used in the visual aids; he also wants to use some off-the-wall images to grab the attention of the audience. Sandra prefers to keep the visual aids as simple as possible, to avoid distracting the audience. David persists, and as he talks, Ross can see that Sandra is getting more frustrated. Exasperated, she interrupts David and reminds him of the importance of keeping it simple. An argument then takes place; even Lucia jumps in to suggest a compromise by using some of David's ideas. Ross, as the project manager, intervenes. He thanks David for his contribution in order to draw attention to his creative thinking; he then acknowledges Sandra's point of view, which he broadly agrees with, before setting out a compromise inspired by Lucia's contribution. He explains, very clearly, which colour and font he thinks they should use; he then asks David to re-think the images because he doesn't think they complement the ideas the team are trying to communicate. In this way, Ross brings the team back together by finding a middle way.*

Ross is an effective leader of the group; he demonstrates a number of the personality traits we highlighted earlier. First of all, he is well-organised; the timing of the final meeting only two days before the pitch is sensible since it provides enough time for changes to be made. The agenda is also a good idea – something that a good leader would use in every meeting – largely because it is designed to give each team member an opportunity to get across their point of view. Ross clearly values communication. David offers some creative ideas, which are clearly worth discussing; but Sandra, perhaps due to the pressure of the upcoming pitch, strongly disagrees and urges caution in the way the presentation is set out. Lucia attempts to intervene by suggesting a compromise, but Ross takes hold of the situation by setting his view, as the leader of the team, and by explaining his decisions. In doing so, he effectively reunites the team and the focus on the pitch is restored.

The difficulty in the scenario set out here lies in the conflict between David and Sandra. This is not unusual; we've mentioned already that one of the greatest challenges facing you when participating in group work is the need to resolve conflicts to allow the team to function properly. One way you can enhance your performance in group work and maximise the value of the experience to your personal development is by building an awareness of different personality types. There is a lot of literature on this in the discipline of psychology; we don't intend to cover all of it here. Instead, we want to highlight the 'big five' factors often discussed by academics in the field. These factors are sometimes collectively called the OCEAN model (McCrae & Costa, 1999); the acronym refers to each of the factors:

- openness
- conscientiousness
- extraversion
- agreeableness
- neuroticism

Each of these factors refers to a personality type. Openness corresponds to creative thinkers or 'innovators'; conscientiousness refers to organisers; extraversion are those people who are good at communicating; agreeableness is characteristic of mediators; and neuroticism refers to those who are realists. Which personality type do you think applies to David, Sandra, and Lucia? David can be associated with openness; he's an innovator. Sandra is linked to neuroticism because she's a realist. Lucia's actions are characterised by agreeableness. What about Ross? He's clearly got leadership qualities, but it is his communication that stands out. We would suggest that his behaviour is characterised by extraversion. Which personality type best describes you? You might need to ask a friend!

Task: Reflecting on your own contribution to group work

> Have you recently completed a group activity? It doesn't need to be an assessment task. Have you worked in a small group during a tutorial, for example? If so, how might you assess your own contribution? Using a three-stage reflective cycle, like the ERA one we met in Chapter 9 (Jasper, 2013), reflect on your performance. Pay particular attention to the personality traits and behaviours we've highlighted in this section. Also consider the personalities of the other team members. What types were they? How well did you interact with them? By the end of the reflection, try to decide which of the OCEAN personality types best describes you. We suggest discussing your reflection with a friend.

Optimising your performance in group work

How can you ensure that you perform as well as possible in group work? We would make several suggestions, based on our discussion of group work.

1. Ensure that you have an understanding of the learning objectives associated with group work. Beyond any assessment involved, consider what the experience might offer to you as you seek to become a graduate. Remember, it's about process not product.
2. Focus on communication. Make sure that your views are clear and that they are heard, and do your best to encourage other team members to do the same.
3. Listen to, as well as hear, the views of others; respect opinions that contrast with your own. It's group work; each team member's view is as valid as any other's.
4. Act as a responsible team member. Fulfil whatever role you're given conscientiously. Approach the tasks in the way you would expect others to do so.
5. Mediate between team members when necessary. You should all be working to the same objectives; conflicts between team members only undermine those efforts. Use your understanding of personality types to inform your interactions with others. Adopt an empathetic approach and always focus on moving forward.
6. Remember the practical aspects of group work: stay focused on the task; adopt an organised approach; manage your time.

Summary

Presentations form a key part of your learning experience at university. Tutors like to set them as assessments, in part to add some variety to types of assessments used. Very few students enjoy the experience of creating and then delivering a presentation. Nasser is not alone in being overwhelmed by nervousness! But it's important for you to recognise the broader value of the experience, however painful it might be at the time. Presentations give you valuable experience of what is a key element of selection processes when you're looking for employment and a core feature of many professions. Use these opportunities to develop this aspect of your graduate identity. When it comes to creating presentations, there are a number of points to keep in mind. Planning is key, as is research; if the content is underdeveloped, you're unlikely to do well. Delivery is important, as are the visual aids you might use; bear in mind the importance of communicating clearly and designing effective visual aids. Remember to learn from the experience, as well; it might not have gone as well as you had planned, but how might you do it differently? Group work can also be challenging, but it's just as important with this type of activity to reflect on your experiences to improve your performance. Like presentations, group work is used by tutors to help develop those aspects of graduate identity sought after by employers. However frustrating or difficult it might be to participate in group work, try to see its value in relation to your personal development. By recognising the part played by both presentations and group work in the process of becoming a graduate, you'll be better placed to hit the ground running when you enter into your chosen profession.

Reference

Jasper, M. (2013). *Beginning reflective practice.* Cengage.

McCrae, R., & Costa, P. (1999). A five-factor theory of personality. In L. Pervin & O. John (Eds.), *Handbook of personality: Theory and research* (2nd ed.) (pp. 139–153). Guilford.

Chapter 12

Learning by doing
Practice- and work-based learning

In many disciplines, you'll be expected to engage in practice or work-based learning. Undergraduates in biosciences, for example, will be doing laboratory work; students in art and design-related disciplines will spend lots of hours each week in a studio or workshop; sport science students will be in the gym or on the sports field training. Students studying physiotherapy or podiatry will engage in clinic-based learning, while disciplines like social work and teaching incorporate placements. The purpose of this type of learning is to bridge the gap between the theoretical learning which you might do in a classroom setting and its real-world application.

The potential impact of such learning is vast. What better experience is there for a student teacher to learn about classroom management techniques than to actually work in a classroom with schoolchildren? Presentations and group work provide you with opportunities to develop competencies sought by employers in authentic but often mocked up settings. Practice- and work-based learning, on the other hand, give you the chance of developing these competencies in the environment in which you will be working as a graduate. It's important therefore that you make the most out of this type of learning, just as you should do with presentations and group work.

This chapter is about how to do just that. We'll begin by setting out the broad range of activities that sit underneath the terms practice- and work-based learning. This is followed by an explanation of the theory of experiential learning and a more detailed look at how tutors assess practice- and work-based learning. We'll then consider the importance of reflection to this mode of learning and, through an example, show you how you can apply Kolb's (1984) 'Experiential Learning Cycle'. This process of reflecting on experiences is key not only as a form of assessment, but also as a means for you to use experiential learning to support your personal development.

Learning Objectives

By the end of this chapter, you will have gained:

- an understanding of the value of practice- and work-based learning to your personal development;
- an appreciation of experiential learning and its core principles as the theoretical foundation of this mode of learning;
- an understanding of how this mode of learning is assessed;
- insights into how you can make the most out of such learning experiences.

Keywords

practice-based learning; work-based learning; experiential learning; Experiential Learning Cycle

Defining practice- and work-based learning

Practice- and work-based learning covers a broad range of activities relevant to an equally wide set of disciplines. Broadly speaking, this type of learning is focused on professional practice; it involves the application of theory or knowledge learnt in classroom settings to the way you do something, whether you're a student nurse or teacher, or you're an artist developing your craft. The learning takes place largely by reflecting on these experiences. It's only by considering what took place, the decisions you made, and how well you performed, that insights are gained into how you can improve your performance.

Given that practice- and work-based learning is integrated into so many different degree courses, it's difficult to provide a comprehensive list of all those activities involved. In the list below, we've tried to highlight the main ones. Not all of them will be relevant to your discipline.

Laboratory work

Common among STEM (science, technology, engineering, and mathematics) disciplines, laboratory work usually requires you to engage in experiments and the application of scientific methodologies with the guidance of laboratory technicians. For example, biology students might conduct guided dissections to better understand anatomical structures.

Studio/workshop-based learning

In art and design-related disciplines, students will often be based in studios or workshops where they will be expected to practise their craft with guidance from technicians. For example, students in ceramics might be based in workshops where they can produce examples of their work.

Field work

Students from a broad range of disciplines might be involved in field work, where they will be expected to work off site in real-world settings. For example, biology students might be observing animals in their natural habitats, or archaeology students might be working on a dig anywhere in the world.

Simulation-based training

Some students might be expected to work within scenarios intended to replicate real-world situations. For example, student nurses might practise patient care procedures in mocked up wards.

Project-based learning activities

This type of activity engages students in extended, real-world projects that often require the application of knowledge from several different disciplines. Such projects often involve research, problem-solving, collaboration, and presentation skills. For example, engineering students might design and then build a sustainable energy system for a local community as part of a capstone project.

Industry placements and internships

Students work directly in a professional environment for a specified period of time. The purpose of placements and internships is to gain hands-on experience relevant to their discipline and chosen profession. More and more degree courses integrate placements and internships into the learning experience. They offer students valuable opportunities to develop professional networks and to define a career path within their chosen profession. For example, marketing students might intern at an advertising agency.

Professional practice conferral

Courses which integrate traditional academic learning with practical application. Such courses often involve work-based learning which is in part designed by stakeholders from industry. Examples include courses on auditing.

Workplace observations

Opportunities for students to observe professionals working in their discipline; such experiences provide insights into daily tasks, workplace dynamics, and industry practices.

Apprenticeships

Training programmes that combine on-the-job learning with formal education. Apprenticeships typically involve a combination of paid work, classroom instruction, and mentorship. Apprenticeships are becoming increasingly attractive in the context of rising tuition fees because they allow students to earn while they work. They also provide students with a clearer career trajectory; once the apprenticeship is completed, employment often follows.

What are the benefits to you of practice or work-based learning?

The guiding principle behind practice- and work-based learning is that you learn through experience. But how are such experiences going to benefit you? What part does it play in helping you to become a graduate?

The first point to make about its purpose is that it offers authentic, real-world learning experiences which open you up to the workplace environment in which you intend to move into as a graduate. By real-world, we're referring to both simulated learning experiences, where you might be working in conditions intended to replicate an authentic setting (e.g. a mocked-up clinic with pretend patients) and learning in the workplace itself. It doesn't matter which definition of real-world is used; the benefits to you are the same. You can use examples drawn from these experiences to enhance your CV and graduate profile when it comes to apply for graduate positions. They give you something to talk about! In addition, such experiences give you a flavour of the workplace, a sense of what you will be doing on a daily basis, the routines involved, the variety of tasks, and the challenges that you might face. These might also form examples for you to use in a job selection process as evidence of your competencies and experience. Practice- and work-based learning offer opportunities for you to apply theoretical knowledge. In this way, they help to deepen your knowledge and understanding by making such theory 'real' through its application in workplace settings. There will also be opportunities for you develop individual literacies, such as communication and critical thought. This development occurs within relevant professional contexts and as such is enhanced and given greater value. Applied critical thought, for example, leads to improved decision-making skills, something that employers look for in graduates. The learning itself is structured and supported. You will almost certainly have a mentor, for example, or the support of an experienced member staff with the relevant technical knowledge, like a laboratory technician. The student-mentor relationship is a vital one if you are to make the most of practice- and work-based learning. A conscientious mentor often makes the difference between a successful and less successful learning experience. Just ask any student teacher. Beyond the student-mentor relationship, practice- and work-based learning also gives you opportunities for building professional networks of contacts which will be useful to you as you look for employment. Finally, the experiences you gain through this type of learning are also useful if you need to work towards professional recognition.

How is practice- and work-based learning assessed by tutors?

The next fundamental question is how do tutors assess what you do in practice- and work-based learning? In truth, it can be difficult for tutors to assess such learning. Workplace environments or settings inspired by the workplace are inherently complex and dynamic. The learning involved takes place within a network of professional relationships involving numerous stakeholders. Each workplace has its own culture that makes it difficult to implement standardised assessment criteria. The environment is also unpredictable with the possibility of unexpected problems impacting upon student performance. In addition, in work-based learning, where a mentor or another professional in the field is acting as an assessor (for example, in teaching), it might be difficult for a university to recruit and then adequately train and support such people. These individuals are often volunteering their time and expertise which means that there is often a high turnover among them. This only compounds the difficulties of recruiting and training these people.

In general, assessment criteria reflect the workplace environment in which the learning is taking place, including its inherent uncertainty and complexity. This requires moving beyond what can be described as reductionist approaches that attempt to break down practice into discrete, measurable skills. Instead, assessment tends to capture more sophisticated ways of knowing, doing, saying and relating that reflect the complexities of professional practice. In practice, this means that tutors often value things like decision-making and professional judgement, together with explanations of the rationale behind both.

Assessment usually revolves around reflective practice. It's by reflecting on these experiences that you gain insights into your own performance and the workplace environment in which you're working. Both sets of observations can then be used to support your personal development so that the next time you find yourself in a similar situation you can perform at a higher level. In some practice- and work-based learning, assessment includes a practical element. For example, student teachers are observed by tutors and qualified teachers. Work you do on a placement might be reviewed by a supervisor or mentor, someone who is already qualified in that profession. But reflective practice remains the most commonly used form of assessment associated with this type of learning. It also holds value as a means for you to make more sense of practice- and work-based learning experiences, regardless of whether it is used as a formal means of assessment. Reflective activities linked to this type of learning are usually underpinned by David Kolb's (1984) 'Experiential Learning Cycle'.

Experiential learning and Kolb's Experiential Learning Cycle

Experiential learning refers to the idea of learning through experience. As a concept, it embraces both practice- and work-based learning, since both ultimately rest on experiences – in the sense of the actions you take – as the currency of learning. The most well-known proponent of experiential learning is David Kolb who developed the four-stage Experiential Learning Cycle, depicted in Figure 12.1.

How do you use this cycle to draw meaning out of practice- and work-based learning experiences? Let's look at how John, our education student, uses it to structure his reflection on a recent school placement. Set out below is his reflective account organised around the four stages of Kolb's cycle.

Experiencing

Leading up to the informal observation by my mentor, I spent several days working on my lesson plan for the Year 5 class. The lesson was about ICT. Its purpose was to give the children experience of how digital technologies like Google Meet can connect people together and create digital communities. The subject chosen for discussion was linked to another subject the children were learning about: history and the Second World War. I developed the lesson plan, stating the learning objectives clearly and how I was going to meet those objectives. I decided to split up the

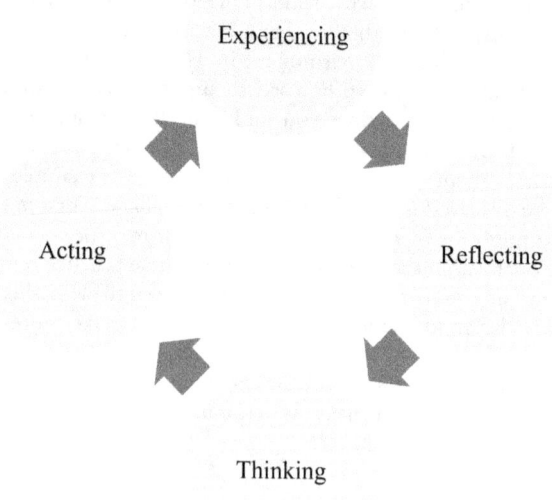

Figure 12.1 Kolb's experiential learning cycle.

class into small groups, each one based at its own table. Each group was asked to think about what questions they might like to ask a historian about life in London during the Blitz – a topic we'd looked at earlier in the week. We would then start a video call with a historian from the local university who would answer the children's questions. Each group was asked to write down what the historian said; we would then review the questions and answers together. I would then ask the children how the video call with the historian had helped us to develop our understanding of the Blitz, what were the benefits of using Google Meet and what were the drawbacks.

Reflecting

Overall, the activity worked quite well. I made the learning objectives clear to the children at the start, that we were going to use Google Meet to speak to an expert on the Second World War, but in order to make the most of our conversation, we need to think carefully about what questions we were going to ask. When I separated the children into groups, which I did randomly, there was some commotion as friendship groups were split up. Some of the children were quite excited by being mixed together and it took a few minutes longer than I had planned to get them to settle down. When it came to coming up with their questions, two of the groups set about the task very well. One group, however, didn't really make much of an effort. I attempted to video call the historian but to begin with I couldn't connect with him. Then, once I did, the connection dropped! I decided to re-boot the PC, which had the effect of losing the attention of some of the children, but once the PC had restarted I was able to restore the connection and the conversation began. The children were quiet as the historian was speaking; the sound wasn't very loud. Sometimes, the picture pixelated, which distracted some of the children. He answered all of the questions and took care to praise the children for their knowledge, which was nice. After we ended the call, we had a discussion about the answers he had given. The boys tended to be very impressed by the detail he had given about the number of planes shot down. One of the girls commented that she understood more now about why the Blitz happened. In our discussion of the video call, the children tended to focus on the technical difficulties; this led some of them to say that it wasn't very good. Others though showed some understanding of how the video call had brought them together with the historian. As a result, they now knew a lot more about the Blitz and many of them seemed to realise that this had only occurred because of the use of technology.

Thinking

When it came to separating the children into groups, I should have thought more about the make-up of each one. The group that had little to say would have benefited from having at least one of the higher achieving children in it. The decision to organise them randomly had seemed like the fairest thing to do to begin with, but I think it worked against the development of the children's understanding. There was little I could do about the technical difficulties. The internet speed isn't great at the school; perhaps I could have tried to explain to the children why the pixelating was happening. Although I wasn't surprised by the technical problems, I didn't have a plan for what I would do if anything had gone wrong. I must, in future, be ready for anything! Similarly, the sound might have been an issue for one of the children who has a hearing impairment. I didn't expect it to be so quiet; I should've tested the equipment more thoroughly first. The historian was brilliant. He had a great way of engaging the children and offered lots of praise when each question was put to him. I think this really helped to make the experience a success. If he had been cold towards the children or not really given sufficiently detailed answers, the experience would have suffered. The children's knowledge of life in London during the Blitz was clearly enhanced by the video call. I think it was a good idea to get the children to write down the answers because by doing so the new knowledge stuck. The children also recognised how the video call had helped to develop their knowledge. Despite the technical problems, the benefits of digital communication and the opportunities to establishing digital communities were clear.

Acting

The next time I design a similar lesson I will put more thought into creating the groups. There needs to be at least one group member who can take the lead in coming up with questions and encouraging others to focus on the task. I would test the technology, more than I did, to ensure that technical problems are kept to a minimum. I might also make sure that transcription is turned on so that all the children can easily follow the conversation. The technical problems highlighted to me the importance of making arrangements in case technology fails. You always need a back-up plan. The impact of the historian's contribution to the lesson highlights the importance of selecting the right contributor. I would make sure in future that I find someone as good as the historian we used. Although the discussion went well, in future, I will set a small number of questions in advance to direct the children's responses. I was a bit too laid back about this part of the lesson. It might have been more effective had I done that.

What does this example tell us about how to use Kolb's cycle to structure reflection on experiences? In keeping with the principles of reflective writing, Kolb's cycle gives John a structure to organise his thoughts. In the first stage, 'experiencing', John sets out the experience, beginning with his preparation for the lesson. In the second stage, 'reflecting', he considers what happened and why. For example, he notes that one group weren't as good at coming up with the questions as the others. In the third, 'thinking', he assesses what he might have done differently to improve his performance in the experience. In the fourth and final stage, 'acting', John sets out clearly the actions he would take in order to apply what he has learnt the next time he engages in a similar experience.

By using Kolb's cycle, John has gained greater understanding of the experience as well as insights into what didn't go to plan. He can then use this understanding and these insights to learn more about himself and to shape his approach to any similar tasks he might undertake in the future. It's in this way that practice- and work-based learning holds value to you, as a student, as you seek to become a graduate. You will learn more about yourself and how you might work effectively in your chosen profession through these learning experiences than you would if you hadn't been exposed to the workplace environment.

Getting the most out of practice- and work-based learning

John's lesson on digital communities and the Blitz points to some of the ways you can maximise the value of practice- and work-based learning experiences to you and your personal development.

1. Immerse yourself in the experience. If these experiences are going to be useful to you, there's no other way! Engage fully in all aspects of it.
2. Approach the experience as a professional. Adopt the conduct of someone who is already qualified in that profession. John is working as a teacher, even though he is still a student; he's doing all that he would be expected to do as a teacher in relation to lesson planning and teaching.
3. Exploit the experience of those around you, particularly your mentor. If you're in the workplace, make the most out of the contacts you make. The mentor is particularly important if you have one; use their guidance to shape your approach to tasks. Other colleagues might also be able to offer words of advice. Actively cultivate these relationships; they hold value to the practice or work-based learning you're doing, as well as to your future employment in the profession.
4. Test theoretical knowledge by putting it into practice. The testing of such knowledge and any reflection you do on its application will provide invaluable insights which will not only help to develop your expertise but will also give you examples to discuss in job interviews.
5. Adopt a reflective mindset when taking part in practice- and work-based learning. Reflection might form part of the assessment for such learning, but reflective practice holds greater value beyond the immediate requirements of assessment. Always reflect on what you've done in order to better understand the experience and how you might improve your performance in future.

Summary

Practice- and work-based learning has become an important part of the learning experience in higher education as more tutors seek to develop links with industry and professional practice. The experience of learning in this way can be daunting for new or less experienced students because it is very different from other modes of learning on your course and in which you might have engaged before coming to university. It's important to appreciate the value of these experiences, however unusual they might seem. Opportunities to learn in the context of the profession into which you intend to move hold special importance since they allow you to develop your competencies in authentic settings. Learning of this type is about experience; reflecting on these experiences using Kolb's 'Experiential Learning Cycle' will reveal many new insights about yourself and your ability to work effectively in professional contexts. Always take the time to reflect on such experiences, even if only informally; doing so will help to support your personal development and shape the graduate identity you're trying to form.

Reference

Kolb, D. (1984). *Experiential learning: Experience as the source of learning and development.* Prentice Hall.

Chapter 13

Revision and exam strategies

Another form of assessment which many of you will experience on your learning journey are exams. Exams provide opportunities for showcasing the depth of your disciplinary knowledge and understanding, as well as your ability to engage critically with the relevant discourse, within a formal assessment structure.

For many students, exams cause a great deal of anxiety. Yet preparing for an exam and then sitting it constitute important learning experiences that can act as catalysts in improving academic performance and enhancing personal development. An effective revision strategy creates pathways to academic success. Implementing some of the revision techniques set out in this chapter can therefore have a very positive effect on your chances of excelling.

This chapter will explore revision strategy and techniques for heightening its effectiveness. The emphasis will be on active learning, activities that help you to develop deeper levels of knowledge and understanding. We're also going to discuss exam anxiety and different ways of offsetting the stress induced by the exam experience. Strategic use of effective revision techniques transforms the potentially challenging experiences represented by exams into pathways for meaningful academic and personal development.

Learning Objectives

By the end of this chapter, you will have gained:

- an understanding of the importance of seeing exams as learning tools designed to support academic and personal development, rather than as obstacles to excelling;
- an awareness of the different forms of exams used in higher education;

- an appreciation of why you might feel anxious in the build-up to an exam;
- an awareness of the techniques available for alleviating that anxiety;
- an understanding of the role of active learning principles in shaping an effective revision strategy;
- insights into effective exam strategy.

Keywords

cognitive resilience; revision strategy; active learning; active revision techniques; time management; targeted revision; exam strategy

The purpose of exams

From a tutor's perspective, exams are tools of assessment used to benchmark academic achievement. They tend to test similar criteria as other forms of assessment: the depth of knowledge and understanding, for example, evidence of your ability to critique relevant discourse, the clarity of your communication – and so on. However, expectations are slightly different with exams because of the conditions in which they're taken; for example, you won't be expected to include in-text references. For the tutor, exams are a leveller, in that they allow the tutor to review student performance at the level of the cohort (i.e. all of the students taking the module), with all students undertaking the assessment at the same time and in the same conditions. They also provide insights into the performance of individual students. These insights, when considered next to observations made on performance in other types of assessment, help to build up a picture of a student's academic progress; any feedback provided can therefore support that student's personal development. For you, as a student, exams allow you to measure your own progress against the objectives you've set for yourself; you can also use your performance in exams to assess your progress against that of your fellow students. Like any other form of assessment, you can use the experience of preparing for and taking an exam as a means of supporting your personal development. By reviewing your performance – and any feedback provided by the tutor – you can identify aspects of your academic literacy that require further development. It should also be noted that exams, as a form of assessment, also provide an effective means of testing professional capabilities like time management. Revising within a limited time span and then writing an answer to an assessment question in exam conditions is challenging for lots of students. As such, exams provide a unique experience of working effectively in time-sensitive conditions.

Exams take different forms, depending on the discipline in which you're studying, your year of study, and the intended learning outcomes of the relevant module. You might meet more than one form of exam on your course.

As with the different genres of writing, if more than one form of exam is used, it's important for you to develop the agility to meet the different expectations associated with each one. There is an emphasis, for example, within multiple-choice question exams (MCQs) on the recall of disciplinary knowledge, whereas in essay question exams, there is a greater need to demonstrate an ability to build an argument and engage critically with disciplinary knowledge and discourse. The different forms of exams you might meet include:

Essay question exams

Essay question exams are perhaps the most challenging, since they require an argument and critical engagement with knowledge and discourse. You must evidence an ability to construct a coherent argument under time pressure. This requires quick analysis of complex questions, effective planning of an answer and the development of a clear line of argument. You will need to engage with different interpretations as well as disciplinary knowledge, and your writing will need to be clear and precise, just as it would be in an essay written outside exam conditions.

Multiple-choice question exams

When taking MCQs, it's important to recognise that these exams aren't just about picking the right answer. You must interpret the questions correctly and understand the subtle differences between possible answers. This requires you to evaluate each answer and select the correct one. By doing so, you demonstrate disciplinary knowledge and understanding.

Open book exams

An open book exam can represent a complex challenge that goes beyond straightforward recall of knowledge. You must effectively manage all of the knowledge available to you if you are to make effective use of different academic sources efficiently during the exam. There's a greater emphasis here on finding a way to organise and access relevant knowledge effectively. It's essential to understand that these exams are testing your capacity to synthesise and apply knowledge under time constraints rather than just recall it. The challenge lies in demonstrating your ability to evaluate academic sources critically while creating a coherent and analytical answer.

Short answer exams

Short answer formats require you to distil complex themes and ideas into clear and succinct answers. You need to write effectively in order to present key ideas with maximum efficiency. You should aim to develop your ability to balance detailed knowledge with concise written expression.

Technical exams

Technical exams require you to demonstrate both an understanding of procedure and conceptual understanding. Your aim should be to develop your skills in applying systematic approaches to problems by demonstrating your ability to recognise and apply appropriate methodological frameworks. The process necessitates paying attention to underlying theoretical concepts, applying precise analyses of methods and techniques, most often in the context of problem-solving. Excelling in technical exams requires you to demonstrate not only technical accuracy but also the ability to present solutions with academic rigour and practical precision.

What form do the exams used on your course take? If you don't know, check in the module handbook. What do the descriptions set out above of each form reveal about how you might prepare for your exams?

Exam anxiety

The elephant in the room when discussing exams is the anxiety many students feel at the prospect of taking on such a challenge. We've already mentioned how important it is to see exams as learning tools and opportunities for supporting your personal development. You might have already decided to view exams in that way, but that doesn't mean you won't feel at least some anxiety in the build up to an exam. At its worst, exam anxiety can have a paralysing effect; yet there are techniques for minimising any stress you might feel, beginning with the way you plan and conduct your revision.

Before we look at these techniques, let's consider the example of Natalie, who is very anxious about an upcoming exam. Read the scenario below; what causes her anxiety?

> *Natalie has given herself a week to revise for her first exam. She was meant to start her revision on Saturday, but she went away for the weekend. This means she doesn't start until Sunday evening when the library is closed. She doesn't know where to start. She missed a special session put on by the tutor last week on exam preparation. One of her friends has suggested looking at past exam papers to see what sort of topics come up, but Natalie doesn't know where to find them. She looks in the module handbook and makes a list of all the lecture topics. She missed some of these lectures, but most of the topics are covered in the course textbook. However, she hasn't been able to get a print copy of the textbook because they're all on loan, but she can read the digital version online. She navigates to it through the library's discovery service and begins to read the first chapter relating to the lecture topics. She realises it's going to take time; the textbook is three hundred and fifty pages long! She starts to read, hoping that it'll give her enough information to use in the exam.*

Natalie's anxiety can be attributed to a number of factors. First, she hasn't given herself long enough to revise for the exam; she's even shortened this time period by going away for the weekend! She has no revision strategy in place. Attending the special session put on by the tutor might have helped, but it's been and gone now. She gives up looking at past exam papers even before she's started because she doesn't know where to find them. This means that she can't target her revision properly on the likely topics that will come up. Instead, she simply makes a list of the lecture topics and then tries to use this list to inform her reading of the textbook. But this is all very ineffective because she begins reading what is a lengthy book at page one! To sum up, Natalie lacks a revision strategy. She hasn't thought about it enough and so her chances of excelling are limited at best.

Alleviating exam anxiety is about putting into place a revision strategy that gives you enough time to deepen your disciplinary knowledge and understanding, and, at the same time, boost your confidence about your chances of excelling. Such a strategy is based on (i) your use of time and (ii) your ability to identify gaps in your knowledge and understanding. You clearly need to give yourself enough time to revise properly. Using these elements as its foundation, building an effective revision strategy will minimise the stress you'll inevitably feel as you prepare for exams.

Developing an effective revision strategy

An effective revision strategy is built upon these two elements: (i) your use of time and (ii) your ability to identify gaps in your knowledge and understanding. The process underpinning its development can be broken down into five main stages. Let's look at each one in turn.

1   How much time is available?
    The first stage in devising the strategy is to identify how much time is available. In the example above, Natalie allowed for one week to prepare for her exam. This isn't to say that she only had one week available; rather, she thought that one week would give her enough time to do her revision. Natalie was being naïve and unrealistic. It takes longer than a week for most students to prepare thoroughly for an exam in part because most students have more than one exam to prepare for! Plot your exams in a calendar and then review how much time you have before and during the exam session. In addition, consider how many exams you have. How much time will you need to prepare for each one? Is one exam likely to be more challenging than another. Do you therefore need to allocate more time to that one than to others? Above all, be realistic in allocating time for revision. Revising is not

something you can do twelve hours per day. Try to figure out when you are likely to be more engaged in your revision. Is it the morning, afternoon or evening? Will you be fitting in your revision around other commitments, like a job? How many hours can you realistically devote to revision?

2 Where are the gaps in your knowledge and understanding?

Once you've established how much time is available, it's important for you to reflect upon the depth of your knowledge and understanding relevant to each exam you have coming up. This might involve reminding yourself of lecture and tutorial topics; you might also be able to identify which topics are likely to come up in an exam by looking at the past papers, often held in the library. Which topics do you feel less confident about? Once you've identified these problem topics, you'll be able to target your revision on those areas. This will help to make the most of the time available. Rather than spending time reading about a topic you already know pretty well, devote that time to building up your knowledge and understanding of these gaps. This is a really important stage in the process since it focuses your efforts and in doing so determines how effective your revision will be.

3 How much time should you allocate to each revision area?

Now that you've built up a picture of your knowledge and understanding relevant to each exam you've got coming up, you can make informed decisions about how much revision time to allocate to each exam. Logically, if you've got more gaps relating to one exam, you need to allocate more time to revision for that one; equally, if the topics for another exam are more difficult to get to grips with, spend more time preparing for it. Try to allocate shorter periods of time for more intensive revision sessions. For example, rather than blocking off three hours one morning to revise for one paper, break it down into smaller chunks and make sure you take breaks between each one. Set clear objectives for each one and be sure to review your progress against them. If you need to allocate more time, consider how you might do it without undermining your revision preparation for other exams.

4 What techniques will you use for each revision area?

You can use a variety of active revision techniques – discussed in more detail below – to help to develop your knowledge and deepen your understanding. These techniques allow you to test yourself; in this way, you can evaluate the effectiveness of your revision strategy and amend it if necessary. For example, you might find it useful to summarise knowledge of a particular theory by creating a poster. In order to create this poster, you'll need to process the relevant knowledge and understanding; in this way, active revision techniques help to ensure that you retain knowledge and that you develop an understanding of it.

5 How will you monitor the effectiveness of your revision strategy? It's important that you constantly monitor the effectiveness of your revision strategy. You can do this by testing yourself using active revision techniques, as we've just noted. But it's also important to consider whether you've allocated enough time, whether you've uncovered any more gaps in your knowledge and understanding, and how well you are managing the pressures associated with exams and revision. The ability to stay focused on objectives whilst managing these pressures is called *cognitive resilience. Monitoring the effectiveness of your revision strategy is essential if you are to sustain your cognitive resilience.

Task: Developing your own revision strategy

> Using this five-stage process, develop your own revision strategy. Working with a friend, discuss your responses to the questions linked to each stage of the process set out above. Use your answers to shape your own strategy. It's best to have a go at this task as you prepare for an exam.

Active learning and revision strategy

The ineffectiveness of Natalie's approach to revision lies not only in her disorganisation; it's also a function of the passivity of it. Her attempt to deepen her knowledge and understanding of the course content, for example, involved reading a textbook from beginning to end. Whilst she might pick up some useful knowledge doing this, it's unlikely that it will develop her understanding of the topics because it is such a passive experience. Adopting an approach based on *active learning principles would have the opposite effect. Making use of what she's reading by, for example, self-testing, would help to ensure that the knowledge she picks up sticks and that she gains deeper levels of understanding. Active learning, when applied in the context of revision, holds the key to successful preparation for an exam; try to enrich the revision strategy you started to design in the task above by using some of the techniques we discuss in this section.

Let's consider the example of Jess. She uses a revision strategy based on active learning. Consider her approach next to Natalie's; how is it different?

> Jess has set aside sixty hours over the next two weeks to revise for the upcoming exam. She's identified aspects of her knowledge and understanding which she feels need further development. She intends to target her revision on these areas; most of these sixty hours will be devoted to filling in these gaps. She uses the library's discovery service to find academic sources

related to these topics. Most of these sources are textbooks; some of them were included in the module's recommended reading. She allocates a set number of hours to each topic. Any reading she does is complemented by tasks in which she is expected to reproduce this knowledge. She uses a variety of techniques: she recreates theories in diagram form; she sets herself test questions on another topic; she designs A4 posters in which she arranges relevant knowledge; she even records herself on her phone explaining certain theories. As a result of using these techniques, she feels more confident about the level of her knowledge; she is also surprised by how clearly she can explain some of the concepts involved. She goes into the exam feeling well-prepared.

The most striking feature of Jess' approach is her active engagement with the learning and the creativity she uses in designing different ways of testing herself. Whereas Natalie relied on reading, without putting herself under any pressure to recreate or even recall relevant knowledge, Jess takes the time to ensure that any passive learning exercise, like reading, is accompanied by another revision technique which requires her to apply that knowledge in some way. She sets out theories in diagrammatic form. She designs information posters where she can summarise key bits of knowledge. She explains theories aloud by recording herself on her phone. By forcing herself to test her own knowledge, all of these techniques help to deepen her understanding. The variety of techniques she uses is also significant: some are visual, some are auditory. The fact that she switches between different techniques helps to maintain her cognitive resilience.

The challenge is to turn a passive revision strategy into an active one. You might, at the moment, be used to revising by reading textbooks and reviewing lecture notes. How might you turn what is likely to be a rather monotonous and uninspiring exercise into one that deepens your knowledge and understanding? Use active revision techniques. These techniques fall into three categories, as indicated in Figure 13.1.

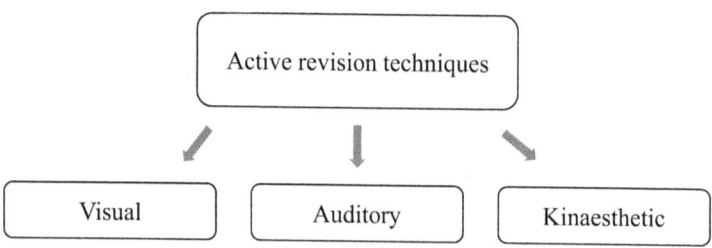

Figure 13.1 Active revision techniques.

Visual

Visual learning techniques incorporate imagery, lettering, colour, pattern and spatial understanding. Examples include:

Mind mapping

Mind mapping involves setting out processes and structures of disciplinary knowledge and understanding through visual representation. It makes it easier to recognise links between key bits of knowledge; in this way, it develops understanding. Mind mapping is designed to let you build on what you already know. Placing a central idea at the core and developing branching subtopics creates clear visual pathways between related elements of knowledge. This approach supports deeper understanding of complex subject matter. Visual elements enhance the effectiveness of mind mapping. Using colours, images and keywords differentiates between concepts, creating distinctive memory triggers that strengthen recall during exams. Connecting elements with arrows or coloured lines highlights relationships within the topic area. The process allows for deeper understanding of how concepts interact and influence each other. For visual learners, this method provides reliable frameworks for accessing information during assessments.

Visual note-taking

Transforming written notes into visual formats not only enhances your ability to retain knowledge; it also helps you to develop a deeper understanding of complex ideas. Different visual formats align with distinct types of information, enabling you to use tables, flowcharts, diagrams and timelines effectively. By experimenting with different approaches, you can develop personalised systems for organising complex knowledge structures. Making use of icons and symbols might also help to trigger the recall of knowledge in exams. Creative use of colours and patterns can work in the same way, while the use of arrows helps to illustrate conceptual relationships. Creating visual notes using digital tools extends the possibilities for making use of coloured icons and symbols.

Flashcards

Flashcards help to create powerful visual associations that can act as recall triggers during exams. Using both sides of a flashcard allows you to pose questions on one side while providing corresponding answers on the reverse. While creating physical flashcards remains valuable, digital flashcards can also be created which have the advantage of being easily available on a phone or other device. This format is especially valuable for memorising diagrams illustrating specific structures, processes or conceptual relationships within your study areas. Flashcards work particularly well when integrated with other learning techniques. For example, verbally describing content while studying cards in different physical locations creates multi-sensory memory associations. Placing challenging concept cards in specific rooms enables repeated testing opportunities, embedding recall triggers through combined visual, verbal and spatial learning pathways.

Visual mnemonics and acronyms

Creating memorable images and symbols representing key academic content can aid knowledge recall in exams. Acronyms can provide structured frameworks for organising visual memory systems. Associating letters with both concepts and memorable images creates multi-layered memory triggers. Incorporating colour-coding and striking imagery strengthens these frameworks, while upward eye movements aid recall through multi-sensory engagement.

Posters and infographics

Posters and infographics translate complex disciplinary knowledge into accessible visual representations. Such images can help to retain knowledge and deepen understanding. Posters also allow you to synthesise key bits of disciplinary knowledge. Careful placing of posters and infographics in your study environment helps to ensure that you see their content repeatedly. This visual reinforcement strengthens your ability to recall and apply complex disciplinary knowledge in exams, while supporting both immediate learning needs and longer-term academic development.

Auditory

Auditory learning approaches draw on listening and speaking as ways of engaging with disciplinary knowledge. Examples include:

Reading loud

Reading aloud is an effective strategy for reinforcing memory and deepening your understanding of key concepts. Articulating knowledge verbally helps you to process information while, at the same time, helping you to recall it in exams. It also helps to refine your use of discipline-specific vocabulary. In this way, reading aloud supports revision as well as your longer-term academic development.

Audio recordings

Audio recordings allow you to revise during otherwise unproductive time. Listening to recordings during commutes or relaxation periods allows you to strengthen your grasp of essential knowledge through repeated exposure. Use of audio recordings provides valuable opportunities for consolidating knowledge and understanding outside formal study periods. By integrating auditory approaches into your learning strategy, you develop additional means of reinforcing knowledge.

Discussion groups

Interacting with other students through structured discussion strengthens your grasp of complex ideas. Teaching concepts to others and engaging in academic dialogue helps you to process disciplinary knowledge. A collaborative approach also helps to develop your critical thinking.

Kinaesthetic

Kinaesthetic techniques use physical movement and tactile sensations to enhance learning and memory retention. More specifically, these approaches are particularly effective within practice-based disciplines requiring specific process-oriented competencies. Such approaches enable you to develop deeper understanding of an experience through active engagement with disciplinary practices. Use of kinaesthetic techniques allows you to develop procedural knowledge during revision. As such, integrating such techniques into your learning strategy supports both knowledge recall and longer-term academic development.

Spatial placing

Physical locations provide powerful frameworks for developing memory associations. By connecting academic content with specific places in your environment, you create recall triggers that support knowledge retention during exams. Regular engagement with these locations through daily routines and activities help to sustain knowledge retention.

Role-playing

Acting out academic scenarios allows for deeper engagement with complex disciplinary knowledge. Physical enactment often draws upon auditory techniques and can help to develop a richer understanding of a topic whilst creating memorable learning experiences. This approach transforms abstract theoretical ideas into tangible explorations and expressions that can enhance recall during examinations.

Physical movement

Physical movement during revision sessions provides effective means of enhancing cognitive resilience. More specifically, activities like walking enable you to engage both mind and body, optimising your ability to process and retain disciplinary knowledge. Physical activity promotes mental clarity and creative thinking. By incorporating movement into your learning routine, you can develop enhanced capacity for synthesising complex ideas and integrating new knowledge with existing understanding. Movement between different study environments also offers valuable opportunities for maintaining focus and motivation, offering further 'hooks' with the learning materials. Outdoor revision sessions provide refreshing perspectives while breaking up extended periods of desk-based study offering both immediate learning and longer-term retention of knowledge.

Interactive models

Physical objects and models can transform abstract concepts into tangible learning experiences. Direct manipulation of models strengthens understanding through multi-sensory engagement. This hands-on approach accommodates diverse learning preferences while building practical comprehension. By integrating multiple physical approaches into your revision strategy, you develop strong frameworks for accessing academic knowledge. These techniques enhance both immediate recall and long-term retention during examination conditions.

Task: Using active revision techniques

> The challenge, as we've said, is to turn passive revision activities into active ones. You can do this by implementing some of the techniques outlined above.
>
> Working with a friend, reflect on any revision you've done recently – it doesn't have to be at university; you can use experiences from school or college, for example, or the workplace. Discuss the way you revised with your friend. Were your revision activities passive or active? For those that were passive, which techniques in the list above might you use to turn them into active ones? Justify your selection. If you've been using active techniques already, how successful were they? Could you use any of the above techniques instead to improve the effectiveness of your revision? Your answers to these questions will reflect what type of learning appeals to you: visual, auditory or kinaesthetic. It's likely that techniques from all three categories will appeal to you.

> Once you've identified which active learning techniques you're going to use, apply them. Meet up with you friend again to review their effectiveness after you've tried each one. If one or more were less successful, which techniques will you try next?

Exam strategy

You've done your revision and you feel fairly well prepared for the exam itself. How do you go about working effectively in the exam? Let's consider the contrasting examples of Natalie and Jess to better understand how to maximise your performance in exam conditions.

Natalie arrives at the exam hall just in time. She checks her name on the list outside the venue to find out what seat number she is in and then bursts into the hall to find her desk. Most of the more than five hundred students taking exams that day are already in their seats. Natalie is embarrassed walking to her desk as the senior invigilator reads out the regulations. She takes her seat and panics when she realises that she's only brought one working pen with her. She writes her name on the answer booklet but leaves out her student number because she's forgotten it. The invigilator announces the start of the exam; she turns over her question paper and very quickly scans the questions. She recognises a keyword from her textbook in question four and immediately sets out to answer that question. She's in a rush – she hates being in the exam hall; the quicker she can finish, the better – and so she writes down as much as she knows about that topic in her answer book. This takes her more than an hour of the two-hour time limit. She then tries to answer question six. She doesn't really understand the question, but she writes out as much as she knows about what she thinks the question is addressing before she has to stop when the invigilator announces the end of the session.

Natalie gets a lot of things wrong in her approach to this exam. She arrives just in time, which immediately heightens her anxiety; note that she is embarrassed when she walks to her desk in front of all the other students who are already settled. The fact that she's only got one working pen provides her with another worry at the outset which also distracts her. She doesn't read the questions properly. She recognises a keyword and then falls into the trap of simply writing out all that she knows in relation to that term. There is no discrimination here; she is almost certainly only providing a descriptive response which doesn't effectively address the question. She spends too long on this first answer – more than half of the duration of the exam – which leaves her with less time to answer the second question. She adopts a similar approach to this one but is almost certainly less successful. In this case, she doesn't understand the question, which makes it highly unlikely that she'll be able to answer it properly. She is stopped before she has had time to finish. Natalie's exam strategy – if it can be called that – is chaotic. A more organised and thoughtful approach is needed. Let's look at how Jess approaches the same exam.

> *Jess arrives in good time and sits outside the venue reading through some reminders she's made for herself. After a few minutes, she sees one of her friends, and they have a quick catch-up which helps to put Jess at ease. She is one of the first students to enter the hall. She finds her desk number on the board and walks to the desk. She lays out her pens, pencil and ruler; she puts a bottle of water on the desk as well, and some mints which she hopes will help her to concentrate. She fills out the front of her answer booklet and carefully reads through the instructions on the exam paper. It clearly states that she needs to answer one question from section A and one from section B. This means that, in a two-hour exam, she should aim to spend one hour on each answer. She makes a note of the timings on the front of her question paper. By 10am, she needs to have moved on to the second answer. She allows ten minutes within each hour for thinking and planning. She doesn't intend to make detailed plans, but it will help to set down the key points in a brief list, so that she knows what she is going to argue. The senior invigilator begins the exam and Jess checks the time before beginning her plan. At 9.10 am, she stops and begins to write. Just before 10am, she moves on to the second question. She spends ten minutes planning that essay; at 10.10, she starts writing. As the exam comes to an end, she realises that she isn't going to be able to finish. She summarises her final point before offering a brief conclusion which reiterates her argument. She finishes it just as the senior invigilator calls for everyone to stop. She is pleased with her efforts.*

Jess' approach is clearly all that Natalie's isn't. She is organised – she arrives early, spends some time reviewing some reminders, and then takes the opportunity calm herself down by having a chat with her friend. She finds her desk quickly and sets out all that she needs. She reads through the instructions on the front of the exam paper – a valuable exercise which reminds her that she needs to answer one question from each section – and plans her time accordingly. She then keeps an eye on the clock as she creates a plan for the first answer before writing it out. She moves on to the second and does the same. She is flexible enough to recognise that she needs to wrap up her answer so that she finishes it within the two-hour time period. She does this and then leaves the venue satisfied that she has done her best. Jess' approach is more considered. She is better prepared and more confident, as reflected in the ease with which she completes the second answer with time against her.

What do these scenarios tell us about exam strategy?

1 Avoid adding to the anxiety you already feel. Give yourself enough time to arrive at the venue early so that you don't put yourself under any more pressure.
2 Bring all that you need with you; if drinks or sweets will help to keep you calm, take some with you.
3 Use the time before the start of the exam to read the instructions on the front of the exam paper and complete any administrative requirements (e.g. adding your details to the front of answer booklets).
4 Allocate enough time for each part of the exam paper; include time for basic planning and consideration of each question.
5 Keep an eye on the clock at all times; take a watch with you.
6 Write to time – avoid spending too long on one answer; be disciplined enough to finish an answer even if it's not quite as developed as you would like.

Summary

Most of you will encounter exams at some point in your learning journey. It's important for you to see exams as learning tools, just as we've said in relation to assessment tasks more broadly. They are not obstacles to excelling; they are valuable opportunities for you to learn more about your progress and yourself, and in this sense contribute to your personal development as you seek to become a graduate. That said, exams quite naturally make most of us nervous. Do your best to offset this anxiety by adopting an organised and methodical approach to revision. The aim of a revision strategy is to deepen your knowledge and understanding. In practice, you need to manage time effectively and target revision sessions on gaps or weaknesses in your knowledge and understanding. Use active revision techniques rather than passive ones. These techniques are proven to aid knowledge recall in exams; they will also help to develop your understanding far more than passive and uninspired revision activities. Once the day of your exam arrives, make decisions that will alleviate anxiety and stress. Your objective should be to stay calm. Read the instructions on your exam paper carefully and – once again – manage your time effectively during the exam. Don't lose sight of the obvious: take several pens into the venue with you and always wear a watch!

Chapter 14

Conclusion

Becoming a graduate

This book is about excelling at university: what you need to do in order to exceed your own expectations about what you can achieve while studying in higher education. In the process of exploring what excelling means in practice, we've set out guidance on your approach to learning and we've provided a fresh perspective on what we call the literacies associated with successful academic practice. Excelling is about these things: working as a self-regulating learner and conceiving of what are traditionally labelled 'study skills' as literacies which hold a broader relevance beyond the academic work you do on your course to that overriding objective of becoming a graduate.

To conclude this book, it's worth reminding you of the importance of these two related concepts to your ability to excel. Self-regulated learning, as an approach towards the learning on your course, is vital if you're going to excel. We talked, in Chapter 2, about the role of goal setting, motivation, and mindset in your approach to learning; self-regulated learning is built upon these elements, together with the need to monitor your performance and personal development through reflective practice. This approach doesn't come easily to all students; some learners struggle to realise that it is up to them to take responsibility for their learning rather than the tutor largely because at school or college they haven't had to think that way. The sooner you make this transition into learning at university, by recognising that you, and you alone, are responsible for your learning and personal development, the greater your chances of excelling. Become a self-regulating learner first and then you'll find it easier to become a graduate.

The second of these concepts concerns the literacies we've discussed. We conceive of them as something more than 'study skills'. If you're going to develop your competency in relation to each one, you need to understand how to write for assessment, for example; but you also need to understand tutors' expectations in respect of this literacy and why it's important to develop it, not just in the context of your learning, but also, looking beyond university, to the process of developing your graduate identity. In other words, you need to recognise the broader value of each literacy and what part it plays in making you a highly employable graduate. We've tried to

DOI: 10.4324/9781003217527-14

emphasise this point in our discussions of each of these literacies, but it's easier to do in relation to some of these literacies. Presentations and group work (Chapter 11) and practice and work-based learning (Chapter 12) are directly related to experiences you might expect to have in the workplace, but this isn't to say that some literacies are more important or relevant than others. The challenge for you, as a student, throughout this book, has been to recognise how each literacy relates to that process of becoming a graduate, and to your graduate identity. Writing for assessment, for example, in the context of the learning on your course, is about understanding tutors' expectations when it comes to writing, as reflected in marking criteria, and how your writing is shaped by disciplinary conventions. In relation to your graduate identity, the literacy of writing for assessment is more about developing an awareness of and an ability to write across genres and meet different expectations. It's about the mental agility required to do that, something that is valued highly by employers.

It's with this in mind that we turn to the final section of this book, which is about how to relate the literacies we discussed and the experiences of practising each one to your growing sense of graduate identity. To do this, we want to look at Michael Tomlinson's (2017) work on *graduate capital as a means of helping you better understand this process. For Tomlinson, as for us, graduate 'capital' – in the sense of 'resources' – is about more than the acquisition of disciplinary knowledge or the learning of specific ways of doing things (e.g., how to search using the library's discovery service). In addition to these elements, graduate capital is also built out of social and cultural awareness, self-identity, and your psychological make-up. You develop your graduate capital in part by engaging in your course but also by recognising the value of the literacies you're practising and the learning experiences you have to your graduate identity.

Tomlinson's (2017) ideas have informed the creation of a framework for helping you to make sense of your own graduate employability. He conceived of a set of interrelated forms of capital which together underpin your graduate employability: human, social, cultural, identity, and psychological (as set out in Figure 14.1).

Human

Human capital sits at the core of Tomlinson's framework; it includes the knowledge and competencies acquired through formal education which allow you to apply discipline-specific theory and transferable skills in professional contexts. It's also about the literacies we've been discussing in this book which employers look for in graduates: the ability to think critically, problem-solve, communicate, and conduct research. Graduates who are able to demonstrate an understanding of the relevance of these literacies to the workplace will boost their employability.

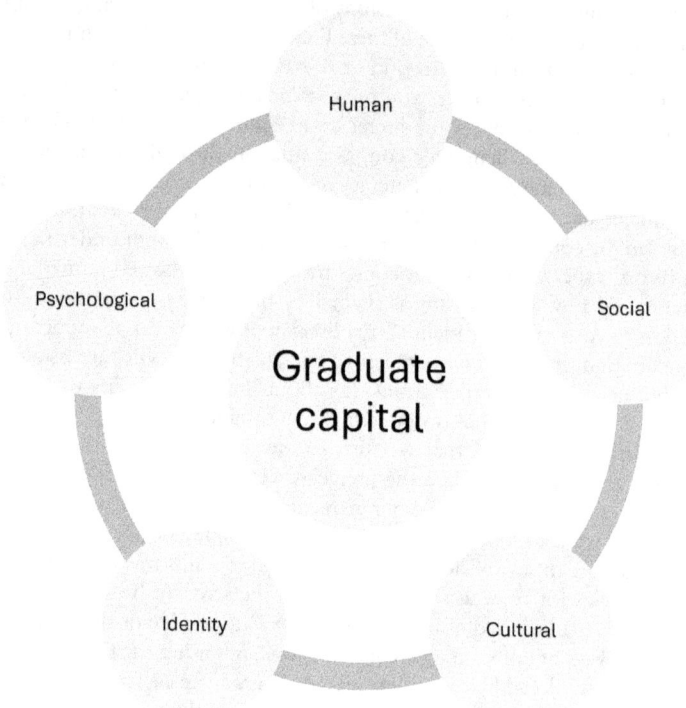

Figure 14.1 Tomlinson's graduate capital framework.

Social

Social capital refers to the relationships and networks you cultivate with peers, tutors, and industry professionals (perhaps via work-based learning). Such connections provide access to employment opportunities, guidance via mentorship, and pathways to employment. These connections aren't necessarily cultivated in person; it's more likely that you will develop them through social media networking platforms liked LinkedIn. To enhance your employability, it's worth building up your online presence.

Cultural

Cultural capital is something that you might pick up and develop through work-based learning. It's about your awareness of the way the culture associated with your chosen profession works; the culture within companies or organisations, expected behaviour, the way professionals communicate – and so on. Graduates with cultural capital are usually very successful at presenting themselves, building rapport with others, and working effectively in teams. You might develop cultural capital by working as an intern or by volunteering; such experiences help to broaden your understanding of the work environment.

Identity

Identity capital is about your self-identity as a professional. A graduate with strong identity capital has a clear understanding of the value of their personal experiences to their career aspirations. As a result, these graduates have more clearly defined goals and are better placed to articulate their potential value to employers. To develop your identity capital, reflect on your experiences (as you should have been doing throughout your degree course), identify transferable skills, and present yourself in a compelling way through your CV/resume and any covering letters you have to write.

Psychological

Psychological capital is about your mental capacity: your resilience in the context of change, for example, your adaptability and emotional intelligence – and so on. Graduates with strong psychological capital are more likely to overcome obstacles and disappointment in the workplace. To develop it, cultivate your self-awareness, develop mechanisms for coping with pressure, and seek support from mentors or colleagues.

Task: Assessing your employability through your graduate capital

> In light of Tomlinson's framework, how would you assess your graduate employability? To do this, you need to consider your graduate capital. How strong is your capital in each of the five areas? You can answer this question by considering the questions underneath each one in the list below.
>
> #### Human
>
> - How do the literacies we've discussed in this book relate to practice in your chosen profession?
> - Which are the most significant literacies?
> - Where do your strengths lie? Which literacies do you need to develop further?

- Can you identify any examples which can evidence your answers to the previous question? How might you explain these examples to a potential employer in a way that draws out their significance to professional practice?

Social

- What links do you have with professionals in your field?
- Are you able to tap into a professional network as a means of supporting your attempts to find graduate employment?
- If you did any practice or work-based learning as part of your course, how did you use these experiences to build up your social capital?

Cultural

- What have you learnt about the culture associated with your chosen profession? Did this learning come about as a result of practice or work-based learning experiences?
- How confident do you feel about presenting yourself as a graduate in your chosen profession?
- How confident do you feel about engaging with colleagues in your profession? Do you have a sense of what behaviours are expected?

Identity

- Do you have clearly defined career goals?
- How might you express your potential value to an employer? What experiences and competencies would you highlight as evidence of this value?
- How can you enhance the impact of your CV/resume on a potential employer?

Psychological

- What are your defining psychological characteristics? Are you determined, highly motivated, flexible, and resilient?
- What examples can you find to support your identification of these characteristics?
- Which of your characteristics might an employer value – and why?

You might like to discuss these questions and your answers with a friend. Once you've done that, the next step is to identify how you might develop your capital in each area. For example, building social capital might involve developing an online presence via LinkedIn. Adding to your identity capital might require you to think more carefully about your career aspirations. Again, you can discuss what you might do with a friend. Once you've identified ways of developing your capital, you'll have established some important next steps to take as you seek to enhance your graduate employability. It will also be worth considering how you will articulate your graduate capital to potential employers. You might like to role-play this with a friend, with one of you assuming the role of a new graduate, while the other plays the part of the potential employer. What sort of questions would an employer ask about your graduate capital and how might you answer each one? The more you prepare now for such experiences the easier they will be when you encounter them in reality.

This discussion of graduate capital and employability provides a fitting way to conclude this book. Our ultimate goal in writing this book and its focus on excelling and academic literacies has been to help you to become a highly employable graduate. Excelling, at a basic level, is about marks and performance in assessment. But, as we've stressed throughout this book, it's also about successfully making that transition from student to graduate. Whether you're sitting in a lecture, completing a formative assessment, or discussing your research proposal with your tutor, all of the experiences that form part of the learning journey we've described in this book contribute to the building up of your graduate capital. How is this experience – however tedious or boring it might seem at the time – going to help you become a graduate? It's this goal that should drive your engagement with the learning on your course and underpin your approach to developing the literacies that will help you to excel.

Reference

Tomlinson, M. (2017). Forms of graduate capital and their relationship to graduate employability. *Education & Training*, 59(4), 338–352.

Index

academic integrity 6, 185–187; and plagiarism 187, 188, 192; and referencing 79, 188, 191–193; and research data 187–188; values of 184, 185–187
academic literacy 2–3, 31–32; and discourse community 30–32
analysis 113–114, 119–120
assessment 4–6, 31, 39–41, 60–62, 67–73; formative 41–42, 61, 62–64; forms of 65–67; and generative AI 6; self and peer 66–67; summative 41–42, 62–64

citation searching 110–112
cognitive resilience 237–238, 242
critical engagement with sources ('being critical') 78–79, 117, 118–120, 157, 194–195; active and passive approaches to 123–127, 159–160, 179–180, 181
critical thought (or criticality) 5, 32, 91, 112, 113, 114–117, 120, 159, 224; in writing 123–133; *see also* journal articles, engaging with; writing, and language of criticality

disciplinary conventions 3, 31, 43; in writing 6, 79, 135, 137–145, 181, 247
discourse 5, 6, 31, 32, 33, 43, 78, 91, 95, 97, 104, 110, 112, 113, 115, 117, 118–120, 121–123, 124, 125, 126, 127, 128, 130, 131, 132, 133, 141, 142, 144, 145, 146, 147, 149, 150, 151, 152, 154, 155, 157, 161, 164, 165, 168, 178, 179, 181, 192, 193, 194, 195, 201, 207, 231, 232, 233
discourse community 4, 11, 28–30, 42–43, 59, 95, 139, 185, 187, 198; and academic literacy 30–32
dissertations 11, 52, 66, 104, 108, 109, 110, 111, 203; and literature reviews 157–160; and research proposals 150–156

essay, the 2, 31, 43, 57, 60, 61, 65, 88, 97–102, 116, 117, 118, 119, 120, 121, 164, 165, 169, 177, 184, 186, 201, 207, 233, 244; as a genre of assessment 145–149
evaluating academic sources 108–109, 121–123
evaluation 114–117, 120; evaluative judgements 6, 116, 120, 122, 126, 127–128, 131, 133, 165–166, 172, 178–179, 180, 215; in self-regulated learning 50–52, 55–57; in writing 67–73, 81–93
exams 7, 17, 59, 60–61, 231; anxiety over 234–235; forms of 232–234; management in or strategies for 7, 243–245; purpose of 232; and revision strategy 235–243
excelling 1, 2, 4, 7, 15–16, 21, 27, 30, 31, 41, 59, 246, 251; and assessment 67; and exams 231, 234, 235, 245; and feedback 75, 86; and goals 23–25; as a mindset 16–19; and motivation 21–23; and self-efficacy 19–21; and self-regulated learning 44, 52, 55–57; and success 9, 10–16; and writing 135, 144
experiential learning 220, 225–229

Index

feedback 4, 5, 7, 11, 17, 18, 19, 41, 42, 75, 76–79, 81, 113, 186, 203, 232; and assessment 59–60, 61–62, 63–64, 67, 73; diagnostic 80; feedback cycle 81–83; forms of 80; making effective use of 81–93; and motivation 21–23; and self-efficacy 19–21

goal setting 4, 5, 11, 16, 23–25, 50–52, 55–57, 246
graduate attributes 13–15
graduate capital 7, 247–251
graduate identity 3, 4, 6, 9, 10, 25, 75, 184, 187, 198, 200, 202, 212, 218, 219, 230, 246–247
group work 6, 7, 200, 212–218, 219, 220, 247

intended learning outcomes (ILOs) 35, 38, 39, 65, 232

journal articles 30, 37, 113, 115, 157, 192; engaging with 33–34, 48–50, 51, 99–102, 103, 107–109, 111, 116–117, 118–119, 121–123; referencing of 196–197; structural elements of 121–123

keywords: in presentations 206, 207, 208, 209; in referencing 191; in revision 239; in searching 57, 96, 99–107, 110–112, 122–123; and synonyms 104; in writing 159, 166–167
knowledge 30, 43; and assessment 67–73, 76, 78, 81–93, 115, 232–234; building knowledge 11, 32–34, 35, 36, 37–38, 45–52, 54, 56, 95, 97, 99–103, 109, 112, 114–117, 118–120, 121–123, 157, 235–242; and discourse community 28–30; and literature reviews 157–160; knowledge structures 30–32, 34, 239
Kolb's Experiential Learning Cycle *see* experiential learning

learning 4–5, 11, 13–15, 16–19, 21–23, 23–24, 25, 27, 32–34, 42, 246–247; active learning 33–34, 237–243; and assessment 59–62, 65–67, 73; authentic learning 65, 204, 223, 230; and behaviourism 37; as change 32; and constructivism 36–37; and critical thought 113, 114–117; deep-level learning 32–34, 51; design of 35–36, 37–39, 67–68; and discourse community 28–30, 95, 185; and feedback 75, 76–78, 80, 93; passive learning 35; and sense-making 32–34; student-centred learning 35–36; surface-level learning 32–34, 35, 51; tutor-centred learning 35–36
learning framework 4, 39–42
lifelong learning 44, 54, 58
literacies 1, 2–3, 4–5, 11, 13, 24, 30–32, 41–42, 59, 66, 67, 95, 113, 146, 186–187, 199, 200, 201, 223–224, 246–251
literature reviews 121–123, 157–160, 203

marking criteria 5, 63, 66, 67–73, 76–78, 79, 81–93, 114–117, 121, 123–127, 151, 164, 167, 174, 178, 180, 181, 188, 192–193, 195, 205, 247
mastery: of discipline 11, 15, 21, 51; and goal setting 23–25, 55
mind-maps *see* knowledge, knowledge structures
mindset 4, 5, 9, 15–19, 20, 21, 22, 23, 24, 25, 44, 58, 81, 246; and 'being critical' 114–116, 133; and feedback 81; and goal setting 23–25; and motivation 21–23; and practice- and work-based learning 229
motivation 4, 5, 15–16, 21–23, 25–26, 49–51, 55, 56, 246; and goal-setting 23–24; and self-efficacy 19–21; and self-regulated learning 44, 45–52, 55–57, 58

paraphrasing 79, 194–195
poster presentations 203
practice- and work-based learning 6, 221–223, 229, 247, 249, 250; assessment of 224–225; benefits of 223–224; and experiential learning 225–229
presentations 6–7, 13, 14–15, 42–43, 60, 65, 67, 201–212, 215–217, 218–219, 222, 247; argument

in 201, 207, 208, 209, 210; and assessment 203–205; common errors in 210–212; designing visual aids for 208–209; and graduate identity 202; as a means of testing communication 202; planning, structuring and designing of 205–208, 209–210; and transferable skills 202

referencing 6, 77–78, 79, 167, 188–198; and *et al.* 190–191; in-text references (or citations) 190; and paraphrasing 194–195; and plagiarism 192; and quotation 193–194; position of in-text references 190–191; purpose of 191–193; reference format 195–198; references list 78, 121, 122, 139, 160, 164, 174, 191, 192, 193, 195–196; referencing styles 188–189
reflection and reflective practice 6–7, 63, 213; and learning by doing 225–229; and self-regulated learning 44, 50, 52, 53–57, 58, 246
reports 160–161
research 5, 11, 12–13, 15–16, 17–18, 24–25, 31, 33–34, 59, 61, 66, 68, 77–78, 95, 96–97, 113, 139–145, 157, 169; and critical thought 114–117, 118–123, 133; and handling data 187–188; and literature review 157–160; and presentations 202, 206–210, 218; and referencing 192; *see also* searching
research proposals 150–156
revision 7, 235–243

search strategy 5, 31, 33, 41, 95, 97, 110–111, 112
searching 96–102, 116–117; and Boolean logic 105–106; and databases 110; and discovery service 104–108; extending searches 110–112; key principles of 97–102; and limiters 99–102, 103, 106–107, 108, 111, 112; and planning 102–103
self-efficacy 10, 19–21, 22–23, 24, 50–51, 57
self-regulated learning 5, 13, 44, 45–50, 55–57, 58, 62, 99–102, 115, 187, 246; as a process 50–52;

and reflective practice 53–57; and self-efficacy 20
success 10–16; and academic performance 11–13; and personal development 13–15
synthesis 30–32, 89, 123–127; and literature reviews 157–160; and poster presentations 203; and revision techniques 240, 242; in writing 128–129, 131, 149
systematic reviews 110

transferable skills 200; and graduate capital 247, 249; and presentations 202

video presentations 65, 204

writing: active and passive voice in 175–176; arguments in 31, 77, 78–79, 86, 89, 91, 115–117, 123–128, 133, 143–144, 145–149, 159–160, 167–168, 170, 177–179, 181, 193; for assessment 6, 135, 136–137, 181–182; common errors in 172–174; conventions 6, 79, 135, 137–145, 181, 247; within disciplines 6, 137–145; and discipline-specific vocabulary 131–132; essays 145–149; expression in 174–177; flow in 130, 159 (literature reviews), 179; forming judgements in 127–128, 165–166, 172, 179; four pillars of effective writing 164; genres 6, 145–164; integrating academic sources into 179–180; and language of criticality 5, 127, 129–133, 159, 181; literature reviews 157–160; in practice 164–181; reflective writing 161–163; reports 160–161; research proposals 150–156; structure in 79, 146–149 (essays), 159 (literature reviews), 165, 177–179; student assumptions about 136; voice(s) in 125, 179–180, 201; writing critically 123–133, 181
writing cycle 164–172; and creating a first draft 169–170; and editing 170–172; and planning 167–169; and proofreading 172; and understanding the task 165–167
working in groups 212–218; challenges of 212–213, 216–217; and personality types 215–217

For Product Safety Concerns and Information please contact our EU representative GPSR@taylorandfrancis.com
Taylor & Francis Verlag GmbH, Kaufingerstraße 24, 80331 München, Germany

www.ingramcontent.com/pod-product-compliance
Lightning Source LLC
Chambersburg PA
CBHW071406300426
44114CB00016B/2197